SHOUTING AT
THE CROCODILE

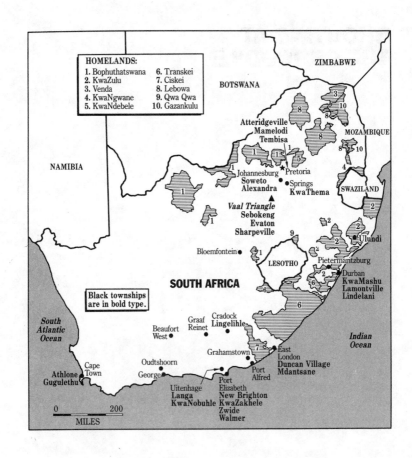

HOMELANDS:
1. Bophuthatswana
2. KwaZulu
3. Venda
4. KwaNgwane
5. KwaNdebele
6. Transkei
7. Ciskei
8. Lebowa
9. Qwa Qwa
10. Gazankulu

ZIMBABWE

BOTSWANA

NAMIBIA

MOZAMBIQUE

Atteridgeville
Mamelodi
Tembisa

Johannesburg ★ Pretoria
Soweto ● Springs
Alexandra **KwaThema**

SWAZILAND

▲
Vaal Triangle
Sebokeng
Evaton
Sharpeville

Ulundi

Bloemfontein ●

LESOTHO

Pietermaritzburg

Durban
KwaMashu
Lamontville
Lindelani

SOUTH AFRICA

Black townships
are in bold type.

*South
Atlantic
Ocean*

Cradock
Graaf **Lingelihle**
Reinet

Beaufort
West ●

Grahamstown

*Indian
Ocean*

East
London
Duncan Village
Mdantsane

Oudtshoorn
Athlone
Cape
Gugulethu Town
George ●

Port
Alfred

Port
Uitenhage Elizabeth
Langa **New Brighton**
KwaNobuhle **KwaZakhele**
Zwide
Walmer

0   200
MILES

SHOUTING AT THE CROCODILE

POPO MOLEFE, PATRICK LEKOTA, AND THE FREEING OF SOUTH AFRICA

ROSE MOSS

BEACON PRESS
BOSTON

Beacon Press
25 Beacon Street
Boston, Massachusetts 02108-2800

Beacon Press books
are published under the auspices of
the Unitarian Universalist Association of Congregations.

97 96 95 94 93 92 91 90   8 7 6 5 4 3 2 1

Text design by C. J. Petlick

Library of Congress Cataloging-in-Publication Data
Moss, Rose.
    Shouting at the crocodile : a trial for the future of South Africa / Rose Moss.
      p.   cm.
    Includes bibliographical references.
    ISBN 0-8070-0210-0
    1. Lekota, Patrick—Trials, litigation, etc.   2. Molefe, Popo Simon. 1952–   —
Trials, litigation, etc.   3. United Democratic Front (South Africa)—Trials, litigation,
etc.   4. Trials (Treason)—South Africa—Pretoria.   I. Title.
LAW <SOUTH AFR 9 Lekota 1990>
345.68′0231—dc20
[346.805231]   90-52585

To those who cross the river
and shout at this world's crocodiles.

Contents

Those who would show the light must first go through the fire.

Proverb in The Struggle

Nebuchadnezzar the king made an image of gold.... Then an herald cried out aloud, To you it is commanded, O people, ... that ... ye all fall down and worship the golden image ...

And whoso falleth not down and worshippeth shall the same hour be cast into a fiery furnace ...

Wherefore at that time certain Chaldeans came near and accused ... Shadrach, Mesach, and Abednego ...

Then Nebuchadnezzar in his rage and fury ... said unto them, Is it true.... Do not ye serve my gods nor worship the golden image which I have set up? ... if ye worship not, ye shall be cast into a fiery furnace; and who is the God that shall deliver you out of my hands?

Shadrach, Mesach, and Abednego answered ... If it be so, our God whom we serve is able to deliver us from the burning fiery furnace.... But if not, be it known unto thee, O king, that we will not serve thy gods, nor worship the golden image which thou hast set up.

Then was Nebuchadnezzar full of fury, and the form of his visage was changed ... therefore he ... commanded that they should heat the furnace ... seven times more than it was wont to be heated ... and to cast them into the fiery furnace ...

Because ... the furnace was exceedingly hot, the flame of the fire slew those men that took up Shadrach, Mesach, and Abednego. And these three men, Shadrach, Mesach, and Abednego, fell down bound into the midst of the fiery furnace.

Then Nebuchadnezzar the king was astonished ... and said, Did we not cast three men bound into the midst of the fire.... Lo, I see four men loose, walking in the midst of the fire, and they have no hurt ...

Then Nebuchadnezzar came near to the mouth of the burning fiery furnace ... and said ... ye servants of the most high God, come forth ...

Then Shadrach, Mesach and Abednego came forth of the midst of the fire. And the princes, governors, and captains, and the king's counsellors, ... saw these men, upon whose bodies the fire had no power, nor was an hair of their head singed, neither were their coats changed, nor the smell of fire had passed on them.

Then Nebuchadnezzar ... said, Blessed be the God of Shadrach, Mesach, and Abednego who hath sent his messenger and delivered his servants that trusted in him and have changed the king's word.

Daniel 3:1–28

Preface

I started this book with reluctance and misgiving and I finish it in hope and gratitude. I had given up on South Africa and expected nothing to come of the conflicts there but continuing repression until a black tyranny replaced the white. That despair was so hard, I tried to turn my back on the country and came to understand why people do turn their backs on apparently hopeless misery. I looked from the inside of indifference.

A decade ago, when I was teaching at Wellesley College, a student who knew I was born in South Africa and guessed that I still cared invited me to attend a meeting of the Trustees Committee on Social Responsibility. Knowing how massive, complex, and hopeless the task was in South Africa, believing that the injustice there is meshed in the self-interest and misunderstanding of powerful people throughout the world, and wary of efforts of distant, optimistic Americans, I joked, "I haven't got time to save the world this year." Then, as now, I saw South Africa as a microcosm of our world where a few, mainly white, have much, and many, mainly nonwhite, want much. Today, from the hope that has replaced my despair, I might joke, read this story. It's about how to save the world.

In spite of my wisecrack, my student exercised enough optimistic persistence to get me to serve on the Committee for a few years.

I was drawn out of despair about South Africa by a series of incidents that felt like chance.

While I was writing a movie treatment set in contemporary South Africa, two South African friends visited me in Boston. I asked them how to find out what is going on there now, and one said, "Read this." He gave me part of the testimony of an African leader charged with treason in a major political trial of the most important internal anti-apartheid organization, the United Democratic Front. Skeptical about whether testimony from what was called the Delmas Trial would really give me the feel and texture of things, I read.

It seemed dry stuff at first—although it came alive when Popo Molefe, one of the two key defendants, talked about his childhood. But something else had started to happen. I was hearing an echo of someone else whose words I had read long ago, a leader with a tragic vision and a tragic task, who cared, deep as bone, about democracy and knew how it works; who longed for unity, and who understood that it might have to be achieved by civil war; who understood that the civil war, if it cannot be avoided—and he wanted to avoid it—must be conducted in a spirit of reconciliation at the same time it is fought. Was I really hearing Lincoln's tone in Molefe's words?

That was a surprise. I said, tentatively, "It might be interesting to write about this man." My friend offered to show me more.

Reading the testimony of the other key defendant, Mosiuoa Patrick Lekota, my surprise was different. Here was this audacious voice, telling the court that when he had been imprisoned for six years, he had found it "a golden opportunity." A what? How can a system of government survive if its prisons are turned into golden opportunities? Lekota said that on Robben Island, South Africa's Alcatraz for black male political prisoners, he had learned "on the knees of Mandela," and what he had learned there was "the secret path of my people's history." He talked a lot about history, about Afrikaner history as well as about black history. His tone was full of warmth, and reverence, and gentleness and joy. His words turned that island, dark as dead blood in my mind's eye, into a golden time. An alchemist. I read on.

I came to a passage where Lekota speaks compassionately about the sufferings of whites who enforce apartheid through the barrel of a gun. Was this man loving his enemies?

Curious, I asked friends about the trial. They called it the most important trial since Mandela was sent to prison in 1964, likely to last longer than the marathon Treason Trial of 1956–61 that accused the most important antiapartheid leaders of their generation and acquitted them. This trial was an attack on fundamental human rights. The United Democratic Front had marshaled nonviolent, nonracial opposition. It had tried to act within the law. If the defendants were found guilty, it would mean that there was no room left for nonviolence.

The Universal Declaration of Human Rights, a lawyer told me, protects nonviolent protest because, without it, people see no recourse but violence. Total suppression invites terrorism and civil war.

His fears would be fulfilled in the short run. After more than three years on trial, some of the Delmas defendants, including Molefe and Lekota, were found guilty of treason and sentenced to long terms on Robben Island. The judge did not believe that the UDF was independent of the African National Congress, and, the African National Congress was, by the apartheid regime's definition, a banned organization. Membership in the ANC was in and of itself proof of treason and commitment to violence designed to make the state ungovernable and lead to its destruction.

The verdict, which did not find any direct connection between those judged guilty and specific acts of violence, condemned them for acting for the same purposes as the ANC and its banned allies like the South African Communist Party. Although the defendants had acted nonviolently, they were found guilty of treason. The verdict seemed to close off nonviolence as a method that could command respect among a large following. It seemed to move the agenda back, from issues of fundamental human rights called for by Molefe and Lekota, to a brute struggle for power.

Many political leaders in South Africa heard the verdict with deep gloom, as though it had taken them by surprise, as though the work of the UDF, the personal esteem many felt for Molefe and Lekota, and the hopefulness displayed by the defendants during their trial had led these observers to expect a different verdict.

Their hope was one measure of the change the UDF had helped to bring about, in spite of harsh government action against it, culminating in restrictions in February 1988 that, in effect, banned the UDF, many of its affiliates, and other antiapartheid organizations. In spite of the trial, continuing deaths of people in police custody, and bombs in shopping malls and offices, people from all over South Africa seemed to know that they would have to work out how to live with each other. The unflinching unity and self-righteousness of the apartheid's supporters seemed to be yielding, here and there, to the recognition that South Africa would have to create a new society, and to a zest for that endeavor. The arts were alive and questioning. The academic community was turning to the intellectual tasks of preparing for a post-apartheid society. I had not seen such life and hope during earlier visits in the seventies and early eighties.

The hope for a lenient verdict leaned on a recent precedent. Under a skeptical judge, a treason trial of sixteen UDF and trade union leaders charged in April 1985 in Pietermaritzburg had collapsed by December. (Four union leaders among the sixteen were held a few months longer.) If Molefe and Lekota had been detained in February, when many of the sixteen were detained, and charged with the other leaders, they might have been free within the year. Instead, arrested April 23, they sat through one of the longest trials in South African history. The judge did not begin to read his verdict until three and a half years later, November 15, 1988.

The charges in the Delmas case were more difficult for the defense than the charges against the Pietermaritzburg defendants. In the Delmas Trial, three UDF leaders were indicted with nineteen defendants from the Vaal Triangle, an area south of Johannesburg where there had been murder, arson, and rioting beginning in September 1984. The Delmas defendants were charged with five counts of murder, as well as with treason, terrorism, subversion, and sedition. At the end of the prosecution's presentation of its case, charges against three defendants were dropped—they had not even been mentioned in the year of testimony.

On appeal, the verdict of the judge, Kees van Dijkhorst, would be upset. He had volunteered to take the case promising to dispose of it in a few months, and by the time I saw him in the bench in August 1988, with the case approaching its fourth year, shifting from buttock to buttock, leaning forward and back, resting his bald forehead on three fingers, he seemed to be writhing slowly in pain. The appeal ruling would be on an apparent technicality, but the ground of appeal called the judge's neutrality into question. The sentenced men were released on December 15, 1989, to a country whose political climate had changed deeply during the year of their imprisonment. There was a new State's President, F. W. de Klerk, who came into office with violence but soon started to allow rallies and protests. He released prisoners who had served long terms with Mandela. The UDF was still formally banned but had been organizing under another name, the Mass Democratic Movement, and soon started to work again in its own name. People were taking no pains to disguise their allegiance to the ANC; even skeptics were beginning to believe that Mandela would really be released soon. Molefe and Lekota resumed their work.

Many I spoke to before my visit in 1988 talked about the trial less as a politically and legally important event, more as a place where extraordinary things were happening. The defendants were cheerful, visitors came to see them constantly, bringing their babies and children to meet them. Children played quietly during the proceedings. It sounded a bit like a Jewish wedding, or like an orthodox

Sabbath service where the prayers are conducted with due reverence by people nodding in silky prayer shawls at the same time as
others in the synagogue aisles ask after each other's health and family
and how's business.
   By this time I wanted to see for myself. What I had been seeing
in the media suggested that the policies of apartheid had worked to
exacerbate divisions, bury the majority in ignorance and helpless-
ness, and license petty tyrants to any exercise of corruption and
violence their imaginations invited. The pseudo-independent homelands had become, if anything, more vicious than Pretoria itself.
Nothing seemed to be effectively changing apartheid. The blacks
were killing each other, the whites were killing them, and most of
those who couldn't stomach living in the tyrant camp were emigrat-
ing. There was some good ironic and tragic writing coming out of
the country, but joy? Zest? Serenity? Reconciliation? I had not read
about it.
   One person, in the State Department, described the defendants
as "like a rugby team," cheerful, even boisterous, and, in passing,
compared Molefe and Lekota to Gandhi and Martin Luther King. Bill
Finnegan at *The New Yorker* said people were telling him to go to
the Delmas Trial because "something extraordinary is going on
there." Scholars and journalists were describing Molefe and Lekota
as the Mandelas of their generation.
   After my visit to the Palace of Justice in Pretoria during the closing weeks of the trial in August and September 1988, I heard similar
testimony from others. Edward J. Perkins, U.S. Ambassador in South
Africa during the trial, returned to the United States saying, "It was a
privilege to meet these men." David Bonbright who visited South
Africa for the Ford Foundation during the UDF's first years said,
"They ennoble everyone they touch."
   I went to observe the trial in 1988 with mixed feelings. Since
leaving South Africa in 1964, shortly before Mandela and the others
tried with him were sentenced in the very courtroom where Molefe,
Lekota and seventeen others were being tried for treason, I had returned a few times, mainly for family visits and time with friends. I
did not see much change from the time before I left, and in spite of
my delight in the beauty of the country, I had heard and seen things
I could not forget. One night in 1963, I was roused from sleep by
hearing a man being dragged along the corridor outside my apart-
ment whimpering and protesting in an African language. I heard the
elevator go down, and when the prisoner and police emerged be-

low, I saw the police beating the prisoner with truncheons. He was screaming now. I could not see the number on the police car. I called the police, but I felt a hopeless idiocy in complaining to the offender about the offense. My sleep murdered, I resumed grading papers on *Macbeth*, wondering whether Birnam Wood would ever come to Dunsinane Castle, whether justice would ever come to South Africa.

At that time the newspapers were full of stories about prison laborers beaten to death on farms and policemen who forced their prisoners to drink water from a hose until their stomachs burst. When the policemen were tried for murder, they were given short suspended sentences, and there was some outcry about the harshness of this punishment. Working in Pretoria, among white colleagues and friends, I felt all alone in distress. I wondered whether I was going mad to take it all so to heart.

During my last spring in South Africa, in 1963, I planned a visit to see the brilliant, flowering fields of daisies at Barberton, but engine trouble stranded me and I found myself at a mission station where the hospital was full of children dying of measles. The dead lawn in front of the hospital was studded with mothers sitting on the ground. They were waiting to hear whether their children had died. Many did. Many lived, blind. The mission did not allow the mothers to visit their children in case they spread the contagious disease to the rest of the starving population, and parents were threatening to kill people at the hospital. On our way to the mission, my companion and I had passed the camp where the parents and children lived—a scattering of tents along the side of a dry canyon. At supper, we heard how, because there was no other water, they used the same desiccating puddles for washing and for drinking. They had been forcibly moved in accordance with the Group Areas Act, a law used to move blacks off fertile land into desert. After that, I didn't much want to look at fields of flowering daisies.

But during the three weeks I observed the Delmas Trial in 1988, what had begun for me as a trickle of interest, and then a stream, became an irresistible current. I sat on the chipped pine benches without backs that, like the peg-board lining the walls and hung with video equipment, mar the gracious architecture decorated with pilasters and arches. When I tried to take notes, one of the six policemen guarding the trial told me that the judge had forbidden notes. I watched, and started to see how a new South Africa is coming into being.

One afternoon after lunch, Lekota opened a roll of candy. He offered it to Molefe on his right, and to Moses Chikane, UDF secretary for Transvaal Province, on his left, then he turned round to offer it to the police sergeant standing near the dock. I had seen the sergeant walking behind the defendants, peering over their shoulders to see what they were doing, letting them know he was keeping them under his eye. The sergeant took a candy from the roll Lekota had offered and handed the rest back. Friendly. As though they were all in this tedious trial together. I thought Lekota's gesture both street smart and principled. It prepared me for the letter I quote in chapter 16.

I saw similar friendliness in the lobby a few days later when defendants out on bail greeted a policeman with warmth. He had been their guard in the farming town of Delmas where the trial was held for its first years to avoid large demonstrations of support for the men in the dock. "How's the case going?" he asked. "Good luck." As though he were really on their side.

One day, I saw a woman bring her baby to the court. One of the three African policemen was standing near the dock. I had seen him staring at his hands—palms, backs. What does one do for hours on end? During that morning's hour-long session he stared at the baby. I do not know whether he was cut off from his family by apartheid as many Africans are. I do know that he seemed to see nothing but that white baby.

Human warmth seemed to be leaking through the dikes. One day, a young policeman who had seen a defense lawyer on his feet all day offered him a piece of fudge. Blacks and whites, supporters and opponents of apartheid, seemed to be fraternizing with each other, as though they were all compatriots and were creating a way to live together in the same country.

I knew it was happening outside the courtroom too. One night I heard a story about eleven young men arrested after conflicts between high school students and police in 1976. At first, the "Soweto Eleven" were heavily guarded by police with automatic rifles. Gradually, their guards relaxed. One day, a young guard sitting with the prisoners, youths his own age, started to show off his gun. He aimed. He broke it open and showed how to unload it and reload it. He handed it to one of the prisoners. The prisoner broke it open, unloaded, reloaded. He handed the gun to his neighbor, who held it, aimed, broke it open. The gun went round the circle of prisoners.

They handed it back to the guard. All the young men had admired the same artifact, felt its power, not used it against each other.

Hostages often come to sympathize with their captors. In South Africa, it is the hostages who are winning their captors over, and the hostages are the majority. The Soweto Eleven story, many years ago, seems a foretaste of what has been happening throughout the society.

Others observing the trial saw it as a presage of a new South Africa. As police sirens cleared the road for police motorcycles preceding the yellow police van that rushed the UDF officials to and from Pretoria Central Prison, Frances Potter, one of the young lawyers on the defense team, said ironically, "The next time they get this treatment, it'll be as heads of state."

Molefe and Lekota, preparing for the new order, saw and acted as though the new order must include structures that protect human dignity and the rights of all—the policeman who took Lekota's candy, the one who could not take his eyes off a baby, and even the judge and prosecutors. The testimony speaks of a society where all live together and must learn how to do so in peace. They speak of reconciliation. In their daily behavior as well as in their testimony during the Delmas Trial they demonstrated what they say.

The testimony of the whole trial fills more than 250 volumes. I have had access to less than 5 percent of it, most of it transcript given to the Ralph Bunche Institute on the United Nations, for its collection of documents in the history of resistance to apartheid. The Ralph Bunche Institute will eventually have the whole Delmas Trial transcript. During the writing of this book, the complete transcript was not available in the United States. I have worked from most of the testimony of Molefe and Lekota, the only full-time, paid officials of the UDF and the highest-level defendants; the indictment; some of the verdict; the documents filed during the dispute between Willem Joubert, one of the two assessors, advisors to the judge in cases where a death penalty is possible and by the judge about the dismissal of Joubert as assessor; a few pages of testimony about the other defendants; and some of the defense argument at the end of the trial. Even this small percentage amounts to more than ten volumes.

The materials I have used present a picture of the two leading defendants, their principles, and those of the United Democratic Front. To me, the stand Molefe and Lekota took, arguing their case on grounds of human rights, transcends the specific issues of apart-

heid and the political struggle in South Africa. They speak for the
dignity of all, and for the hope that work for justice will not be in
vain. Their words reach out to all who look for a moral dimension
in public life.

The strategies of nonviolence they followed reveal powerful political techniques of interest to all who seek to marshal nonviolence
against repressive regimes.

Because Molefe and Lekota are important leaders of the anti-
apartheid struggle, and their trial dealt with issues critical to South
Africa and the events of the tumultuous mid- and late eighties, their
testimony speaks to those who have a specific interest in South Africa.

I have worked to present a readable and coherent narrative
mainly composed of quotations from the testimony. For the sake of
coherence, I have arranged quotations thematically, drawing on material that appears and disappears in the indictment, the evidence in
chief, the labyrinthine cross-examinations, the defense argument,
and the verdict. I give a context where passages of testimony do not
explain themselves. Although I have edited some passages for brev-
ity, I tried not to change the meaning. Occasionally I comment on
implications that may not be self-evident. I hope this book presents
a vivid picture of the work, beliefs, and quality of two leaders who
have restored my hope for the country where I was born.

Acknowledgments

This book would not have come into being without the initial inspiration of Molefe's and Lekota's testimony, and then the privilege of meeting them in person and experiencing the warmth and dedication they inspire in people. Throughout the writing of the book, I have received help from people who supported the project because of their own respect and friendship for Molefe and Lekota. I want to thank them on my own behalf. Many others helped because of their respect and affection for the legal team. Some were my friends before I started on this project, some have become friends during the project. I want to thank especially Lorraine and Arthur Chaskalson, George Bizos, Frances Potter, Gilbert Marcus, Karel Tip, and Zak Yacoob.

Thabiso Ratsomo, one of the defendants, gave me a copy of his own account of the trial and some material in print in South Africa but unobtainable in the United States.

Willem A. Joubert also gave me materials published in South Africa and showed me great kindness in discussing his role as assessor. Edwin Cameron helped me get materials important in the trial that were not in the record of Molefe and Lekota. Hennie Sterkfontein encouraged me to look at clippings he had collected during the trial that pointed me to some of the most important aspects of the testimony and incidents I would not have guessed at from materials accessible to me in the United States. Matthew Chaskalson gave me his insights and some of his research materials.

Ron Wells and Enid Gort at the Phelps Stokes Institute, which granted me the status of Resident Scholar, offered important moral and logistical support for the project.

When the verdict was read, Philip van Niekerk called and read me the wire service accounts. In his reading I heard Lekota's comment about those who go through the fire. Slightly more than a year later, when the appeal ruling came out, Ellen Bartlett read me the wire service accounts.

It was John Hall's interest in South Africa and his sympathetic insight into the key values at issue there that led to my initial reading of the testimony. Jill Paton Wash and John Rowe Townsend received me with tolerance and practical friendship when I returned from observing the trial almost unable to talk about anything else. Margaret Ann Roth, who published a long article of mine on the trial in *The Boston Review*; Keith Henderson, who accepted an op-ed piece on Ramakgula's door in *The Christian Science Monitor*; Sandy Close at Pacific News Service; Kitty Axleson at the *Valley Advocate* in Hadley; Rebecca Rickman, who read the piece in *The Boston Review* and invited me to give a reading at the Institute of Contemporary Art in Boston; and Gay MacDougall who reprinted an op-ed piece for members of Lawyers Committee for Civil Rights under Law all helped me overcome warnings from myself and others that "No one in the United States cares about South Africa." Janice Jones at *The Los Angeles Times,* who recognized the unique character of Lekota's voice, Roger Thurow, whose account of the verdict in *The Wall Street Journal* identified Lekota and Molefe as heirs to Mandela's legend, the interest of Bill Finnegan at *The New Yorker,* the lively curiosity of Steve Atlas at WGBH, who looked at the testimony, also reassured me that the book would be worth the work.

Constance Parvey, who immediately recognized that, as a fellow Lutheran, Popo Molefe had a special claim on her attention and care, and who saw how Lekota's testimony witnesses to values that focus much of her life, introduced me to Deb Chasman at Beacon Press, and helped cut short the time of doubt about undertaking the project at all.

During the writing, I have continued to receive irreplaceable help. Tom Karis, at the Ralph Bunche Institute, has been a fund of gracious and intelligent support and information. He read some chapters with meticulous care for accuracy, clarity, and readability. He sent me some valuable material, including a copy of the speech by Edward Perkins that led me to another friend of the defendants. Betsy Spiro, another friend of Molefe and Lekota in the State Department, also read several chapters and invited substantial and useful revisions by her comments.

Stephen Ellman at Columbia sent me the verdict and answered questions about South African law. Karl Beck and Tony Marx encouraged the project and gave valuable advice. Laura Farmello sent materials, answered questions, and suggested that I look at the Mayekiso verdict, and Marvin E. Frankel sent me a copy of that verdict at the request of Richard Goldstone.

Ken Carstens, a friend who has worked long in exile, shared my feeling that Molefe and Lekota tell an important story, and he gave me copies of International Defense and Aid publications that helped me understand the context of the trial, and Jeff Wisner, also at Defense and Aid, gave me more materials and answered questions.

Edith Pearlman read the manuscript, clarified the needs of an American reader, demanded that I write as well as I am able, and gave me food and wine during many evenings of supportive criticism.

Florence Ladd helped arrange a reading, with music by Tod Machover, for Oxfam America. Claire McKeowan, Anuradha Desai, and Rachel Zoll made the benefit happen and introduced Molefe and Lekota to new audiences.

Many of my friends, some with South African connections, have shown continuing forebearance as I read them passages of testimony. I want to thank them for their friendship, and for keeping me in touch with other things in life during this year. Janet Levine offered her own perspectives on Molefe and the UDF. Michael Padnos cheered, amused, and revivified me week after week. Rachel and Alexis Belash, who have shown their own understanding and will to work for a new South Africa, offered sage advice on managing the project. Frank O'Neil implicitly warned me against programmatic and partisan sympathies and kept my eye on the importance of making the story clear and vivid. Libby Blank, Maria Georgeopolis Mackavey, and Bill Mackavey showed me how eagerly Americans may understand and welcome news of people like Molefe and Lekota. Lex Kelso helped keep me sane with his friendship and skepticism. Barbara Grizzuti Harrison and Ellen Levine recognized the story as important and offered publication advice. Alan Bomser helped me with legal advice when I was anxious that untimely leaks of confidential material might damage Molefe and Lekota. Pam Sacks offered understanding and wisdom on matters connected with the trial, the book, and people who care about South Africa.

Many who know Molefe and Lekota have said they want to know about the progress of the book and look forward to its publication. Their interest has also sustained me. I want to thank especially Elizabeth Barad, David Bonbright, Michael Clough, Jonathan Cohen, Jan Jaffe, Jeanne and Paul Simon, Laurence Tribe, and Donald Woods.

Duncan constantly told me that what I was doing was good and helped me through times of doubt.

Deb Chasman at Beacon Press has become a friend as well as an editor. Her faith in the project, editorial skill, and understanding of South Africa have been irreplaceable.

Chronology

1910   Act of Union creates South Africa, excluding almost all blacks from government.

1912   January 8, South African Native National Congress, forerunner of the African National Congress, is formed.

1913   Natives' Land Act divides South Africa into "white" and "black" areas.

1923   South African Native National Congress changes name to African National Congress.

1936   Natives' Trust and Land Bill restricts Africans to 13 percent of the land.

1948   Nationalist Party wins election.

1950   Population Registration Act identifies every South African by race. Group Areas Act restricts each population group to "own" area.

1952   ANC launches defiance campaign. Nelson Mandela is Volunteer-in-Chief.

1953   Bantu Education Act segregates schools, syllabuses, and examinations.

1955   Congress of the People adopts Freedom Charter.

1955–   Treason Trial of 156 activists, most of them ANC members.
61

1959   Pan-African Congress formed.

1960   Protests against pass laws. Sharpeville massacre. State of Emergency. ANC and PAC banned.

1961   Albert Lutuli receives Nobel Peace Prize.
       ANC founds Mkhonto We Sizwe to pursue "armed struggle."

1963   Mandela and others arrested in Rivonia.

1966   Prime Minister Verwoerd assassinated. B. J. Vorster becomes Prime Minister.

1969   South African Students' Organization founded by Steve Biko.

1974   Colonial liberation struggles provoke revolution in Portugal; Angola and Mozambique become independent. South Africa sends troops to Angola.

1976   Students march in Soweto to protest Afrikaans as medium of instruction. Hundreds killed. Molefe among many detained. Lekota sentenced to six years on Robben Island and meets Mandela.

1977   Biko killed in detention. 17 anti-apartheid organizations and two newspapers banned. W. Krugel disposes of their assets.

1979   P. W. Botha becomes State's President.
        Zimbabwe becomes independent.
        Black trade unions are officially recognized.

1981   Molefe calls for united front against apartheid.

1982   P. W. Botha proposes new constitution.

1983   January 8, ANC President Oliver Tambo calls for united opposition to new constitution.
        January 23, Allan Boesak, head of World Council of Reformed Churches, calls for united front opposing new constitution.
        August 20, national launch of United Democratic Front. Molefe named general secretary, Lekota named publicity secretary.
        November 2, white referendum approves new constitution.

1984   School boycotts in Atteridgeville, near Pretoria, Cradock, and other parts of the country. Student killed in Atteridgeville. UDF conducts Million Signature Campaign against new constitution.
        June 16, UDF and AZAPO supporters clash about commemoration at Regina Mundi.

July 15, rioting in Tumahole. Lekota detained for several hours.

August 19, UDF one-year rally.

August 20, children in Sharpeville overturn bus.

August 21, 35 UDF officials detained, Lekota among them.

August 22, Coloureds vote under new constitution.

August 28, Indians vote under new constitution.

August 29, student protester in Daveyton (near Johannesburg) dies. Serious rioting. Three other children shot by police.

September 3, violence in Vaal sparks nationwide violence.

October 2, Molefe detained. October, Bishop Tutu awarded Nobel Peace Prize.

November 5–6, UDF and unions acting together organize work stay-away.

December 10, Molefe, Lekota, and others released from detention.

1985   January 31, Botha offers Mandela conditional release.

February 10, Mandela refuses conditional release.

February 19, police swoop on UDF officials. Molefe and Lekota go into hiding.

March 21, twenty-fifth anniversary of Sharpeville. Police kill more than eighteen mourners at funeral in Langa. New cycle of violence begins.

April 19, Botha says in Parliament that UDF is part of an ANC–SACP alliance. Molefe and Lekota issue immediate denial and emerge from hiding.

April 23, Molefe, Lekota, and Moss Chikane are detained.

May 20, sixteen UDF and affiliate leaders are charged with treason in Pietermaritzburg court.

June 11, Molefe, Lekota, and twenty others are charged with treason in court.

June 27, Mathew Goniwe and three others are found killed.

July 21, State of Emergency is imposed.

November 4, Delmas Trial begins.

1986   March 7, State of Emergency is lifted and new security regulations are imposed.

June 12, stricter State of Emergency is imposed.

1987   March 10, Judge Kees van Dijkhorst dismisses W. A. Joubert
        as assessor in Delmas Trial. August, Molefe takes the stand.
        September, Lekota takes the stand.

1988   February, UDF and other organizations banned in effect.
        August, defeated South African troops withdraw from An-
        gola.
        November 15–18, van Dijkhorst reads verdict.
        December 8, Molefe, Lekota and three others sentenced to
        Robben Island. ·

1989   Namibia granted independence. Banned organizations de-
        clare themselves unbanned.
        September 6, F. W. de Klerk's Nationalist Party wins election.
        September 13, massive peaceful rally in Cape Town fol-
        lowed by rallies throughout South Africa.
        October 15, Walter Sisulu and other Rivonia prisoners re-
        leased.
        November 27, Appelate Division hears appeal of Delmas
        verdict.
        December 15, Delmas verdict is overturned. Molefe, Lekota,
        and three others are released.

1990   February 2, de Klerk promises to release Mandela, unban
        ANC, UDF and other organizations.
        February 11, Mandela walks out of prison.

A Note on Sources

Page references to quotations from the transcript may change as the transcript is compiled. Lawyers assure me that those who want to check quotations will be able to find them with the references given. These references come in several main sets:

3894–3929 refer to transcript of a prosecution witness who testified in camera.

13: 110–14:933 refer to transcript when Molefe was on the stand.

15:441–17:048 refer to transcript when Lekota was on the stand.

VD 1–Annexure Z refer to the verdict by van Dijkhorst.

I have corrected spelling and other obvious errors, and indicate omissions to avoid repetition and colloquial looseness.

1 Introduction: In the Jaws of "the Big Crocodile"

On the morning of November 15, 1988, a young ex-policeman, Barend Hendrik Strydom, drove past Church Square. He was looking for someone to kill. Someone black.[1]

Outside the Palace of Justice where ambassadors and church leaders, television crews and celebrities, lawyers and family members were gathering to hear the judge deliver his verdict on those accused in the Delmas Trial, Church Square was full of policemen and Strydom saw few blacks. He drove on, looking for more. Two blocks from the court, he found some. He parked, taking care to pay the meter. He did not want to do anything illegal. Then, laughing, he shot an eighty-eight year old woman, an Indian storekeeper, and another woman waiting in a hospital bus. He shot twenty-two people. Seven died.

A week before, he had practiced at a squatters camp, shooting two women, "to see if I was physically capable of killing people." One died.

At first most people thought the rampage had nothing to do with the Delmas Trial, but at Strydom's trial another picture emerged. Strydom had come to Church Square looking for friends of the Delmas defendants. He hoped to kill Allan Boesak, President of the World Alliance of Reformed Churches and a patron of the United Democratic Front, the organization the trial was designed to crush.

Strydom, son of a policeman and an ex-policeman himself, belonged to a political party, the AWB, that admires the Nazis and holds rallies displaying three-legged swastikas. He said he was head of a secret society called the White Wolves, which has claimed credit for bombing the headquarters of the South African Council of Churches, the Southern African Catholic Bishops Conference, and other buildings housing anti-apartheid organizations. (The police had been noticeably unable to bring to court people responsible for violence against anti-apartheid institutions and people. Some believed the police themselves were responsible.)

Strydom explained, "Each black person threatens the continued existence of whites, even an eighty-eight-year-old woman. They are known to breed very fast." He added, "Scientists have shown that oxygen is decreasing. They are threatening the life of the entire planet."[2]

Strydom is not alone. Supporters attended his trial wearing the nineteenth-century dress of the Voortrekkers, the forebears whose penetration of the interior sets the patterns of Afrikaner myth and identity. Another supporter, inspired by the trial, threatened to shoot black workers at the plant where he works as a supervisor. When Strydom was found guilty, newspapers received letters calling him a "martyr of the third freedom war," and demanding that his death penalty be commuted.[3]

On the morning of the Delmas verdict, while Strydom was doing his bloody business nearby, a few minutes before the defendants went up to the courtroom crowded with observers and police, Lekota, one of the prisoners in the holding cell under the courtroom, was writing a letter to a friend.

Today we are receiving judgement. Earlier on I had some anxiety for my family. All my years are going to our struggle, and the question must cross their minds as to whether I still remember my obligations toward them. But now, all that has suddenly changed into unbridled rage with this system of South African law. This past week, an Afrikaner bully, Jacobus Vorster, was fined [$1,200] for tying an African laborer to a tree and beating him to death. He was then released to go back to his farm with an order that he pay the widow [$43] per month for five years. The laborer (deceased) had accidentally killed Vorster's one dog and injured another one ... African life remains extremely cheap in this country.

That "system of South African law" was about to pronounce on him and eighteen others tried on capital charges of treason and other crimes listed in an indictment of more than 360 pages. Charges against three defendants originally included in the indictment had been dropped.

Some observers waiting to hear the verdict believed that the United Democratic Front, the most important internal anti-apartheid organization in South Africa in the 1980s, had acted within the law (unlike the African National Congress, banned in 1960, which acted outside the country, and sent members to South Africa to further the policy of "armed struggle" it adopted in 1961. Members of the ANC inside the county also worked underground to mobilize, organize, and politicize people so that they would engage in mass action. Many UDF members were ANC members. As the conflict of the eighties developed, some made no bones about their allegiance. For them, the issue of the trial was not whether the UDF had complied with essentially illegitimate laws prohibiting political expression and actions. It was whether the government would allow any political action against apartheid). Under a banner proclaiming, "UDF unites, apartheid divides," the United Democratic Front had brought together about 600 affiliated organizations ranging from sports clubs to church choirs, labor unions to political protest lobbies. Its members included all South Africa's racial and linguistic groups. It brought its diverse constituencies together in focused opposition to apartheid, and especially to its latest incarnation in a new constitution that created new, racially based, "junior" houses of Parliament for Indians and Coloureds [people of mixed racial lineage]. The new constitution excluded Africans from anything but weak, local government on the grounds that Africans had "homelands" outside South Africa. These "homelands" had been part of South Africa before "grand apartheid" redrew the map to deny Africans any legitimacy or rights in South Africa.

With its affiliates, the UDF had held rallies and press conferences, organized boycotts and petitions, and called for a national convention to redesign South Africa's constitution. It organized mass protests, insisting that the majority would never be content with anything less than full citizenship and equality in the country of their birth and that political rights for the majority did not mean anything the minority need fear. It called for a nonracial, democratic, unfragmented society.

Founded in August 1983, the UDF had initially seemed too weak to be worth suppressing. Within a year, it had become the most powerful voice of opposition in the country. To the government, it seemed impossible that this strength had only local, lawful roots. The UDF, the prosecution would allege for the government, must be working hand in glove with South Africa's enemies, taking orders from the banned African National Congress, conspiring with the banned South African Communist Party to bring about violent revolution. The prosecution amassed documents, videos, and witnesses to prove this relationship, and, in the eyes of the judge did prove it, although his verdict shows signs of having to reach over the weakness of the prosecution's case to what he knew must be true. He believed it impossible for leaders as skillful as those he condemned, as successful, as thoughtful, and as well informed, could really be acting in isolation from the ANC for which they confessed open respect (although they said they differed from it on the issue of violence).

There had been violence in South Africa before the UDF was formed. The UDF said it wanted to end violence. Molefe, General Secretary of the UDF, claimed the UDF had worked for a future that would make reconciliation, peace, and cooperation possible.

All we are saying is that you cannot perpetually deny people a vote in the country of their birth. You cannot forever suppress people through force when they speak out against your policies. You cannot forever deny them a share in the wealth they have built with their own sweat and labor. If you do that, inevitably you have a situation where an increasing number will lose hope in the methods of peaceful struggle. They will go and join those who have taken up arms. That is the reality of our situation. We do not see ourselves working for that. We see ourselves playing the role of persuading the government to move away from these policies. (14:335–36)

The UDF, the defendants said, was prodded into being in 1983 by proposals for the new constitution that firmly excluded Africans from representation in Parliament. At the same time, the constitution would create "junior" houses, less powerful than the minority Parliament, for South Africans of Indian descent and Coloureds.

We are saying in the United Democratic Front, if this new constitution is allowed to go on, we are allowing them to create a worse situation. We are allowing them actually to deepen the amount of racial and violent conflict that is in the country. That is why we are taking the risk of mobilizing the people, of calling upon them not to go and vote. We know we can go to gaol. We will lose our jobs, our families will be left starving, but it is a bit

that we can do ... If this government is stopped now ... our country, many lives can be saved. That is why we are taking this risk.
We are asking you to join up ... Refuse with your vote, but join us
as well. Mobilize more and more people to say with us, apartheid
is unacceptable. Let the world know ... That is the nature of our
contribution. If that does not happen, the scale of dissatisfaction
must lead to a deepening amount of armed conflict. (14:336–37)

During the years in which the UDF became the voice of opposition, the violence that had started before it was formed flared out
into the country. On September 3, 1984, rent protests in an area near
Johannesburg called the Vaal Triangle escalated into five mob murders and days of arson and looting that stimulated a new level of
violence throughout the country. Black city councillors and other
government officials were killed. Government offices, courts, police
stations, and stores were bombed.

The government sent the army to supplement police power by
cordoning off and occupying the black townships. There, unequal
battles, with stones and Molotov cocktails on one side, and bullets
and tear gas on the other, produced large numbers of dead and
wounded.

Opponents of apartheid had long pleaded for sanctions against
South Africa: now each evening's newscast made sanctions more
likely. The government knew it had to do something to stop an economic crisis that could bring minority rule to an end.

The Delmas prosecutors charged that the UDF had caused the
violence. Its leaders, "the conspiratorial core inside the UDF apple,"
had plotted with the banned African National Congress and with the
banned South African Communist Party to make the country ungovernable, to foment revolution, and to engineer black rule.[4]

Within a few months of the United Democratic Front's launch,
August 20, 1983, its meetings were banned. Soon after, its leaders
were being detained. Despite frequent official denials by UDF leaders, government media described the UDF as the internal wing of
the African National Congress, and, therefore, as proponents of violence.

In October 1984, while South Africa seemed to be approaching
a condition of civil war, Bishop Desmond Tutu, a patron of the UDF,
was awarded the Nobel Peace Prize.

As the violence increased, the government blamed and denounced the UDF more fiercely and took more people into deten-

tion. Some UDF leaders sought refuge in the British embassy. Pressured by international criticism, President P. W. Botha, nicknamed "the Big Crocodile," offered to free Mandela, the leading patron of the UDF—if Mandela accepted conditions. At a UDF rally, February 10, 1985, to celebrate Tutu's Nobel Peace Prize, Mandela's daughter read an answer: Mandela would renounce violence if the government renounced violence.

In less than two weeks, February 19, 1985, sixteen senior leaders of the UDF were arrested and charged with treason. Molefe, the General Secretary, and Lekota, the Publicity Secretary, the only two full-time paid officials of the UDF, escaped that haul. A few months later, they were arrested and indicted for treason. They, and twenty others, not all members of the UDF, were accused of working through the Vaal Civic Association to instigate violence in the Vaal and so to begin the revolution by making the country ungovernable.

At the opening of what would be named the Delmas Trial, on June 11, 1985, policemen with automatic weapons surrounded the court, blocked off a road leading to it, and took videotapes of observers.

Setting the tone of incivility and coldness between the lawyers that characterized the trial, the prosecution refused to translate the 361-page indictment into English, although English is one of the two official languages of South Africa. The trial itself was conducted in Afrikaans when the prosecution took the lead and in English when the defense took the lead. Testimony in African languages was interpreted into either English or Afrikaans.

The indictment cited 911 co-conspirators. It charged that UDF policies and campaigns inspired events in the Vaal Triangle in 1984 where protests reached a boiling point and the murders of four councillors and another man. The charges were so comprehensive that one of the defense lawyers, George Bizos, said, "If we understand the indictment correctly, or some aspects of it, it would appear that because the UDF campaigned against the Black Local Authorities, you . . . as an office bearer of the UDF, are responsible for everything that happened in the country, even during the period that you were under detention." (15:780) The period of indictment included periods in which the defendants had been in prison.

The prosecution alleged that the actions of the UDF were treasonable because its actions, although purporting to be nonviolent, were in fact violent. These actions were part of a "sinister web" of overlapping organizations, of a conspiracy with a "revolutionary alliance" of the ANC and the South African Communist Party to overthrow the state by violence.

Although the Delmas prosecution nailed its case firmly to allegations of violence, it did not allege that any of the defendants personally and physically participated in the murders in the Vaal, and it never proved other violence done or planned by the defendants. An American legal observer in 1986 noted that the prosecution felt its case to be particularly difficult, because it was essentially a case of "psychic treason," as contrasted with "physical treason." (Kees van Dijkhorst would cite an analogy with spying in his judgment. Spying is treason without violence.)

During the years Molefe and Lekota spent behind bars, as violence deepened and spread throughout the country, the government imposed states of emergency that superseded the rule of law. More than three thousand people, many of them children, were taken into detention. There are reports that many were tortured. Several died in prison and in continuing violence outside. Much of the violence was described by the government as "black on black" and attributed to tribal conflict. Some allege that violence was fomented by the police. Numbers and accurate information are hard to come by—severe censorship forbids accounts of police action and disturbances.

Vigilante killings supplemented official power. Old resentments, private feuds, and tribal conflicts found camouflage and fuel in the widespread turmoil.

The world watched as people torched and axed each other, as policemen attacked children scaling school fences, as enraged mobs attacked those they identified as collaborators and "necklaced" them with burning tires, and as government officials (explaining that all this was the work of outside agitators and communists) promised that they would soon restore order. They promised to "reform" the system, and they said that they rejected apartheid. They still intended to keep the minority in control of the country.

Leaders of the UDF died in prison, on country roads, and in vigilante killings at their own homes. Most foreign media reverted to cursory coverage of the dangerous and discouraging story.

In the courtroom, the slow legal battle was conducted by teams that seemed to embody the principles at stake. The defense team seemed a model for a South Africa made up of all races, languages, and genders—the kind of South Africa Molefe and Lekota want to create.

Arthur Chaskalson, head of the team, tall, dark, and sober in demeanor, is known and honored internationally for his human rights work. He heads Legal Resources Center, an organization that has fostered public interest law and helped make the law one of the bastions of the struggle to create a post-apartheid South Africa where human rights will be respected. George Bizos, portly and grizzled, a veteran of political trials in South Africa, was the other eminent senior lawyer, famous for his skill at cross-examination. He and Chaskalson were part of the team when Mandela was tried in 1964.

Bizos was born in Calamata in Greece. When he was a boy and the Germans occupied Greece, his father decided that they could not live under Nazi rule. They set off in a small boat for Crete. A British destroyer stopped them in mid-Mediterranean to ask what they thought they were doing, told them that Crete was temporarily occupied by the Germans, and took them off to Alexandria. A while later, they were sent to South Africa: refugees traveled first class; prisoners of war, economy.

Bizos described the defendants' stance as like Socrates' rather than Gandhi's. Gandhi admitted breaking laws for higher principle. Molefe and Lekota said they obeyed the laws. Perhaps Socrates' case was not a happy omen of success.

Karel Tip, younger than Chaskalson but with something like his tall, dignified demeanor, was born in Holland. He had been president of the National Union of South African Students, an organization that continually criticized apartheid. He and five other student leaders had been tried on charges of terrorism, in a trial prosecuted by Philip Jacobs, head of the Delmas prosecution, defended by Chaskalson, and acquitted. The experience persuaded Tip to take up law. Several of the younger defendants in the Delmas Trial now talk of taking up law.

Like Bizos, Gilbert Marcus, in his early thirties, enjoys good stories. He has worked on several important censorship cases, including one that secured open publication of the ANC's Freedom Charter. Frances Potter and Caroline Heaton Nichols, a graduate of the same exclusive girls' prep school, used to go into the townships at night looking for witnesses. Most whites would have thought they were risking their lives. Zak Yacoob, from the Indian community in Natal, is blind but compensates. He cross-examined a witness using graphic exhibits, saying, "If you look in the top left hand corner, you will see . . ."

The prosecution team, led by Philip Jacobs, with gray hair and gray skin, reminded me of the kind of middle manager in a large corporation who knows where all the bodies are buried. Paul Fick, with a thick neck and stout body, younger, and more energetic, looked to me like an ambitious salesman.

The judge, Kees van Dijkhorst, had a reputation for brilliance and had made judgments in labor law that won him the praise of union leaders. He had never handled a political case before. From his bearing and demeanor, Lekota immediately guessed that van Dijkhorst was a "Dopper" and had his guess confirmed. The "Doppers" are Afrikaners whose ancestors, hearing about the Enlightenment in Europe, the American Revolution and the French Revolution, perceived that the ideas fueling these changes would undermine the fundamentalist values of their own lives and resolved to extinguish these ideas. Resisting the Enlightenment, they called themselves Extinguishers, "Doppers." A *dopper* is, literally, the metal hood that snuffs out a candle flame. In Afrikaner history, the "Doppers" are those who chose darkness. The "Dopper" church was founded in 1859 "by fundamentalists who objected to the singing of hymns in church."[5] Dopper culture tends to be severe, abstemious, legalistic, and focused on individuals. It has held aloof from the virtually total identification of state and church that characterized the other two Dutch Reformed churches. Lekota, gregarious, fond of good food when he can get it, politically adroit, and rooted in a highly communal culture that expresses its vision in singing, believed that he had been judged guilty before he was tried.

It was not the lawyers or the judge, imprisoned in a high, canopied oak bench, who caught the eye in the courtroom. Molefe and Lekota were the visible focus of energy. Seated in a long dock specially constructed for Mandela's trial a generation ago, they talked quietly with each other, passed notes to counsel and other defendants like irrepressible school children, looked at newspapers, journals, and catalogs from which they could order clothes—they had been in prison more than three years—turned round to see observers, waved to friends and smiled. Sometimes defendants out on bail dozed off in the dock. During the Byzantine processes of the law there was not much for them to do most of the time except, perforce, be present. Lekota and Molefe never seemed tired or bored. They were working. For a few minutes before and after sessions they talked with those who had come to see them—nuns, scholars, political leaders, alumni of other political trials, business executives, un-employed men, government spies, ambassadors. Supporters from the Vaal came by bus twice each week, simply to be there, support, representatives of thousands throughout the country.

During the first days of the trial, these visitors had traveled even farther when the trial was moved to the small town of Bethal and then to Delmas, an hour's drive from both Pretoria and Johannes-burg, and a 40-mile drive each way in a closed police van for the prisoners. The prisoners, many the sole support of their families, some confined since September and October 1984, were even far-ther away from their families. Several suffered health problems. One had been hospitalized for severe depression. During the long months when the proceedings in Delmas slipped from the front pages to obscurity, the defendants wondered whether they had been totally forgotten and abandoned. But they thought it important to show indomitable spirit to their supporters, and in court, they im-pressed almost everyone who came to the proceedings by their cheerfulness, confidence, and friendliness. By the last days, when I visited, the trial had been moved to the Supreme Court in Pretoria, and the police detail had been reduced to six.

Most of the foreign visitors talked first with Lekota. Built bigger than Molefe, and with a constant and unmistakable smile that shows a center tooth missing, he is the United Democratic Front's publicity secretary and has an "American" political style: a few days after we met, during the closing weeks of the trial, he gave me a UDF pin. Molefe, smaller boned and darker, sometimes wearing glasses, ini-tially comes across as quieter. Both give an immediate impression of deep warmth, of delight in the people they talk with. It was not difficult to imagine, in the courtroom where Mandela had testified in 1964, the qualities of leadership that lead people to describe Mo-lefe and Lekota as the Mandelas of their generation.

After more than three years of court proceedings, Kees van Dijk-horst took four days to read an abbreviated version of his 1,521-page decision. During the latter part of the trial, he had granted bail to all except Molefe, Lekota, and Moses Chikane. On the first day of read-ing the verdict, he rescinded bail for eight others. On the last day of reading, he found Molefe, Lekota, Chikane, and a fourth, Thomas Manthata, not a member of the UDF, guilty of treason. He found seven others guilty of terrorism.

Archbishop Tutu said, "If this is treason, then I am guilty of trea-son." Helen Suzman, a veteran Member of Parliament and opponent apartheid said, "It narrows the margin in this country between lawful dissent and what is considered treason."[6] The U.S. State Department said South Africa had perverted the judicial system for political ends.

At the time of this writing, Molefe and Lekota are out of prison. They are likely to play an important role in a new South Africa and become widely known abroad as well as at home.

The kind of society they want to create is suggested by Lekota's words on hearing the verdict: "We are not ashamed of anything we have done. Not one thing. We will correct things in this country." Gesturing to the judge and prosecutors, he promised a new order that would protect them and their role. "Those of us who have gone through the fire will be playing the very role of defending these people."[7]

Part One
The Defendants

2 "Chief" Molefe

The defense introduced the evidence in chief of Molefe, Lekota, and other defendants by having them give a brief description of their lives. The defense hoped that these biographies would show the character of the defendants, and how they had been drawn into political activity by personally experienced and legitimate grievances, not by theoretical commitment to abstract ideology.

The defendants' descriptions of their lives became testimony about what apartheid means to those who suffer it and became an education to some who heard it. W. F. Krugel, one of the two assessors who sat with the judge in place of a jury to assist him in judging matters of fact, a magistrate paid by the government, a man who had helped dispose of the assets of anti-apartheid organizations banned in 1977, reputedly a member of the Broederbond, a secret society dedicated to Afrikaner supremacy, said after listening to the testimony of one defendant, Ephraim Ramakgula, that it was the saddest story he had ever heard.

At the time of his arrest, Popo Simon Molefe was thirty-three, the father of two children, one born a few days before his confinement in April 1985 on charges of treason. His story takes him from penury to a leadership position in the largest opposition organization in South Africa.

He was born April 26, 1952 in Sophiatown, outside Johannesburg, the fourth of eight children. His father, an ordinary laborer, and mother, a domestic servant, could not afford to maintain all the children. He was handed over to his paternal aunt who brought him up with his three sisters. When his uncle died in 1960, his aunt found work as a live-in domestic servant.

She had to occupy a backyard room in her employer's yard. She would only come home once per month. So the children were

cared for by my aunt's eldest daughter and other members in the
home like the step-daughter of my aunt.... I personally grew up
under very very difficult conditions, conditions that one could describe as of extreme poverty, and as a result of that I learned to
fend for myself at a very very young age. I had to do various
things to earn a living. Among these things were selling apples and
peanuts at the football grounds, selling apples at the railway stations on weekends and late in the afternoons when workers were
coming back from work. I also had to look for jobs as a caddy at
various golf courses on weekends. (13:114)

During those days we had to travel every morning to the golf
course. There were a lot of youngsters from various townships of
Soweto who were also going to the golf course, [and] every morning there were very long queues [lines] of those who stood there
to caddy. Therefore it became necessary for us to wake up very
early to catch the first train so that we would be the first in the
queue. This meant waking up at about three in the morning, and I
remember [that] when I went to the course I was chased around
by a group of thugs who wanted money from us. One night I was
so terrified I had to go back home. But on other occasions I man-
aged to run away, but there were other occasions on which they
actually got me and I had to part with the little cent I had.
(13:125)

At the age of ten, Molefe went to school for the first time but
could not afford the compulsory school uniform and dropped out.
At twelve, an older brother who had started working paid for his
education and he started right from the bottom of the ladder.

One had to go to school very hungry, sometimes without
even having had breakfast. I remember very specifically one day
on my way to school, I was so hungry that I became dizzy on the
way and I had to stop and lean on the fence, and finally I collapsed
and fainted because I was very hungry. (13:116)

He remembers a day it snowed in Johannesburg, in 1964:

It was a very terrible morning. I had no pair of shoes and only
a short pants and a shirt and a jersey [sweater]. I had to walk to
school that morning without shoes on. It was such a terrible day
in my life it has left a very indelible impression in my mind.

There were many other young boys and girls who also had to
walk to school without shoes on. (13:116)

For four years he did not have money to pay school fees so his class teachers paid and gave him books. At a new school in third grade, he was unable to pay.

Every time those who did not have money to pay were sent home to go and look for that money. Every morning we got into class and we were asked, "Why are you not paying?" How could our parents send us to school without paying for us? I felt so much embarrassed and so much humiliated that I finally decided I was no longer going to go to school. After a couple of weeks, the teacher sent some boys to call me back to school. (13:117)

A company selling condensed milk ran a competition for collecting milk labels and gave notebooks as a prize. That year he worked very hard to be able to get as many books as possible.

After fifth grade Molefe won education scholarships every year and used the money he earned to pay for younger sisters to go to school. He was twenty-four when he reached the final year of high school.

Really that kind of situation typifies the lives of the black people in the township. You find many young people at the age at which they should have completed their university studies still at high school. (13:118)

Molefe's home was devoutly Christian. Almost every Sunday everybody went to the Lutheran church. Molefe was confirmed in church, and he sang in the choir. He participated in the Student Christian movement and a church-sponsored Teen Talent Club. He considers himself a Christian and, like many of the supporters who came to the trial, sees connections between his religious and political principles.

CHASKALSON: Have your religious attitudes had any influence on your political involvement?

MOLEFE: That is so. I was influenced wisely by the principle of love for one's neighbor and love for one's fellow man. That is the principle that really influenced me. And I have always believed that conditions should develop in which the love for one's neighbor can find a practical manifestation in the day-to-day interaction in life. (13:122)

Molefe sometimes went to visit his aunt.

MOLEFE: Black domestics were allowed to live with their employers in the backyard room, they were not allowed to bring their children or members of their family to that yard. It was very difficult. Those who were going there had to stay for a brief time and they were not supposed to be seen by their employers. So when I visited my aunt, very often I had to hide in her backyard room so that her employers should not see me.

I remember on one occasion travelling through a white suburb in Johannesburg, Westdene. I was going to my aunt. On my way, I saw a young child playing in the street, a white boy, about my age. When I passed there, he started taunting me, calling me *kaffir* [nigger]. I ignored him because I was very scared. As I ignored him, he went on taunting me, calling me a *kaffir, swart gat* [like "kaffir," a term of contempt; literally, "black hole."] and so on. He ended up slapping me in the face with an open hand. I hit back at him.

There was an adult white woman coming from the opposite direction. She threatened to assault me for doing what I did to this white boy. I felt very angry, perturbed and terrified. I could not understand why this adult white woman should have treated me the way she did when she should have reprimanded this boy.

CHASKALSON: Did you notice any difference between white living conditions and black living conditions when you would move into white areas to visit your aunt?

MOLEFE: Oh yes. I know of no white area that has got no tarred [paved] roads. I know of no white area that has got no electricity. I know of no white area that has got a shack. I know of no white area that has got no properly built house. There is a marked difference. Even before you enter any white house, you see these things. There are parks. There are nice hedge trees around some fences. There are lawns in the yards. There are road signs at every important intersection. These things are not there in the black townships . . .

CHASKALSON: I want to ask about other possible influences. While you were growing up in Soweto, did the police ever come to the house?

MOLEFE: Yes, they did on a number of occasions.

CHASKALSON: Why would they come?

MOLEFE: During those days there were policemen called the Black Jacks. It seems to have been a routine job of theirs to go

from time to time at the wee hours of the morning, going into
houses to check for permits, seeing if there were not any illegals
in the houses.... First when they came into the house, they
would knock on every door, or sometimes knock on windows,
lighting with [flashlights] through the windows, and once they got
in they would get everyone out of bed. Sometimes when this happened, people had to get out of bed undressed, or dressed only in
nightdresses and so on. It was very humiliating to see this happening in front of children, but that is how it happened very often,
and they would insult people, "Get up!" "Do this!" "Who are you?"
"Where is your permit?" ...

CHASKALSON: Were you ever arrested?

MOLEFE: Yes, I was.

CHASKALSON: How old were you when you were first arrested?

MOLEFE: I could have been about twenty, twenty-one. I am
not sure.

When I was arrested, I was standing right in front of my home.
I was arrested for not having my reference book with me. I told
the policeman, I live in this house. If he would allow me the opportunity, I would go and fetch it and show it to him. He refused
to allow me to do that. Instead, he handcuffed me and insisted
that I must accompany them. We walked some distance, possibly
five kilometers, and after that they decided to release me and un-
cuffed me and told me to go back home.

CHASKALSON: Did you ever spend time in jail?

MOLEFE: Yes, I did ... I was on my way to Krugersdorp and I
was travelling by train. I alighted at the Langlaagte station, and I
was supposed to buy a ticket there. Just when I got out of the sub-
way, there were policemen outside. They asked me for a reference
book. I did not have it with me, and they decided to arrest me.
They took me to the Langlaagte police station. I was locked up
there in a cell until a friend of mine who was with me at the time
went to my home to fetch mine, and I was later released.

CHASKALSON: Did you know whether white people had to
carry reference books?

MOLEFE: I know of no white person who was required to
carry a reference book.... I know of no white man who was arrested for not carrying a reference book. (13:125–27)

In 1973, when Molefe was twenty-one and in high school, the
government was enforcing the policy of ethnic differentiation. In

pursuit of that policy, it sought to take all the Zulu-speaking children out of his school and send them to another. The students called a meeting to discuss the issue and resolved to tell the principal that they were unhappy with the decision and to ask him to communicate their opposition to the Inspector for the region. The outcome was that those children were not sent away.

The following year, Molefe became assistant head boy. He helped organize senior students to tutor juniors.

He joined the Youth Hostel Association and took trips to Lesotho and Botswana. He was a member of the South African Student Movement whose main activities were organizing book discussions for the students on the subjects with which they had problems and on methods of improving relationships between students, parents, and teachers.

He also joined the Black People's Convention, without formally enrolling.

MOLEFE: As I understood it at that time, the philosophy behind the Black People's Convention was to develop the attitude of mind that would enable black people to overcome the attitude of feeling inferior to white people. They should strive to demonstrate that they had dignity [like] any other human being, and they were capable of doing anything that any other human being was able to do. Really, it was a response to apartheid . . .

CHASKALSON: Were you in Soweto in 1976?

MOLEFE: That is so. [Molefe was due to write the state examination for high school graduation, called the "matriculation" examination or "matric."]

CHASKALSON: And you were Head Boy of your school?

MOLEFE: That is so.

CHASKALSON: Was that the year of the school protests in Soweto?

MOLEFE: That is correct.

CHASKALSON: What was the protest? Why did they spring up all over?

MOLEFE: The fundamental cause of the protest was the attempt by the government to impose . . . [both] English and Afrikaans in Black schools as . . . media of instruction . . .

CHASKALSON: Did the schools remain open or did they close down?

MOLEFE: They closed down.

CHASKALSON: Was there violence in the township?

MOLEFE: There was.

CHASKALSON: Did you yourself witness any violence?

MOLEFE: Yes, I did.

CHASKALSON: Were people killed in the township?

MOLEFE: There were several people killed and several injured. I know at least one boy who was a very bright boy, who I know very well from Diepkloof, Abion Lebelo, who died round that period.

CHASKALSON: Was there heavy police presence during that time?

MOLEFE: There was heavy police presence all over. In fact, it was even dangerous for students to walk around the streets because walking around the streets in uniform seems to have been the shortest way of either getting shot or arrested by the police, yet at the same time, it was crucial for students to wear uniforms to ensure a clear distinction between the students and the mobs which were roaming the streets at the time. And it was also important because at that stage, students could only be respected by the mobs if they were seen in uniform. If you were seen as one of them, sometimes you were running the risk of being attacked by the mobs themselves. So, really, one was finding himself in a Catch-22 situation. If you put on school uniform, you got arrested or attacked by the police. And if you do not, you have a problem with thugs in the townships.

CHASKALSON: Did you yourself witness any shootings in Soweto at that time?

MOLEFE: Yes, I did.

CHASKALSON: Were you yourself arrested at that time?

MOLEFE: I was arrested some time in August 1976.

CHASKALSON: Were you kept in detention?

MOLEFE: Yes, I was kept in detention, in solitary confinement . . . for about seven months.

CHASKALSON: Were charges ever brought against you?

MOLEFE: No charges were brought against me. . . . It strengthened my resolve to continue opposing the legislation based on a policy of apartheid. . . . I found it a very humiliating experience, a very bitter experience. . . .

When I came out of detention, I took serious interest, now, in politics, and I started attending meetings of the Black People's Convention . . . I could not go back to school. While I was employed, I studied on a part-time basis, and I wrote my exams and took my matric. Later on, I enrolled at the University of South Africa with the hope of studying towards a degree in Bachelor of Commerce . . . I did not have time to study, and I failed. I could not pass, and I abandoned my studies. But I hoped that I would again, under better conditions, pursue my studies. (13:130–33)

The Black People's Convention was outlawed in October 1977 and the following year Molefe became a founding member of a new political organization, the Azanian People's Organization, AZAPO. At the invited meeting where the decision to found AZAPO was made, a steering committee was set up to lay the basis for the actual launching of AZAPO. A few days after, about five of the people on the steering committee were arrested.

Molefe was elected chair of the Soweto branch. (13:136)

He began to articulate ideas and practices that would be central to the UDF. One was collaboration across ideological divisions. As chair of AZAPO, he initiated a discussion aimed at drawing together organizations to deal with problems of common concern. Several organizations joined to demonstrate against rent increases in 1980 and against celebrating the twentieth anniversary of South Africa's becoming a republic in 1981.

Experience simply tells us that it is only when people are united in a broader sense that they are able to be effective. They can speak with one voice. They can be heard. (13:154)

Since 1976, the official Urban Bantu Council had become ineffective. Critics called it the Useless Boys' Club. A Committee of Ten was widely perceived as the real leader of the community. In October 1977 all members of the Committee of Ten were detained. (This was when Krugel, one of the Delmas assessors, disposed of the assets of newly banned anti-apartheid organizations.) By September 1979, when all had been released, Molefe attended a meeting where the Committee decided to form a broader, more grass-roots organization. It became the Soweto Civic Association and the Committee of Ten became its executive.

In May 1981, addressing the South African Conference of Churches, Molefe called for a united front including a broad range of organizations, like the SACC itself, to work together.

[To expose] political careerists, self-seekers, quislings and sell-outs who daily help the oppressive structure to realize its aims; to heighten political activity aimed at exposing the evil machinery that perpetuates our servitude; to [create] a broad opposition structure to [galvanize] the masses against the common anguish; to rout the system and its agents who operate within liberation movements and black organizations. (13:157)

In developing a strategy to gradually reintroduce people terrified by police repression to political action, the leaders of the struggle in South Africa fostered civic associations throughout the country where people could articulate their day-to-day concerns and begin to act jointly on them. Many of these civic associations would become affiliates of the UDF.

The Vaal Civic Association figured importantly in the Delmas Trial. Its members helped organize a march on September 3, 1984 to protest rent increases in the apartheid ghettoes of the Vaal Triangle, and the prosecution said it had fomented the violence that erupted on September 3. The VCA was an affiliate of the UDF. The prosecution charged that it was a conduit for UDF propaganda to mobilize the masses for revolutionary violence. The judge intervened early in Molefe's testimony to ask:

What do you understand under a civic association?

MOLEFE: I understand a civic association to be a broad, community-based organization that concerns itself immediately with what one could call the bread and butter issues, the problems experienced by the residents relating to housing, services at that level, facilities, health care, problems related to education, high rentals, how these are determined, and so on. A whole range of issues really that affected the community. But I must also point out that very often, because of the interconnection between what happens at a local level and what happens nationally, they tended to be influenced or called to respond to the issues that arise as a result of the national policy of the government. . . .

The civic association is a broad organization that is supposed to cater to the interest of a broad community, and within that community you have people with different backgrounds and different interests, and committed to different ideological positions, and so on. A civic association seeks to bring all those kind of people together. Because of the crucial position that it occupies, it is not in a position to commit itself to a single ideological position. So it would really find itself accommodating all sorts of people on the basis of the problems they experience at a local level. (13:142–43)

In 1981, believing that whites must be included in opposing apartheid, Molefe resigned from AZAPO.

Whilst they accepted the fact that white people had a role to play in advancing the process of change, they did not see that happening by [including] white people in their own organization, or by participating in any joint program with organizations which had white members. (13:169)

Molefe believed something deeply rooted and pervasive in his own values—means must be consonant with ends, and present action must show forth the future it desires.

We had to convince the white people that if we are building the future and the future is non-racial in character, that process, that goal must manifest itself in the course of the structure for that future. (13:169)

In 1982, Molefe was elected to the Committee of Ten.

At the meeting that elected him, there was discussion of upcoming legislation to establish Black Local Authorities. The Soweto Civic Association resolved to boycott elections held in terms of the Black Local Authorities Act and to cooperate with other organizations that had a similar attitude. One of the objects of the UDF would be opposition to the BLAs and to related legislation, called the Koornhof bills, after the minister who sponsored them.

In 1982, the government proposed a new constitution creating two "junior" houses of Parliament, one for people of mixed race, called Coloureds, and one for people of Indian descent. There was to be no parliamentary voice for Africans. The proposed constitution provoked great anger from various quarters in the black community. Many saw it as part of a plan to maintain apartheid by co-opting some blacks and dividing those opposed to apartheid. Dr. Allan Boesak called for a united front to oppose the new constitution. In March, Molefe was invited to join discussions about creating a United Democratic Front. (The prosecution alleges that the United Democratic

Front answered a call from Oliver Tambo, head of the African National Congress, made in his annual address, January 8, 1983.) In May, a United Democratic Front formed in the Transvaal Province to oppose the Koornhof bills and the new constitution. At the end of July representatives of united fronts in several parts of the country decided to launch a national United Democratic Front the following month. Soon after, in August, they appointed an executive with Molefe as a member. They focused on the considerable logistical work; developing a program and working principles; publicizing the launch; consulting with organizations like trade unions; and consulting with lawyers to ensure that they were acting within the law. At the launch, August 20, 1983, there was a conference and a rally. "Prior to the rally, a conference of 2,000 delegates and observers from more than 500 organizations around South Africa adopted the national declaration which [formed] the basis for cooperation between organizations of the UDF." (13:194) Molefe was elected National Secretary. When people first proposed the role,

> **I had a lot of reluctance. . . . I felt I did not have the necessary experience to handle that kind of job . . . it was just too big a job for me. (13:198)**

But he accepted, resigning from his position as a machinist at the processing laboratories of Kodak, South Africa, to become one of the two full-time, paid officials of the UDF. He was thirty-one. He had become a leader in virtually every organization he had joined. Practical, patient, political, choosing the background as comfortably as the foreground, he set about attending to the mundane, essential circumstances that create "conditions . . . in which the love for one's neighbor can find a practical manifestation in the day-to-day interaction in life."

3 "Terror" Lekota

Mosiuoa Patrick Gerard Lekota turned forty a few months before the end of the trial. His third child was born shortly after his arrest and indictment for treason.

He was born August 15, 1948, in Kroonstad, in the heartland of Afrikanerdom. He was the first of seven children. One brother died during the last weeks of the trial.

Lekota was not drawn into political activism by extreme childhood poverty like Molefe.

I had a home, and I had my parents, and I had somewhere to return to when the sun set. (15:444)

Lekota's political involvement seems to stem from his zest for being where the action is, his curiosity, and his lively habit of looking at things from the perspective of others.

In Molefe's testimony, there are many references to "experience" as a source of learning and touchstone of authenticity, but allusions to his childhood are implicit. They come in the rare moments when emotions carry him into eloquence about the sufferings and indignities imposed by apartheid. Lekota's testimony is more openly emotional and often personal. His occasional references to boys stealing peaches, to his experiences as a boy scout calling for attention in front of the camp fire, to soccer, imply a happy childhood not as cramped by poverty as Molefe's. His father ran a soccer team in the early sixties and Lekota played in it. He has been an ardent sports fan ever since. He has other memories too.

When my father had gone to work, and especially if he did not come back on time, my mother would say we must go and look in his jacket or overall . . . It meant we must go and find out whether his pass was not forgotten there, and maybe he might not be coming back because he had been arrested for a pass offense. The fact that the pass was not there, did not imply that he might not have been arrested for it, because people leave home sometimes with a pass and on the way a pickpocket takes it out. But when you go around the corner, and the policeman says, "Where is your pass?" whether you have it or you do not have it. If you do not have it, you get into the lorry, and then you are off . . .

What threatens the family, the fears, filter through to the younger children. You can feel something that is dangerous. If a dog approaches a family, everybody tries to go and stand behind their father because he might do something with the dog. So, the pass had been a threat to me as an individual. (15:445)

I have spent many nights when I have been sitting at home as a little child, and I have been worried when my father was not coming back home, and we did not know whether he was arrested for a pass or what, and we were all terrified. We would sit there with wide eyes wondering what is going to happen, because

if he does not come back, there is no money ... who is going to pay the rent? ... and everybody is uncomfortable, including my mother. (16:670)

After school in Kroonstad, Lekota attended mission schools in the Transkei, and then in Marianhill, Natal where he played soccer so ardently the sports master in 1965 gave him a nickname that has stuck, and sometimes needs explanation: Terror. He would become an amateur middleweight boxing champion, and he played rugby as well as soccer. Steve Biko came to know him as a member of the school soccer team.

He completed high school, winning a distinction in Southern Sotho, taught part-time at Marianhill, and then found work as a court interpreter.

That experience exposed me to the depth of what the pass laws and influx control laws meant in African life, and what it was doing to my community. (15:444)

Lekota has more formal education than other defendants in the Delmas Trial. After his stint on the official side of court procedure, he resigned to attend Turfloop, a university set aside for black students and largely divided from other black universities according to ethnic group.

Early in 1972, his second year at Turfloop, all members of the Student Representative Council, including Lekota, were expelled for supporting a graduating student, Abraham Tiro, who criticized the university administration and apartheid education policies of the government. (Tiro was killed by a letter bomb sent to him in Botswana at the beginning of 1974.)

Although several other members of the SRC were readmitted to Turfloop the following year, Lekota was not. For a few months, he worked in community development projects undertaken by the South African Student Organization, SASO, an organization inspired by Biko. (Biko died in police custody in 1977. The inquest into his death exposed routine police brutality and torture.)

Asked to describe the philosophy of SASO in court, Lekota said it arose more or less parallel with the Black Theology movement. Lekota says he is a practicing Catholic, and among those who visited the courtroom were nuns, priests, and devout lay people. He did not say much about the Black Theology movement during his trial, but many of the leading figures associated with the United Democratic

Front, especially Dr. Allan Boesak and Rev. Frank Chikane, have been active in developing a theology and practice that believes that in South Africa, Christ, who chose a path of poverty and suffering, lives among those who are poor and who suffer, in short, that in this society, Christ is Black.

Fueled by this insight, theologians have led many churches in South Africa to declare apartheid a heresy. Religious figures of several denominations stand in the forefront of opposition to apartheid. Many sent greetings to the UDF when it was launched in August 1984. Some, like the Nobel Laureate Archbishop Desmond Tutu, have won international recognition for their leadership in the conflict they see as spiritual as well as political. Many are the subjects of assassination threats and attempts. In the closing weeks of the Delmas Trial, vigilantes bombed the offices of the South African Council of Churches and the South African Catholic Bishops Conference. Both organizations had been offering assistance to the defendants and their families.

In secular and political language, Lekota describes SASO as Black Consciousness.

> Our concern at that time was that a lot of black people . . . tended to look down on their own cultural heritage, their own humanity. . . . The thinking behind Black Consciousness was an attempt to say, you are black and for you to be a human being, you do not have to be white, you just have to accept yourself as you are. What makes you a human being is not the color of your skin, it is the content of your character. . . . Black Consciousness was defined as a state of mind and way of life in which you say, OK, the white man is a human being, but I am also a human being, just as equal. . . . The teaching of Black Consciousness remains relevant even in our own time. People must still just accept the fact that I am a human being as I am, and that I have got to be accepted as I am, but also that the humanity of black people must recognize the humanity of others as well. (15:448–51)

In 1973, Biko was banned by the South African government. His movements were restricted to a magisterial district more than sixty miles from any major city. (Banning forbids the banned person from being in the presence of more than two people, addressing an audience, or being quoted by the media.) It was too late to silence Biko's message, that "the most potent weapon in the hands of the oppressor is the mind of the oppressed."[1]

At the beginning of 1973, when Lekota saw that he would not be allowed to enroll anywhere as a student, he found work as a teller in a savings and loan bank.

On April 25, 1974 a revolution in Portugal created the first crack in the wall of white-ruled states between South Africa and the rest of Africa. The Portuguese colonies, whose struggle for independence had precipitated that revolution in Portugal, became independent. Black Consciousness groups organized rallies to celebrate the coming to power of a new government in Mozambique, which borders South Africa. The Minister of Justice banned the rallies the evening before they were scheduled. When crowds gathered at the rally sites, police unleashed dogs on them. Black leaders were detained. Lekota and eight others were charged with terrorism. The act that defined their crime describes terrorism as, among other things, an act that embarrasses the government; or that would "cause, encourage or further feelings of hostility between the White and other inhabitants of the Republic."[2]

In the same courtroom where Mandela had been found guilty in 1964 and where the Delmas verdict would be delivered in 1988, the nine defendants were tried:

> I recall quite well that in 1975, when we were charged in this same court, we used to come up here into the dock singing. (15:763)

Lekota used time in the dock to write.

> [One poem] was written in 1976, just where Accused No. 3 is sitting. I wrote it from there. [It] reflects what was said there in the [news]papers. Students were marching, and then all of a sudden, police let go with the shooting. Then for a while students were bewildered, because they had not expected anything of this nature. They started rioting, throwing stones, and things like that. There were pictures in the newspapers in subsequent days of some of them holding dustbin lids, because the teargas was being thrown around, and the bullets were being shot. So this poem details what took place, but I was sitting just here. (16:467)

During the 1974–75 trial, Lekota married Cynthia. They have three children.

The defendants were found guilty of what one newspaper described as "terrorism of the spirit."

Because really, we had not done anything. We had held public meetings, and we had made speeches, but there was no question of any kind of violence or encouragement of that. (15:447)

Biko testified at this trial in his last public appearance before his death.

Lekota was sentenced to six years on Robben Island, where he met Mandela, Sisulu, and other heroes.

These are names and these are men I had grown up hearing about. I had been told by my elders, uncles, aunts, grandparents and so on that these are the leaders of our people. So when I landed there it was a golden opportunity. For me it was important to learn the secret of the path my people had travelled, to find out from the men who had given everything, almost, that they had for the cause of freedom. I had come to the well of the history of my people. These are men who lived for nothing else, I discovered, but for the dream of a future democratic South Africa. From them I learnt the history of the century-long struggle of blacks in South Africa for political rights. . . .

There is a lot to learn from the history of the various people of our country, and I think that if the future of the country is to be shaped in a direction which will benefit all of its people, it is crucial that one understands the contribution of every one of the sections of population in the country.

Even more important, if one is going to reconcile the people of South Africa, it is important to understand them, and to understand each and every group in its historical context, to understand their fears, to understand their aspirations, to understand the path they have travelled to the present. It is for that reason that I busy myself with reading the history of the people of our country, discussing it where occasions arise. To formulate a perspective on the future path I think our country must ultimately take. (15:452–53)

The habit of reading history acquired on Robben Island continues. It is part of Lekota's lifelong purpose.

I have told the Court here I take particular interest in history, not only of the African people. I read extensively on the history of the white people, the Afrikaners, the English, the Indian people. I have read their history from India into this country. I have read the history of the African people from long before the white people came here. Even just the ordinary stories of the cultural background of the African people. When it is history, I just eat the books up.

Now I have a reason why I do that, because I concern myself with the social dynamics of our society, and I believe that if I have to make a meaningful contribution to the creation of a democratic society in this country, one in which the various racial groups of our country will be reconciled, I must first and foremost understand the people that I am talking about and talking to, understand their fears, and so on. It is imperative for me to know their history. I must go back to the Slagtersnek Rebellion.[3] I must come down like that with the history of the Afrikaner people, the origin of the language of the people. I eat it up, because I also believe that it is only when I know the people of my country and understand them that I can actually develop a love for them. It is very difficult to love people you do not even understand, and you do not know, and I seek to do that. (15:866)

In addition to being "a golden opportunity" to learn the history of South Africa, Robben Island became an opportunity for Lekota to rethink his adherence to Black Consciousness.

Some Black Consciousness followers argued that blacks should not have anything to do with whites. For Lekota, this view raised "immediate practical problems." It is clear from the context that these practical problems first present themselves as religious.

Some of us came from Catholic traditions, the Catholic Church, others from the Anglican Church, non-racial churches ... I have always felt that it would be more realistic to accept that there must be cooperation between black and white. (15:463)

Lekota does not reject Black Consciousness.

There must be a basis of equality. As long as the position remains in which we are underprivileged, in which we do not enjoy the humanity that others enjoy, this thinking that there must be equalization makes it necessary that there must remain talk of Black Consciousness. (15:463–64)

He was released on December 20, 1982, joined a Release Mandela Committee in 1983, and soon heard discussion about the formation of a United Democratic Front. He responded to this talk with skepticism. He did not think that enough organizations would support such a broad front, and he did not think the timing right. He debated against the idea but "the flood was moving against me." (15:466)

It was hard for him to resist the call to political action. He was invited to speak at a meeting commemorating the protests in Soweto in 1976, and he prepared a speech but had to cancel for an appendicitis operation.

In spite of his skepticism about the UDF, Lekota's name was put forward for the position of Publicity Secretary.

I myself was not keen at all to take up a position of that nature. I, just being released from prison, felt I needed to get a bit more orientation to the outside world. I also was of the intention to spend a bit more time with my family, which I had not been able to do for many years. (15:469)

He agreed to represent the Natal region at the national launch, went to Cape Town a few days early, and acted as one of several spokesmen at a press conference to introduce the UDF. At the launch, he accepted the position of Publicity Secretary and became Molefe's full-time colleague. He may have known that, whether he obeyed the law or not, by opposing the government he was risking another term in prison.

Asked in the trial whether he had ever considered exile, he answered:

No, I did not consider leaving the country. My view is that those of us who would like to help the process of change must remain at home.... My loyalties are to this country, and ... I cannot reconcile myself with the idea of leaving my country when I might never be able to come back to it. I have very strong ties with South Africa. As I have grown older, I have grown to understand that various other sections of the population other than the African population of which I form part, and my ties to the country are very strong....

Even if I got arrested, I would still have access to my people. I would still be in my country. If anything happened to me, I would go to the graveyard of my grandparents.... I belong here at home. The problems of the country are the problems of all of us. (15:605)

Part Two
The UDF

4 The Launch

Like the Pietermaritzburg Treason Trial, the Delmas Trial was aimed at the UDF through its key leaders. The prosecution presented the UDF as a sinister, conspiratorial body, the internal wing of a banned organization aiming to seduce the masses into the arms of international Communism and to destroy South Africa by mayhem leading to a black coup. This grandiose vision of the purpose and power of the UDF did not mark original government perceptions. At first, the UDF seemed harmless enough to merit no more than everyday reminders of who is in charge, like banning rallies, and taking leaders into detention.

To its supporters, the UDF seemed to promise more, from the first. The launch on August 20, 1983, was an occasion of hope. Many present felt that they were changing history. They were implementing a strategy that had begun with the creation of civic and special interest organizations. These organizations brought people together around common causes like high rents, poor schools, and inadequate sports facilities. Initially, in a society terrified by the repressions of the sixties and seventies, these organizations did not seem political to themselves or others, but they were nurseries of leadership where a new generation was learning how to speak for itself and for the people it represented. They were developing the skill to act together. The process had been systematic and incremental, building on successes. The people had been mobilized and organized. In 1983, the proposed new constitution was driving the definition of issues toward political action, and the people would come to frame their concerns in terms of political power.

In the UDF, grass-roots organizations affiliated to oppose apartheid, and especially to oppose the new constitution that they believed would perpetuate apartheid by co-opting members of the black community. In early 1983, affiliates first formed regional groups in the Transvaal, Natal, the Eastern Cape and the Western Cape. People who had created new bonds that let them speak together about parochial issues were joining each other to speak to the issues that united all at a wider, more universal level. The process reached a climax in mid-1983, in the decision to create a national UDF where all would speak for all. At the same time, since they were affiliates and not a party, none would have a right to coerce any other. The UDF was determined not to founder on the divisive strife that often characterizes those out of power.

At the launch of the national UDF on August 20, 1983, in Mitchell's Plain, a township near Cape Town, their policy began to take form in concerted national action. Each voice would become stronger by being united with others. In joining each other, they would identify and present the framework that united them. At the launch, they came together on the basis of one, fundamental agreement—opposition to apartheid. They defined apartheid itself nonracially, in terms of justice, as the exclusion of the majority from power. Without allowing internecine conflicts to divide them, without quibbling about ideological differences, members of the national UDF would invite the government to hear and to negotiate. They would invite the diverse peoples of South Africa to listen and to choose. They would invite the international community to see and to help. Speaking together, they were going to demonstrate a new South Africa.

Lekota testified:

> There was very wide interest in the moves to launch the UDF . . . The country was busy with debates about the new constitution. Various personalities had been unbanned. Really, a new spirit was abroad. . . . The National Forum Committee had been launched in April. So when the moves towards the launch of the UDF came up, it also excited a lot of interest, and we went down to Cape Town with all kinds of articles, speculations in the papers . . . (15:469)

Molefe recollects that the UDF was launched in a spirit of freedom and invitation:

> It was really a relaxed atmosphere, one that invited free thought and free action taking. . . . The government was saying that it . . . was in search of reform. . . . The big phrase of the time was power sharing, and therefore, as I understood it, we were being

invited to say what we wanted to see, or how we saw a peaceful future for our country shaped, therefore, as I understood the position, we were obliged to stand up and state our views as honestly as we could, as long as we did not use any violent methods. We were free to say what we wanted, and to put our suggestions forward to the government ... and we availed ourselves of the opportunity. (15:473)

At the same time that it was setting out to recreate the country and give it a new future, the launch needed to be organized in mundane and practical ways. Molefe, aware of both dimensions, had helped coordinate committees that attended to the logistics. Some logistics symbolized the UDF's desire to act within the law. They hired a large tent so that the crowds outside the hall would not break the law by being an outdoor gathering, and they appointed marshals to keep the crowd orderly. Delegates had come from all over the country, from every racial group, from many faiths and occupations. For a day, they would have the kind of community that manifested the country they wanted to start creating. Journalists commented on the unusually efficient organization of the rally.

The crowds were so large they spilled out of both the hall, where participants climbed on the rafters, and the hired tent, but the police did not harass those attending. They watched but did not interfere. Someone had printed leaflets announcing that the launch was canceled. Other leaflets advertised a rock concert at another site in Mitchell's Plain. In spite of the disinformation, the conference of 2,000 delegates was followed by a rally estimated at between 10,000 and 20,000. Describing it at the trial, Molefe presents the harmony and unity of the occasion as if it made real before his eyes the future to which he has dedicated his life.

That was a rally of the people of South Africa. White people were there. Coloured people were there. Africans. Indians. All of them came together in this massive event.... There was great enthusiasm at that rally. People were very happy, and they felt that this was a very, very historical event ... and all of them participated in the rally with great enthusiasm. (13:193)

Lekota had been busy with publicity and, the evening before the rally, chaired a press conference for about forty reporters and media people in a church near the Houses of Parliament. The reporters asked, among other things, about the UDF's attitude to violence. Lekota answered, setting the UDF between those it disagreed with on the one side and on the other, by saying that the UDF did not advocate or condone violence:

Neither in the form of spectacular explosions like the ANC, nor in the form of institutional violence [like apartheid]. (25:493)

The creation of the UDF would transform South Africa by introducing organization into protest that had been spontaneous, sporadic, and strategically null. Previous bursts of resistance, in Soweto, in other school protests, in protests against the local tyrannies of homeland tyrants, had resulted in enormous death and destruction among those already victimized by apartheid while achieving little to weaken the power or complacency of the apartheid regime.

The UDF, basing itself on issues people were already aware of, deepened people's understanding of how to act together toward a unified purpose. It taught them to recognize the political structures of apartheid as the cause of their suffering and the basis for their unity. In identifying compelling issues in local areas, the UDF planted itself deep in the concerns of everyday life and social intercourse. When the government did try to destroy the UDF, it could not stop people from talking about the buses they took to work, the high rents they paid, the heavy sales tax, the poor schools, or any of the other issues the UDF taught people to see as rooted in apartheid.

In accepting affiliates from many areas of interest, many different ideologies, and different ethnic and class backgrounds, the UDF modeled how to attain unity. It developed cadres of disciplined leaders. Its organization in networks of regional affiliates, fundamentally different in conception from the command structures understood by the prosecution, defied government repression. When the regime did try to extinguish this movement, it found the UDF too diffuse to control without massive detentions. In attempting to destroy the work of the UDF, the regime would display such an ugly face to the world it lost the appearance of legitimacy and critical support both abroad and at home.

By the time of the launch, on August 20, 1983, the UDF had united 400 organizations (soon to become 600), including practically every political and social body of note in black communities and some from white communities. It was reaching for the international support Molefe believed important to get the government to hear leaders of the majority. The UDF received messages of support from antiapartheid and church groups in England, Ireland, the United States of America, Canada, France, Sweden, Finland, Holland, Germany, Switzerland, Greece, Australia, and other countries. It knew itself as part of a struggle for human dignity. It received support from religious leaders of many faiths and denominations who saw apartheid as an offense to the human spirit and to God and who believed that the purpose of the front was spiritual as well as political. The President of the Catholic Bishops Conference wrote:

> Your purpose . . . is the intention to educate . . . all South Africans in the matters of human rights and political justice, by every peaceful method available to you. . . . The rights that you plan to promote are God given and sacred. (13:287)

Allan Boesak, a keynote speaker, framed the work of the UDF in terms that both address and transcend the politics of the moment. He said:

> The fear of the gun is always overcome by the longing for freedom. You can kill the body, but you can never kill the spirit and the determination of a people . . .
> We must not allow our anger, which is legitimate, for apartheid to become the basis of a blind hatred for all white people. Let us not build our struggle upon hatred, and let us not seek to quench our thirst for freedom by drinking from the cup of bitterness. Let us even now seek to lay the foundations for reconciliation between white and black in this country by working together, by praying together, and by struggling together for justice . . . If we cannot do it now, we will not be able to do it one day. (VD:315)

At both conference and rally there were speeches, songs, and slogans. Among the speakers—also representing black and white, men and women, young and old—were current leaders and people revered for their courage and suffering in opposition to apartheid. Helen Joseph, a veteran of the Congress campaigns of the fifties, recited a roster of leaders like Nelson Mandela, and Walter Sisulu, and recalled the march of women to Pretoria in 1956 to protest the extension of pass laws to women. Others were present only in name, as designated patrons of the UDF. Again, Mandela and Sisulu headed the list of heroes chosen to educate people in the history of their long struggle for political rights.

Albertina Sisulu, one of the three UDF presidents, spoke about the children of apartheid:

What is happening now? The government wants our children to fight each other. We, as mothers of this country, must stand up and say, No, to that. We are not going to allow our children to be fighting each other. Why should we? If the government of this country wants peace, it must release our leaders, all our exiled leaders, and our children. (14:355–56)

The focus the UDF declared at the rally was simple. It opposed apartheid laws and the new constitution. It called for a national convention to negotiate and create a new constitution. The government had presented the new constitution as a generous concession—whites would share power with non-whites. To the UDF, these concessions were worse than nothing. The new constitution, they said, would divide victims of apartheid from each other. It was another version of the long-standing Nationalist policy of divide and rule. Molefe testified:

The new constitution was not addressing the fundamental problems of the country. It therefore meant that those protests which led to people getting detained would still take place. . . . People will still die in detention. It meant that people might still be banned. All it means is that unless the fundamental issues that give rise to . . . protests are addressed, the constitution could be seen as the surest way of perpetuating the situation that has existed before, if not even making it worse. (13:256)

On the same point, the testimony quoted an article Lekota had published in 1984:

[The constitution] excludes the African majority from government. . . . [It] entrenches white monopoly of power. . . . Racism remains the cornerstone of the new constitution. . . . The Minister of Transport has already assured the official opposition even the Blue Train will be divided into racial coaches so that white MP's [Members of Parliament] do not mix . . .
More than this, the new constitution is unacceptable for the fundamental reason that it is not the constitution of people of South Africa. . . . Only whites voted to decide whether it is accept-

able or not. What we call for is a constitution for the entire people of our country, black and white.... Over the centuries ... all the people in this country have contributed to the present shape and face of South Africa. All have a rightful claim to the heritage of wealth, culture and residence ...

A constitution such as the present one can only intensify African, Indian, and Coloured frustration at their failure to attain effective political rights. Such a constitution amounts to fuelling the fires of anger at the government's stubbornness and insensitivity to their aspirations ...

It is generally considered that the next logical step ... is to conscript Indian and Coloured youths into the army ... to strengthen the South African Defense Force as a tool against African resistance.

The SADF's [South African Defence Force's] role ... has cut a threatening image in African eyes. When African students refused to study in Afrikaans [in 1976] because white students were not forced to study in Sotho or Zulu, it was the SADF and police units which came and shot them. Many of them left the country and took to arms in response ... (15:490–91)

The UDF believed the new constitution would have to be abandoned. It said that the transition to a new, democratic society would be achieved through a national convention of all South Africans, black and white. For the national convention to be truly representative, it would have to include those now excluded from the political process by prison, banning or exile. Molefe testified:

Organizations that are banned, and individuals who are jailed, and those who are in exile—all of them ... to whom these things happened because they spoke out against the policies of apartheid.... We believe that if a new constitution has got to be established ... it must also recognize that those people have got a crucial role to play.... They too are part of this country. They belong here ...

It is particularly crucial that those people participate because the raging violence that is taking place in this country is taking place because ... the government had closed all avenues through which they could articulate aspirations of the oppressed people.... This is the reason why there is no peace in the country today. We are simply saying that the necessary conditions have got to be created if a proper constitution has got to be formulated, acceptable to all the people of South Africa. (13:206)

We are not under any illusions that every one of these conditions would be accepted by the government. What was crucial for us was the acceptance of the principle of the call for a national convention and the preparedness of the government to talk to all the leaders of the people. (13:883)

Molefe and Lekota speak of achieving the end of apartheid through a negotiating process likely to take a long time:

I do not think it can be a two year, one year time thing. . . . It is a very sensitive issue. It involves a lot of people. It involves a huge country. And one has to be careful from step to step. . . . We may even begin the process that, at some point we pass into history, and others have to continue to finish it.

The important thing is to begin to find the process, to begin the process. (15:902)

The prosecution presented the demands for a national convention as a mask for a seizure of power:

JACOBS: You did not come clean with the people and tell them right from the start that you [were] going to oppose the government and try to bring in your own structure and take over the government . . .

MOLEFE: It is true that we did not tell the people that we wanted to take over the government because that has never been the intention of the UDF, and it has never been the policy of the UDF. Our call for a national convention testifies abundantly to that position.

JACOBS: But is it not . . . the UDF's policy that the government cannot come up with alternatives? . . . The masses themselves must come with the alternatives?

MOLEFE: We are saying that the best method of dealing with the problem is that of a national convention . . . in which the government would be a key participant. The convention . . . would be called by the government . . . (14:718)

Jacobs moved to another point. But the defense was up against a rock when it tried to present as reasonable the faith of Molefe and Lekota that the government could be brought peacefully to change.

Jacobs would see no ground for hope. He had come up on an un-
shakeable principle: Molefe's will to live in hope and not to plan for
contingencies of despair. At this point in the cross-examination, the
conflict of principles was so strong that it brought even Molefe, far
less confrontational than Lekota, to a point where he challenged the
legitimacy of the proceedings:

JACOBS: How are you going to achieve the destruction of
apartheid if the government is not prepared to agree to a national
convention?

MOLEFE: Well, we are not working on the basis that the government is not prepared to agree, ... and I am not going to accept
being pushed here to say that there is—that the UDF would opt
for violence, in this court, simply because counsel believes that
the government would not agree to the national convention.
We worked on the basis that the day will come that that will
happen ...
[The UDF] operated on the basis that we are capable, through
unity and through struggle, to move the government. (14:405)

The UDF did not have a blueprint of the constitution it wanted
the national convention to draw up:

The UDF was really a very young front. It really had broad
principles. It would articulate a vision, but it had not reached a
stage where it could work out the pros and cons of everything,
the mechanics of everything. (13:890)
[Under these few, broad principles, the UDF became] a loose
conglomeration of organizations, each one of them retaining its
own ideological position, its own constitution, its own separate
membership ... striving for liberation. But it does not regard itself
as a liberation movement. ... A liberation movement would entail
much more than that. It may require one ideological position, [a]
far-ranging program of action, and tight discipline. (14:465)

Although the process might take a long time, Molefe prophe-
sied, it would inevitably come:

A situation is going to arise in the future of this country
where the people of our country, black and white, are going to
have to sit down to try and resolve the crisis that this country has
been going through over the years. The government is going to
call that national convention in the future. I am pretty certain of

that. It is going to happen ... there is no use equivocating now
and prevaricating when we know that in the end we are going to
have to call a national convention and talk about the real future of
the people of our country. (13:329–30)

At the time of the launch, many domestic and international observers treated this certainty with skepticism. Many predicted that
the UDF, so loosely held together would not survive. They described
it as a bubble.

The organizational structure of the UDF was highly decentral-
ized. The structure was consistent with its mission to coordinate resistance to apartheid in organizations that existed already as well as
to encourage the creation of new local organizations and to build
networks of information and cooperation. For Molefe and Lekota,
this structure meant frequent meetings and travel to hear what
people in the affiliates were saying, to consult with other UDF affiliates, and to respond after consultation. At times, this structure
seemed cumbersome and inept. Especially in the actual conditions
of operation, with virtually no staff, continual police raids, intercepted mail, tapped telephones, banned meetings, government disinformation, and the detentions of politically active people, it was
not easy to make or implement decisions. This apparently inept
structure, however, had the strength of a net that tangles lions. It
consisted almost totally of lines of influence with virtually no head.
It was not easily susceptible to destruction when leaders were imprisoned or assassinated. Breaking one thread was of little use.
Breaking many was extremely difficult because the political education of the UDF was so embedded in local issues such as rent,
schools, sports, and shopping for groceries and clothes that it was
virtually impossible to prevent talk about the ideas it proposed. The
UDF's primary means of growth were door-to-door talk, encounters
outside the doors of churches, and neighborly talk about day-to-day
matters. It answered the forces of government censorship with the
human skill at contriving gossip and telling news. It operated partly
through an oral culture largely impenetrable to whites who rarely
trouble to learn African languages. Its ideas seemed to flow around
and through barriers in ways the government could not foresee or
staunch.

The prosecution tried to identify and criminalize this evasive
and pervasive power embodied in children's games and grandpar-

ents' stories and the colors of scarves. They repeatedly questioned Molefe and Lekota about the speeches, songs, and slogans character-istic of the launch and other UDF meetings. Both Molefe and Lekota seemed taken aback by the insistence of the prosecution on ele-ments not usually treated as evidence of treason. Molefe and Lekota answered by descriptions of how things are done in "our" commu-nities. Both said that singing about events of interest and shouting slogans are customary, and that they had never before been treated as revolutionary or criminal.

> In a situation . . . like there at the rally, now we had something in the region of 15,000 people, and people sang. . . . It was just like a public gathering, you know. Anybody just sings what they want to sing there. Anybody shouts what they want to shout, you see. It is not the policy of the organization. But these are communities from which we come, and within these communities, these things happen day in day out and nobody ever raised an eyebrow about it. They are not a crime. We are not saying people must commit crimes . . .
>
> At all those work situations, people sing all round . . . (16:659)
>
> The proceedings were over, and some of the people wanted to leave. . . . So in order to avoid people just going out of the hall, and then the marquee, and then filling the streets, and then . . . consti-tuting illegal gatherings outside, they were asked to remain in-side. . . . It was in that kind of atmosphere that people were just singing . . . dancing, and so on. There was whistling, laughing . . . and that was that. (16:681)

To van Dijkhorst, the "Dopper," that kind of atmosphere was in-tensely alien. He found that the singing and dancing at the launch "evidences a pattern found in virtually all UDF meetings." (VD:317) He saw antigovernment language, songs, and slogans; "Mandela, and others in prison for acts of violence against the state, are throughout glorified and called 'our leaders' and their deeds are never disap-proved of or disclaimed:" the ANC is glorified; the language could be understood as a call to violence because it uses words like "fight"; "Emphasis is throughout placed on oppression and persecution of the people by the government;" and "The Soweto riots of 1976 and their participants are glorified and the unbridled violence thereof is never disapproved of. The riots are called a fight for freedom." This atmosphere is a precursor of revolution. It is treason.

But from the launch on August 20, 1983, to the detention of thirty-five leaders on August 21, 1984, Molefe and Lekota operated as though expressing their opposition to apartheid through nonviolent organization was lawful, as their legal advisers suggested. At the same time, they knew that obeying the law might not, in itself, protect them.

5 The Referendum

For a year and a day, the UDF set about building its organization and organizing opposition to apartheid. Molefe and Lekota, the UDF's only two full-time paid officials, set up an office in a building owned by the South Africa Council of Churches, shared a secretary, and, working weekends and nights, when they could reach people who held full-time jobs, they began to build the UDF through door-to-door campaigns, meetings, rallies, media, church services, vigils, the tolling of bells, and workshops.

The only direct connection between Molefe and Lekota and the Vaal cited in the trial was one of the hundreds of meetings Molefe attended. On September 18, 1983, he talked at the Roman Catholic Church in Small Farms in the Vaal Triangle. He explained the principles of the UDF and encouraged people to form a local association.

Many issues drew immediate attention from UDF affiliates. There were forced removals, including some from squatter dwellings at Crossroads, near Cape Town. There were reports of arrests, torture, and hundreds rounded up and tortured in a soccer stadium in one of the homelands, the Ciskei, where a Catholic bishop disappeared for several weeks. A UDF pamphlet quoted eye-witness reports of ninety people killed by police and hundreds injured.[1] Protests about the quality of black schooling, "gutter education," had been endemic since 1976. In the period 1982–3, the government spent R1,385 on each white student, R871 for each Indian, R593 for each Coloured, and R192 for each African.[2] The almost tenfold disparity between whites and Africans fueled protests which grew even stronger when research showed substantial corruption in the grading of college entrance examinations to favor white students. There was the ongoing daily grinding of apartheid, the pass laws, the group areas laws, the bureaucracy of apartheid, and, doing the dirty work, an expensive police force and army, forces on the borders to prevent

Namibia in the west from developing into an independent state, to prevent Mozambique on the east from becoming peaceful, prosperous, and a haven for the ANC, to exercise constant vigilance against the trickling back into the country of young men who had left after 1976 to receive military training. Apartheid was taking a lot of money, and one source was sales tax. It was taking a lot of young men, and one source was conscription, soon, the UDF warned, to be extended to Indians and Coloureds.

While supporting its affiliates in their diverse efforts, the UDF focused on a whites-only referendum November 2, 1983 on whether to approve or reject the proposed new constitution. The UDF wanted voters to reject the new constitution. The weekend before the referendum, the UDF coordinated a "People's Weekend" of workshops in many parts of the country on the new constitution and UDF principles.

In September, the UDF wrote a letter to President W. P. Botha to present the UDF position. Receiving no reply, they sent the letter again. Molefe and Lekota tried to arrange a meeting with Botha to deliver the letter. The Prime Minister's secretary said he would try to gain them access on the nineteenth. They hoped to speak directly to "the Big Crocodile."

We sent this letter to the President in Natal [Archie Gumede, one of the three co-presidents of the UDF] to sign, and from there it had to go to the Western Cape to be signed by President [Oscar] Mpetha, and then we had to work very fast because the appointment had already been made. And unfortunately for us, the letter ... when it came, had a lot of fingerprints on it. It was just not in a presentable condition. We, therefore, could not take a dirty copy there.... We had to cancel that appointment. (16:550)

They delivered the letter on October 25. They did not meet Botha. They did not receive acknowledgment of their letter.

Even before the launch, police had confiscated thousands of UDF newsletters, and returned them after the UDF threatened legal action.[3] Some UDF meetings were banned in September,[4] and every week in October, the month before the referendum, UDF and affiliate meetings were banned.[5] The UDF decided to challenge this tactic in court and had one banning order set aside October 24, but other bannings and detentions followed. Lekota noted:

Each time we called a meeting, it did not matter where, it did not matter how many people were going to be there, it was just

getting banned ... These bannings took place in spite of the fact
that all the meetings that the UDF had held up to that time had
been very peaceful meetings. Not one of them had ended up in
any kind of violence or any kind of disruptive action. (15:549)

UDF members were held for questioning in Cape Town, and, on
October 24, Lekota was taken from his home in Durban and questioned at police headquarters for two hours.[6]

In the referendum, an overwhelming number of whites supported the government and approved the new constitution. The government lost in only one constituency where voters opposed the
constitution as too generous to blacks.

At the trial, Lekota described his feelings about the referendum:

I felt extremely hurt. I was even more hurt for my own father.
I recall asking some of my comrades. ... "I wonder what the difference could be said to be between my father and Bishop Tutu on
the one hand, and an Alsatian dog that is owned by any ... of our
white citizens in this country."

My father was in [his] sixties. Throughout his life he had never
voted to decide any one of the laws that had controlled his life. I
was in my thirties myself. I had never been able to participate in a
democratic process to decide on any one of the laws of the country that would govern my life, and that would govern the lives of
my children. And in spite of what we had said, our white compatriots were not responding to the pleas which we had made.

My father's contemporaries, the white ones ... had made laws
that he must carry a reference book. They also made a law that an
Alsatian dog must have a certain ticket on his neck [a dog li-
cence], and he must also carry a "reference book." That Alsatian
dog was going to die without ever deciding a law that governs his
life. So was my father ...

The discomfort of prison cells is better than the emptiness of
walking in the streets as if you were free when you are a dog in
the land of your birth. (15:545)

After white voters approved the new constitution by 66 percent,
the UDF needed to decide how to demonstrate black opposition to
it. Some suggested boycotting the elections to the new Coloured and
Indian houses of Parliament, others suggested participating in the
elections to register a "No" vote. A UDF National General Council
meeting in December could not resolve the issue. It established a

commission to take the question to the regions, and a compromise was worked out—the National Executive Committee would suggest guidelines, and the regions retained tactical flexibility. It was all rather cumbersome and inefficient, and it did not please some regions who wanted the UDF to "take a position that forces everyone to toe the line." (Molefe, 13:275)

But Molefe's testimony clearly showed that this process of consulting and working toward consensus was essential, both tactically and as a matter of principle:

> **The very size of the United Democratic Front, the hundreds of organizations that were coming together under this banner, simply meant that it was not going to be feasible to control every component . . .**
>
> **Besides . . . it would simply run counter to the whole concept of democracy, because it is the members of those organizations who must decide . . . the direction that they thought their organization should take. (13:269)**

In the final defense argument, Chaskalson cited this process:

> **It is very clear evidence . . . that the UDF was taking its own decisions, because if the ANC was telling it what to do, the ANC would have issued a directive, "Do this," "Do that," and it would have been implemented. (25:466)**

The UDF's mode of operating through such an apparently unwieldy organizational structure seemed more than implausible to the prosecution. Incomprehensible. Unimaginable.

The UDF seemed hopelessly weak. Its own work to unite the efforts of its many grassroots, autonomous affiliates took hours of careful talk. UDF leaders received information and moral support from affiliates and funneled information and moral support to them.

Different affiliates focused on different issues, bringing them to the attention of others in the network. The specific instances they brought forward connected a wide variety of injuries done by apartheid. Using simple, vivid examples from everyday life to explain the connections they saw between particular issues and the new constitution, UDF leaders displayed the whole interwoven fabric to their supporters. They educated their followers to see the underlying structure of laws and power governing the country. They supported local and specific campaigns around issues that demonstrated the concrete meaning of apartheid in everyday life.

The prosecution alleged that there were no necessary links between the diverse campaigns the UDF supported. The UDF, it said, supported affiliate campaigns in an opportunistic strategy—any issue could serve to implement the larger plot. The main purpose of the UDF was to mobilize the people against the government and to politicize them. Molefe answered:

Those are real problems affecting the community and they have got to be addressed. . . . If we say there are 30,000 people on a waiting list in Soweto, we want more houses, we really mean it. We do not mean that we just want to use that as a public relations exercise. . . . It is a problem. People need houses. And once it is solved, we will not talk about it. . . . Addressing the problems of the people—we did not see that as a strategy. (14:505–6)

Lekota saw that underlying the state's case was a suspicion of any political activity that enabled black people to understand their lives politically and to gain a voice in their own fate:

The UDF was committed to opposing the new dispensation [the new constitution]. . . . The affiliates of the UDF were organizations . . . concerned with issues that affected communities. . . . They supported or joined the UDF to oppose the new dispensation because they saw . . . it was going to continue a situation in which the problems they were opposing would continue . . . never . . . for mischievous ends of a conspiracy, as alleged. (15:998)

There is not a sector of . . . South African society . . . we were not interested in organizing, but naturally . . . in an urgent situation like ours, we tried to reach areas where organization would be quicker and easier . . . so that we could win quick support fast, so that we could . . . talk to the government. We would have been a very dull lot of people if we did not locate areas . . . where we would be able to build our support and make it strong. (16:015)

As far as I am concerned, [these] are obvious activities of any political organization . . . interested in serving its community. . . . Why should it be wrong to link our politics with the day-to-day issues of life? Politics is about governing a society . . . (16:019)

We picked up issues . . . [one] in order that they must be solved; two, to gain definite benefits for our constituents; thirdly, we linked them up with the new dispensation . . . to indicate that apartheid . . . is a source of these problems. . . . If water comes into the house, and there is a [faucet] . . . open somewhere, [while we try] to block the water ... we must also go to the [faucet] so we can close it. (16:030)

The UDF took root throughout the country. Even rural backwaters that had previously been isolated became part of the organized opposition to apartheid. The political education the UDF organized to relate the daily issues and "agony of our life under apartheid" to the overall issue of the vote and the constitution enabled people to see connections between their experience and the experience of their neighbors, between high rents and conscription, forced removals and "gutter education," the plight of squatters in Crossroads near Cape Town, and the humiliations of single sex hostels for workers in the mines. The bonds forged by the UDF through its affiliates campaigning from door to door and person to person seemed elusive and resilient. They were incomprehensible to the government. They survived years of emergency laws, hundreds of detentions and bannings, and barrages of propaganda intended to repress and destroy mass extraparliamentary opposition. Although the UDF was banned, in effect, in February 1988, the political consciousness it helped organize had become a powerful force that resurfaced in 1989 as the Mass Democratic Movement.

The bubble was not bursting. Instead, what might once have appeared to apartheid authorities as an ephemeral alliance between sentimental whites, Christians, human rights activists, and blacks pleading once again for a respite to their sufferings had become an organization that seemed to be connected to every act of protest and resistance in the country and to increasingly noisy and potentially damaging protest abroad. Wherever the government turned, whatever the issue, the UDF seemed to be behind it. The bubble began to look like a dark cloud threatening to cover the whole sky. How could it have happened? How could it have happened so quickly? It must be a conspiracy.

6 The Million Signature Campaign

After the referendum, November 2, 1983 and through 1984, the UDF continued in its main work of building a national network. It built relations with affiliates, garnered new affiliates, and helped to set up new branches.

The UDF worked to build a new South Africa through the style of its work as well as through specific changes in policy and constitution. Its leaders felt that the process toward democracy must itself be democratic. When the prosecution accused the UDF of taking orders from the ANC, Molefe testified:

We made it very clear on many occasions that we do not believe that a small group of activists . . . are the ones who must decide for the people, and use their understanding of issues as a yardstick to determine the understanding of the ordinary people. We must find a way of allowing the ordinary people to participate . . .

Those issues are very crucial to us, as [because] organizations that are operating within our community . . . had never tasted democracy. Our people . . . lived a life of being shunted from pillar to post, either by the bosses in the factories or the madams in the homes where our mothers work as domestics. We do not want to extend that kind of situation where we want to pull around people by their noses. We want our people to taste democracy. And that democracy can be tasted in our organizations. They can begin to develop their own confidence to do things on their own, to decide on matters that affect them in organizations.

If we do not do that, we are merely perpetuating what the present government is doing, . . . where it is denying us a right to participate . . . , where in the factories we are simply shunted around as workers, or as garden boys and washing girls. That, the UDF does not want to approach. It is simply not in line with our approach. (13:800)

Similar attitudes show in the way the UDF launched a Million Signature Campaign in January 1984, to support its program of opposition to the new constitution and the Koornhof laws, and to ask for a national convention. (This campaign resembled, and may have been inspired by, a petition circulated by the National Union of South African Students in 1983.) The UDF guide for those collecting signatures is deeply expressive of the values Molefe and Lekota wish the future society to manifest:

The challenge is to collect signatures, educate the person who is signing, and help build our organization at the same time. We must remember that we are dealing with another person, and not merely another signature . . .

Points to remember. Be polite. Before asking for a signature, greet correctly, and introduce yourself. Say where you are from. Once you have made contact with someone you want to sign, find out his or her interest, especially as regard day to day problems like rent, transport, refuse collection, wages, working conditions, passes, food prices, etc. What does that person feel about these problems, and what does he or she think has caused them. Explain the link between these problems and why we are asking people to sign . . .

Be patient and learn. The person from whom you are collecting is a potential supporter, and not an enemy. This is the case even if they do not understand the issues involved, and even if their point of view differs from yours.

Be patient and do not rush. If a person does not understand, explain slowly. If a person has different understanding, do not push your ideas down their throats. Try to find common ground in opposing apartheid rather than points of difference. UDF unites, even though our views are not exactly the same. (13:339–41)

In addition to gathering signatures, those going out with petitions would be gathering information:

We need to learn about our people. We need to find out about their problems, about how they feel about various issues, their willingness to take part in activity, their level of understanding about the political situation in the country. All this we can only do by speaking to people individually, asking questions, and listening carefully when they speak. (25:503)

The guide warned against violence:

Do not be provoked into arguments, anger, or violence. Discipline is important. (25:503)

It also gave instructions on how to deal with the police. The prosecution asked why this was necessary. Molefe answered:

It has been the experience in the townships that . . . every time people go around doing something, there is always an interference on the side of the police, and that this . . . leads to confrontation. . . . We wanted to avoid any confrontation with the police . . .

The UDF had ... made sure that lawyers were consulted to
advise how a thing should be done, on the legality of the matter.
(13:341)

In spite of these precautions, there were confrontations.

It is a known fact that those who have stuck out their necks to
speak out against apartheid have very often landed up in jails or
under banning orders.... Ordinary people have been harassed.
Anybody who has spoken against apartheid has been harassed....
When we collected the signatures in 1984, people who had
signed the million signatures forms of the UDF were harassed in
their homes. We even had to threaten legal proceedings against
the police to stop that, and to get our forms back. And these
things were happening to the ordinary people, not the leaders of
the UDF ... (14:326)

The prosecutor asked if Molefe was talking about collectors.

I am talking about people who had appended their names on
the signature forms, who themselves were not collecting signatures. In any event, even if it were people who collected signatures, it is not unlawful to do that. Nobody has got any reason to
harass a person who is articulating his own position on a matter
which is the subject of debate nationally, where everybody has got
his own right to express [an] opinion on the matter. (14:326)

When Lekota spoke about assaults on activists in Johannesburg
and how Million Signature forms were taken from them and torn to
pieces "right in the middle of the day, in town," Mr. Fick challenged
him:

FICK: And I presume UDF laid charges against the police for
taking the MSC forms.

LEKOTA: ... If people want to complain about the forms, they
must go to the same man who has taken the forms from them.
And the fact of the matter is, anything happens to them now.
Maybe they get arrested. And people generally are terrified because [of] the treatment which our people get there ...

FICK: Did you personally in any instance go to the police station?

LEKOTA: Which police station?

FICK: Any police station, after a complaint like this.

LEKOTA: I myself have been deprived of property of the organization, like in Kroonstad,[1] and I had to go there on a number of
occasions to go and demand my things. Right now, one of the
T-shirts of the UDF is still sitting with the police in Kroonstad.
. . . One of my books is still with the police in Kroonstad.
(15: 809–12)

During the cross-examination of Molefe and Lekota there is no
hint that a slow fuse, possibly lit during the Million Signature Campaign, had exploded into the trial itself. Six months previously, it had
broken apart the judge's bench when van Dijkhorst dismissed one of
the two assessors acting in place of a jury. Juries were abolished in
South Africa in 1969. In important cases, especially where the penalty might be death, the judge chooses two advisers, called assessors.
They are supposed to have some knowledge of the law, and advise
the judge on matters of fact rather than law.

Before 1985, the hearing of political matters had fallen to a small
circle of known judges in the Transvaal. In 1985, the new Judge President of the Transvaal bench decided to rotate political cases among
all Transvaal judges. Van Dijkhorst, who volunteered to take the Delmas Trial, some say, to show that trials like it need not drag on for
months, had never heard a political case before and had attended
only one political meeting in his life. (This may have been a meeting
of Pretoria University students addressed by Chief Albert Lutuli after
he received the Nobel Peace Prize in 1960. The meeting was broken
up by rowdy hecklers, and van Dijkhorst testified against his fellow
students when they were tried for their behavior.)

He chose his two assessors from very different points on the
spectrum of Afrikaner political opinion. One, W. F. Krugel, a magistrate paid by the government, was reputed to be a member of the
secret Afrikaner Broederbond. It seems safe to assume that he would
not question the assumptions of apartheid. The other assessor, W. A.
Joubert, a professor of law, would bring to the discussion a liberal
point of view. Joubert had known van Dijkhorst as a young man. He
had offered van Dijkhorst his first academic position. He was known
as an Afrikaner who "had played a prominent part in intellectual
dissent on the part of certain Afrikaner academics from the policies
of apartheid."[2]

Joubert had been dean of two law faculties, edited important
law publications, and had received an honorary degree. He was a
founding member of the Progressive Federal Party that eventually

called for a universal franchise. He ran for Parliament on its platform in 1981. In 1983, Joubert opposed the new constitution. Invited to sign a petition opposing the new constitution (perhaps put out by NUSAS, perhaps by the UDF), he signed without thinking the act particularly momentous.

When van Dijkhorst invited Joubert to sit as an assessor, both men knew that their political views differed. Joubert considered this to be irrelevant.

Throughout the trial they perceived the issues and the witnesses differently. Early on, Joubert wrote a note to van Dijkhorst saying that he would be "unhappy if there were to be any political undertones affecting the case."[3] Van Dijkhorst answered, "Willem, you know of course that we are confronted here with an onslaught on our whole system of government."[4] Joubert did not know. "We had heard hardly any evidence as yet against the twenty-two accused." From then on, Joubert found himself excluded from discussions about the case.

Months later, Joubert made the casual remark that he looked forward to hearing what the defendants would have to say in the witness box. Van Dijkhorst said the defense could not and would not risk putting the defendants on the stand under oath. Joubert said, "I could not, at that stage, consider the accused to be guilty criminals of whom it could be assumed that they would be unwilling to put their case to the court and to the public from the witness stand. I assumed that the accused had a story which they wished to communicate to the court. More importantly, I took the view that the court should maintain an open posture until it had heard that story." Van Dijkhorst then "informally bet me a bottle of whiskey that none of the [defendants] would give evidence."[5]

In January 1987, when Chaskalson gave the opening defense address, it became obvious that most of the accused would give evidence in their own defense.

At the tea adjournment I [Joubert] jokingly enquired of the judge whether he had bought the whiskey yet since its price was increasing.[6]

The next day, the judge's clerk gave Joubert a bottle of whiskey.

Several weeks later, Joubert mentioned casually that he remembered signing the Million Signature Petition. He may actually have signed the petition circulated by the National Union of South African Students in 1983, not in the UDF campaign that began in 1984. Van Dijkhorst said Joubert should resign because he was politically prejudiced in favor of the defendants. Joubert said that if he should re-sign from the case, so should van Dijkhorst. The next day van Dijk-horst discharged Joubert without warning or allowing Joubert to state his case.

Joubert believed himself unfairly dismissed and still bound by an oath to give true verdict in the case. He made a report under oath. Van Dijkhorst accused Joubert of giving a distorted picture. Joubert made two further reports. Chaskalson, head of the defense team, asked van Dijkhorst to resign. Van Dijkhorst refused. Chaskalson asked the other assessor, Krugel, to resign because he too was not neutral. As a member of the Broederbond, he was as biased against the defendants as Joubert might be for them. Krugel did not resign. Chaskalson said the court, lacking one assessor, was no longer prop-erly constituted and the case should end forthwith. Van Dijkhorst said that Joubert had made disclosures that were "either improper or unlawful." (10:689) He threatened Chaskalson with contempt of court.

The trial continued without resolving the issues of the judge's prejudice and the legality of the court without one of its assessors. These issues remained for the defense to take up as grounds for appeal.

7 Grassroots

One of the issues in the trial lay half-buried under prosecution charges. The apartheid government did not merely want to impose its will. It wanted no other will to exist. A profound cultural antago-nism surfaces from time to time, and with that antagonism, intoler-ance. The government wanted more than to dominate: it wanted to exterminate any other way of looking at the world. So, when the UDF made connections the government did not want made, the UDF was doing something illegitimate, even if it was not actually illegal.

One of these illegitimate activities was the UDF's work to po-liticize people so that they would connect local affairs and apartheid as a whole, local affairs and the affairs of the country. The govern-ment's charges express an intolerance that required a dizzying chasm of ignorance in the awareness of most whites about the cul-ture and circumstances of the majority in South Africa.

The charges also impute to the defendants responsibility for events that happened when they were in prison, like the turbulence of 1985 and 1986 when many in black ghettoes were refusing to pay rent, government by the minority appointed officials did break down, and local communities created alternative local government structures to deal with the anarchy created in the absence of other administrative power.

At the Delmas Trial, white ignorance about the lives of the majority in South Africa was compounded by van Dijkhorst's lack of experience with political meetings and behavior, his profound distaste for anything that looks to him like disorder, and his habit of turning attention away from what he does not want to know so that he need not acknowledge its existence. One of the concerns of the UDF was the unrest in black schools. The Bantu [African] Education Act of 1953 was designed to teach Africans that "the green pastures reserved for whites are not for them." Africans were to learn only enough English and Afrikaans to be able to take orders. "What is the use of teaching a Bantu child mathematics when it cannot use it in practice? . . . Education must train and teach people in accordance with their opportunities in life . . ."[1] In the eyes of apartheid, Africans' opportunities would be restricted to "certain forms of labor." In 1976, the students in Soweto protested that the proposed use of Afrikaans as a medium of instruction would imprison them in ignorance. School protest had been endemic since 1976.

In the early 1980s a number of school boycotts protested "gutter education," corruption in the grading of national exams, sexual harassment, drunken teachers, and other abuses of power that the UDF saw as part of the overall effect of apartheid, denying students and parents access to effective protest and redress. Scandals and protests had been a matter of national debate, the subject of government inquiries, university research, and reports in the newspapers for many years.

During cross-examination on the attitude of the UDF to education, van Dijkhorst revealed that he did not know that blacks and whites wrote different national examinations and were graded differently.

Lekota saw this type of ignorance among whites about how apartheid works and is experienced as an obstacle to understanding and reconciliation. "It is very difficult to love people you do not even understand, and you do not know." (15:866) Addressing students at Rand Afrikaans University in Johannesburg in late February 1984, he said:

> Come into the townships and see the crowded conditions we
> live in. See the schools where we learn, and find out from the
> people in the townships whether they like living in conditions
> that border on being like those in a pig sty. (15:778)

Students from the university visited Soweto.

During the more than forty months of the Delmas Trial, van
Dijkhorst never visited the Vaal Triangle to see for himself the world
described in the testimony. By contrast, in another high-profile treason trial started in October 1987 and ended in May 1989, focusing
on events in a black ghetto nestled among the prosperous suburbs
of northern Johannesburg, Judge Pieter van der Walt visited the site
of the alleged crimes. "I regard it as important and necessary to be
able to arrive at a better understanding of the events that took place
during the period spanned by the charge."[2] Driving through Alexandra, he found the physical features and lack of amenities were only
too apparent.[3] His verdict found government-supported authorities
improved conditions for themselves but that "squalid conditions"
prevailing in the rest of the area were clearly "the reason why the
community was dissatisfied and developed a lack of trust and faith
in the authorities. Moreover, these factors evidently contributed to
the problem experienced by some of the councillors which led to
their resignations."[4] Judge van der Walt ruled, in 1989, that the defendants in the Mayekiso case, although they often used "intemper-
ate and exaggerated language . . . liberally spiced with current political cliches [were] citizens just striving for a better South Africa."[5]

In striving to create a better South Africa, the UDF supported
affiliates engaged in creating a new society as well as in opposing
the old. It was no longer enough to oppose apartheid. It was important to start building the institutions of a post-apartheid South Africa.
Through the network that was to prove so difficult for the government to control, the UDF worked with affiliates to transcend the normal scope of political organizations by leapfrogging the present,
brushing aside the impediments of custom, assuming a postapart-
heid society, and supporting organizations to function in this new
society.

> We have recommended that people must begin to set up their
> own projects, like . . . mobile clinics. . . . They are projects where
> people are taught to begin to do things for themselves, to make
> decisions and participate. . . . Active participation in a democratic
> way relating to decision making and implementation of decisions

in organizations ... will begin to ... give a vision of a totally alternative society, a society based on popular ... decision making. ...
It laid the basis for the understanding of the processes of democracy. (14:713)

[The UDF enlisted young people] to give them meaningful
programs in which they can be involved, which would begin to
shape them into responsible men and women of the future. But if
they are just left to roam the street, and maybe get into this she-
been [bar] or the other ... they would just be directionless. ... So
we certainly encourage them to join the UDF ... not for mischief,
but so that they can make a meaningful contribution to the better
life of the community. ...

We ... attempted to shape our own youth, organize them into
organizations, pass on to them the heritage of their own people,
both in history and even [in] those squalid houses in the townships. How we have survived in those. How our forefathers have
survived in them. They have got to know these things ... because
they are going to survive tomorrow. ... Those are the things that
make us a people. That is the only thing we have got to pass on to
them. We have got to pass it to them. (15:555)

The prosecution presented these organizations as attempts to
"take over the running of the communities," undermine the Black
Local Authorities, and make the country ungovernable.

That is not so. They are alternative structures insofar as they
allow democratic participation of the communities. The decisions
that they take are the decisions of the people. They do not run
roughshod over the heads of the people. (14:728)

We are the last people to advocate disorder and lack of control. Where there is no control, where there is no order ... who
suffers? Our own communities, our own children, our own
people. ... [We want structures people would be loyal to.] If there
is disorder, anybody could be knocked down with a kierie [blud-
geon] on the head. (15:553–55)

The prosecution alleged that the connections the UDF saw between local and national issues were either trumped up or evidence
that the UDF picked local issues to implement a national and international conspiracy. So the events in the Vaal had been provoked by
UDF propaganda and had nothing to do with what Bizos described
as "the widespread impression that the local government authorities

were subjected to blatant displays of nepotism, corruption, arrogance, and unaccountability on the part of the councillors, and the council as a whole." (25:701) The prosecution turned a blind eye and deaf ear to evidence that similar conditions prevailed throughout the country and that they were an effect of apartheid. When Bizos pointed out that in the Vaal, where people were living in poverty and unemployment had been rising, there had been a 459.5 percent increase in rent in the Vaal in seven years, Fick said, "So what?"

The dangers of the UDF's grassroots approach to building a new society and the character of events in 1984 before the murders in the Vaal are suggested by what happened at Cradock, a small town in the Cape.

The town council in Lingelihle, the African township of Cradock, had been raising rents ever since 1978. Van Dijkhorst said, "The increase was due to the increase in the cost of services about which they could do nothing. The councillors were derogatorily called puppets." (VD:530) In 1980, a meeting called by councillors was disrupted by stone throwing and a beer hall was set alight. (Beer hall licenses are given by councillors, often for patronage. A percentage of beer profits was supposed to fund civic services.)

In 1983 a new teacher, Mathew Goniwe, came to Cradock from Graaff-Reniet, another small Cape town. Goniwe, appointed vice-principal, had been active in politics in the Transkei and had served a four-year sentence there under the security laws. In May 1983, he called a meeting of clergy and professional women and urged them to encourage young people to attend church and form cultural groups. They formed committees for drama, education, sport, and choral music. In August 1983, a mass meeting of parents and young people created CRADOYA and elected Goniwe chair.

On August 25, teachers and nurses called a meeting to do something about high rents. They consulted a lawyer, created an organization, CRADORA, and elected Goniwe chair. In November, CRADORA affiliated to the UDF. They said that "the struggle went beyond the confines of a specific problem. The particular civic issues were seen to be interwoven with, in fact to be emanating from, the general problem of exploitation in our country (quoted in VD:531)."

"Probably as a result of his political activism" Goniwe was transferred to Graaff-Reniet. (VD:531) He refused to go, and CRADOYA and CRADORA tried to have the transfer rescinded. They were not successful and Goniwe was dismissed. Students at his school started a boycott in February, and other schools soon joined them. Police and students came into conflict and primary schools were closed. On March 23, the magistrate prohibited meetings of CRADORA and CRADOYA. "At one of these, Goniwe allegedly rebuked a pupil who had struck a teacher." (VD:532) [In the verdict, van Dijkhorst complained, "Nowhere does one find an instruction to dampen the overheated youths." (VD:207)] The Department of Education and Training threatened to close all schools permanently.

Two days later there was rioting "followed by a large police presence in Cradock." (VD:532). Five days later Goniwe and three others were detained without charges. Within a few weeks the entire student, community, and youth leadership had been detained.

Two weeks later, the nephew of the acting principal stabbed another student to death. The houses of the principal and two councillors were attacked with petrol bombs. "More petrol bombings followed." (VD:553)

Two weeks after that, two youths were shot.

When the mother of the mayor was buried, May 12, the funeral procession was stoned.

On June 16, a consumer boycott was held. It was repeated on July 26.

Van Dijkhorst noted that "the formation of CRADOYA and CRADORA coincided with that start of UDF political activity in South Africa." (VD:531)

Shortly after their first court appearance, in June 1985, the Delmas defendants heard that Mathew Goniwe and three other UDF activists from Cradock had disappeared while driving home from a political meeting. The four burned bodies were found in circumstances suggesting foul play.

The pattern of school boycotts, clashes with police, stonings, attacks on the property of councillors and their associates, deaths, and funerals prevailed in many parts of the country. Molefe and Lekota were traveling, building alliances, making arrangements for rallies, and, Lekota more than Molefe, speaking. Lekota was briefly arrested in January, warned that he might be banned, and released. There was no immediate follow-up.

Some sense of the conditions in which Molefe and Lekota worked is conveyed by testimony about the commemoration of those who had died on and after June 16, 1976. Rivalry between AZAPO and UDF supporters had led to physical clashes, and a group of Christian ministers took over the sponsorship of the memorial.

Before the service in Regina Mundi Catholic church, pamphlets were distributed attacking and demeaning the UDF. The pamphlets seemed to come from AZAPO, but, to deal with what both sides recognized as "dirty tricks," all agreed that an AZAPO office bearer would speak at the beginning of the meeting to deny that AZAPO had written them. He said that AZAPO and the UDF had a common enemy: "We know what our enemy is. We are in no way going to fight for small things, trivial things. We are fighting for the recompense of our country, and on that we are all united." (16:722)

FICK: I put it to you that at this very meeting ... AZAPO and UDF were working together ... against the government:

LEKOTA: No, that is not so.... In fact, as I said earlier ... this meeting was chaired by the Ministers United ... precisely because of the sharp differences that had taken place in the course of that week, almost breaking out into fisticuffs.... This was just an attempt to calm things down. (16:722)

During the meeting competition between UDF and AZAPO members to start songs created problems for the priest:

You had a whole part of the hall being UDF supporters, and then you had the whole wing this side being Black Consciousness. When there is a gap, these ones want to lead a song, and those ones want to lead a song ... and ultimately, the chairman had to say, "O.K., we will have to alternate." (15:767)

Other things tested tempers:

There were units of the riot police who came to the meeting for purposes of observing and keeping law and order, but it so happened that they took positions almost at the entrance of the ... gate ... to the church, and then made it difficult for people who were coming to the meeting to come in, because they were not sure whether the police were there to block the gate or for what purpose. Both [Molefe's] and my attention was drawn to this, and we went up there and discussed the matter with the officer in charge, explaining the problem that the position they were taking was causing.... The police then considered our point, and they retreated, and took a position that allowed for free flow of movement in and out of the church. (15:703–4)

The prosecution cited what was happening inside the church:

FICK: Inside that hall there was singing and dancing and a black, green and gold flag [Colors of the banned African National Congress] tied to something—it is not clear whether it was the barrel of an AK 47 or not—was carried by an unknown black male dressed in khaki. Did you see this at the meeting, Mr. Lekota?

LEKOTA: No, I did not see this. I do not know at what stage [of the meeting] this was. But, you know, this thing that there was an AK 47 there—I do not agree with that. In the first place, you know, the whole place was just teeming with police. I myself had a lot of time with the police just at the entrance of the hall there, pleading with them to give way. I do not think anybody would come here with an AK 47. Unless it was just maybe some of these toys that kids play with, and so on, but . . . throughout the period I was there, there was no AK 47 . . .

FICK: Did you see the black, green and gold flag?

LEKOTA: I did not see a flag there, but there were a number of people with scarves and skullcaps . . . with those colors . . . (16:720)

Lekota continued with the kind of digressive, fond comment about daily life that characterizes his testimony:

You know, it is like if you go to the football ground, if Orlando Pirates is playing, you must find a combination of black and white. If it is Kaiser Chiefs, you will find people wearing clothing with colors of black and gold. This is the kind of thing that is just common, you know. (16:721)

Lekota's testimony often suggests a relish in everyday life and delight in community customs. One focus of that pleasure, greatly disapproved of by the prosecution and the judge, was the songs sung at UDF meetings. Some had rousing words about fighting for freedom, about Oliver Tambo, and about dramatic acts of sabotage, like the destruction of large gas tanks, and the bombing of a court. Both Molefe and Lekota defended singing as an intrinsic element of African culture, not the work of the UDF. They claimed that many of the songs had been sung for years without any subsequent violence. Van Dijkhorst was not convinced, and he saw songs, slogans, and the choice of ANC colors for affiliates as no accident. He saw them as part of a deliberate pattern amounting to treason. Lekota seems to be celebrating his own pleasure, more than trying to convince van Dijkhorst, in his testimony about singing:

> In our community, singing is part of any occasion where people come together in considerable numbers.... As I grew up ... I found that songs were used sometimes to console the people. Sometimes when people are doing a piece of work, to lighten the burden of what they are doing. Sometimes for sheer entertainment.
>
> An example ... I recall very well, is ... called *letsema* ... you will find a member of our community has got some project ... for instance, he wants to thatch a hut. Maybe ... the walls are already built. The owner would ordinarily make a large amount of beer, and he would invite his neighbors to come there and help him do the job—the beer would of course be for consumption while they are working. One finds invariably that once the job starts ... the working will be accompanied with the singing ...
>
> Or sometimes you have an occasion called *pitiki* ... maybe a child is being taken out of the house for the first time.... Instead of just sitting there quiet ... they sit in age groups, and then, after some time, they would begin singing.... Even the elderly men would stand up once in a while and just shake themselves and do something ...
>
> Once somebody starts the song, it is a communal activity. Everybody participates. Everybody responds ...
>
> I found songs ... when the men are digging a hole for the electric pole ... say for instance municipal workers, where elderly men may be working, digging a trench or something. You will find then going in rhythm with the song, and each time they pick the hoes up, they sing or they chant something
>
> You would see a white foreman sitting guarding them, and ... they would be singing, *Abelungu ngo'dam, ngo'dam.* What it means is that the white man is a damn, because he calls us jack ... mostly the white foreman is sitting there. He does not know what they are singing. And they are saying, he is a damn, he is a damn ... [6]
>
> In the townships ... one finds ... young kids ... particularly in the late afternoons and evenings, you will find them playing games, and during the course of those games composing songs ... and at a later stage sometimes you will find them taken up by people even older than themselves ...

Invariably songs went on to deal with our lives. Hymns were converted, or, at least adapted . . .

The one thing we cannot do if we are a large number at the same time is to talk, but we can sing together, all at the same time . . .

This singing is a tradition . . . we are born into it, and it will be there long after we are gone . . .

There is no conspiracy about it. Our fathers were doing that . . . long before us. And at weddings in the townships here, from time to time you will find the father of the daughter who is getting married, as the proceedings go on, especially after he had had two, three tots and he feels nice and warm, he will sometimes stand there and he will also perform for the people who are there . . . and for his daughter who is going away and who may never have an opportunity to see him do this . . . even his contemporaries will also perform and dance. . . . It is an occasion . . . (15: 756–59)

In 1984, it was becoming increasingly difficult for many people to live the ordinary life Lekota celebrates.

8 Violence

When Lekota, child of an intensely Afrikaner part of South Africa and versed in Afrikaner history, first saw van Dijkhorst, he was convinced that he recognized the kind of Afrikaner he was dealing with. There was no point in trying to appease this judge with good behavior. So he felt free to do anything necessary to promote the UDF cause.

One of his first opportunities to put his insight into practice came at the pleading. Each defendant in turn answered the charges with a simple, "Not guilty," making no statement. Even Molefe, the nineteenth to plead, less openly audacious than Lekota, gave a simple, "Not guilty." Lekota was determined to show UDF supporters he was not intimidated. Instead of following the script, "Not guilty," he threw down the gauntlet. The UDF, he said, had always acted lawfully and followed a policy of nonviolence. That was why he was not guilty.

The battle lines were drawn. Lekota had declared for all the world, including the judge, that he would not be obedient and unobtrusive. He would not follow the rules quietly.

Much of the subsequent battle was about "violence" and "non-violence." The prosecution, van Dijkhorst believed, had "clearly nailed its indictment to the mast of violence." (VD:66) The UDF says apartheid is the cause of violence and that the UDF seeks to cure the society of the violence that cannot be eliminated from apartheid.

Molefe testified:

There will really be no peace as long as apartheid exists because apartheid divides people into races. . . . If you are black, you do not qualify for higher wages. You do not qualify for a decent house. You do not qualify to own the land. You do not qualify to own property . . .

All we are saying is that once you have that kind of situation, you must inevitably have . . . protest from people who will speak out. And then they get arrested. They die in detention because a person has "slipped on a piece of soap."[1] They die in detention because "he hanged himself." They die in detention because "he jumped through the 10th floor of John Vorster Square." "He has suffered brain damage," and so on, in detention.

All these things . . . will go on because people speak out, and the police force that is defending apartheid will continue to harass them and lock them in detention, removing them from their families . . .

As long as apartheid continues, the government will have to continue to use force to contain those who are oppressed, because we cannot keep quiet. We cannot die there in the quiet when we are starving without jobs, we are starving in the homelands. [Reservations for Africans. They are the expression of "grand apartheid," the division of the country into tribal areas, as distinct from "petty apartheid," the segregation and Jim Crow laws in "white" areas.[2]]

We cannot keep quiet. We must speak out. When one puts his foot on a red hot iron, he is not expected [not] to say, I am feeling the pain. We will say so. We are feeling the pain. We cannot keep quiet.

We believe it is our right to express our feelings in respect of these things. So that when we say that unless the government calls a national convention to resolve the problems of the country, there will be no peace, we mean that the government will continuously be forced to suppress people. . . . On the other hand, there will be . . . people . . . who have already taken up arms, going on to engage in acts of violence. That is the pain, the agony that the

country has got to go through. We do not want that to be perpetu-
ated....

People have suffered for many, many years under the policies
of apartheid. Others have decided ... to take up arms. We have refused to do so. Now we are appealing to the ... conscience of the
government [to] realize that if it does not address this issue, and it
relies on the army and the police force in the townships to suppress the people, it may well be creating a situation of hopeless-
ness where people ... do not believe that it is still possible to
bring about change through peaceful methods, and that kind of
situation is "too ghastly to contemplate."[3] We do not want it to develop to that point, and we have got to issue warnings from time
to time to the government....

This kind of warning ... is not something that is new and pe-
culiar to the UDF. These are things that have been said even in Parliament ...

I recall ... one [Member of Parliament] even suggesting that at
some stage, South Africa might have to have trials of those who
perpetrated atrocities against the oppressed people, trials similar
to those of Nuremberg ...

These things are said, and they are reported widely in newspapers.... I have listened sometimes to speeches by leaders ... in
the homelands ... where they refer to the South African government, police, and army, as people whose fingers are itching to
"Kill the kaffirs," to "Shoot at the kaffirs." These things are said ...
by people who are ... supporting the government.

When ... we ... say that this conflict will not stop until the
government calls a national convention, we are really saying that
violence is not the option: the option is the national convention.
(13:935–38)

The prosecution said violence was an inevitable outcome of the
UDF's political activity. It charged the UDF leaders in the Delmas
Trial with creating the climate in which conflicts began on Septem-
ber 3, 1984.

The defendants said violence had always accompanied apartheid, and that the UDF wanted "lasting peace." Molefe testified:

If ... a solution that would guarantee lasting peace ... was to
be found, there was a need to bring together respected leaders of
various communities in a national convention where ... a new
constitution for South Africa could be formulated....

This call was made by the United Democratic Front in 1983.... There was a raging conflict in the country, violent conflict taking place.... The UDF was simply giving expression and echoing the views that had already been expressed.... But in making this call in the context in which there was this ... violent conflict ... that involved the government on one hand, and certain of South African citizens who had decided to pursue the noble goal of freedom ... through armed struggle ... [it] had become clear that ... casualties ... are being suffered. Very talented and important young white South Africans were dying ... in that conflict.... There were other people who were not involved directly in taking up arms, who were also dying ...

The UDF saw ... the national convention as a very crucial issue ... to be shouted as loudly as possible to convince the government of the need—and those who had taken up arms of the need—to come together in ... negotiations where this conflict could be ended once and for all, and we could bring an end to the loss of life ... and ... begin to lay the basis for proper reconciliation of different racial groups in the country....

We felt that there was a need to create a climate in which there would be no need for anybody to pursue any violent methods, and we honestly believed that there was no other way of doing it. (13:294)

The prosecution interpreted the UDF predictions of violence as threats, quoting speeches in which UDF leaders showed sympathy with the motives of those who had taken to violence. Lekota had made a speech saying:

If we are not ... carrying arms today, it is not because we do not understand how and what persuaded some of our fellows ... to resort to those methods. We understand very well what pushed our people to that point. And today ... we are reminding the rulers of our country, we are reminding the masses of our people, that if the Nats [the ruling Nationalist party] are allowed to continue with this ... they can only deepen the scale of racial and violent conflict in the country. In that, the disaster will engulf us all. (15:714)

These words, the prosecution charged, were a covert call to violence. Lekota rejected the accusation, quoting a later passage from the same speech:

In the presence of two fighting elephants, the ground suffers. If two men are fighting, you must either take sides or you must stop the fight.... There is no way you can say, "Look, it does not really matter. Let them go on." ... We are in ... a situation where two giants are colliding. We have an obligation as South Africans. We can make a contribution. We must make our choice.... Let them lock us in jail if they like. Let them burn us.... We must refuse to go to the polls [for the tricameral elections].... We must not give approval to this type of thing. (15:714–15)

Molefe said:

It saddens me to read about [bombings where civilians were killed]. They are not something that one derives pleasure from. It worries me. It pains my heart.... I know that I myself could have been one of the people killed. My wife could have been involved in that tragic incident. It could have been my little daughter who is only two years old. I feel once more that the blame should be placed where it belongs ... at the doorstep of the government. (13:362)

Lekota said:

When we go into buildings, or when we go into trains, we are no longer sure whether we will come out alive. We do not know whether somebody has planted a bomb there.... When it does explode, it does not choose whether you are a white or a black, it takes all of us. (15:553)

Concerning his tone of sympathy for the ANC's choice, he answered:

It is very tragic that the African National Congress has had to resort to these methods ... because so many innocent people suffer in the process. It is also tragic because ... a lot of young people from within our own communities ... are lost to our society.... I understand ... the depth of frustration of young people ... who look around themselves and see [a] life without any opportunities.... Young men, young fellows, and mothers, who look around and see that they have nothing to bequeath unto their children except a state of political recklessness.... For that reason ... I have reserved my condemnation for the policies of the government. (15:688)

Van Dijkhorst intervened to make a point. He would come back to it again, and he would use it in his verdict:

VAN DIJKHORST: So, in fact, you are saying that you will never say to the ANC, "Stop your violence."

LEKOTA: I disapprove of their use of violence, and I would say the best path is the one we are pursuing.... However ... I respect them for their dedication to democracy and a just order, and I do not think myself with a right to condemn them. (15:689)

Molefe sees the ANC's accepting violence only as a last resort.

The ANC ... has been ... pursuing nonviolence for close to fifty years, and it is closed down.... People like Mr. Mandela took a clear decision that they were not going to injure people.... They were going to go for buildings which were seen as symbols of apartheid, and they would do that when there was nobody there. They would avoid the loss of life as much as they could. (14:372)

To the prosecution, violence is practiced by the ANC, "terrorists who plant bombs in the middle of streets of our cities and who kill innocent people." (14:372) To the defendants, violence is essential to maintain apartheid. It is the substance of day-to-day life in South Africa, especially for blacks, no matter what their political opinion.

The prosecution cited a meeting where people chanted, "Botha [President and Prime Minister] is a terrorist." Lekota answered:

Here we are in Cape Town.... In winter, when these people did not have house[s], police would come in there, in the middle of winter, and smash down these shacks, plastic shacks that they had.... In the eyes of the people watching these things, it was terrorising them.... It is in the light of experiences of that nature that people say, This is terrorism....

Women sit there in the open with little kids in their arms, they do not know what they are going to do when night comes— people say, This is terrorism....

People are sitting in their homes ... or they are sleeping ... [in] the early hours of the morning, two, one, three. Police come and, "Gagaga," [not a word] hit the doors, "Open," get in. "Everybody wake up!" "Where is your pass?" Kick, "Kom, kaffir, wat?" ["Come nigger, what?"] and throw them in cars....

It cannot be expected that people who live in conditions like that can say every day, "Thank you, baas [boss]. Thank you, baas." (16:670)

Then, characteristically, he offered a bridge back from his harsh accusation:

So it is those experiences which have shaped the perceptions of people . . . and really, there is no problem if the government could just allow for our communities [to] participate in the government of the country. . . . There would be peace. I have said it again and again. We have forgotten and we have forgiven everything that has happened. . . . Can we not make a new beginning, and share the future in this country? (16:670)

Fick moved to the next point.

Lekota frequently says the UDF chose nonviolence for the sake of future reconciliation:

We . . . seek a negotiated settlement because . . . the less bitter the methods adopted to resolve the present problem, the easier will be the process of reconciliation. The longer the government resists a program of guided negotiation, the more it creates the chance for a deepening of the conflict. . . . The process of reconciliation then becomes more difficult. (15:513)

"Lekota speaks from the point of view one who sees himself making leadership decisions to heal the post-apartheid society."

This was a point of view neither prosecutor nor judge could accept.

Part Three
Compatriots

9 UDF and ANC

In 1961, Mandela announced that the ANC had accepted "armed struggle" as necessary to move the South African government to abandon apartheid. Membership in either the ANC or the Communist Party would, in and of itself, have sufficed as proof of high treason and hostile and violent intent. So the UDF's relations with the banned organizations became a focus of the Delmas Trial.

Some of the defense rests on a legalism. No one could prove that the defendants were members of the ANC. The prosecution tried. It cited a speech on January 8, 1983, by Oliver Tambo, head of the ANC in exile, calling for "mass democratic action" organized "into one front for national liberation." Chaskalson said there was no evidence to connect the defendants with Tambo's call.

> There is absolutely no evidence to show that anybody in
> South Africa was aware of the call made by Mr. Tambo on 8 January-
> ary. There is just no evidence. At the best there is speculation that
> somebody who might have been a member of the ANC might have
> heard it over Radio Freedom if that message was broadcast and if
> it was broadcast in a way in which it was received in South Africa
> and not blocked. (25:350)

The UDF, the prosecution said, was formed to lead, organize, and mobilize the masses inside the country, because the banned ANC could not do so itself.

Ever since the National Party has held power, it has attributed internal protest and unrest to "outside agitators" and to people inside the country influenced by "outside agitators."

Bizos, leading Lekota's evidence in chief, exposed these assumptions:

> BIZOS: It is suggested in the indictment that you really were
> doing the bidding of the ANC and the Communist Party, and were

75

in secret conspiracy in opposing the Black Local Authorities. How do you feel about that?

LEKOTA: That is absolutely untrue. . . . I do not need anybody to come from Russia to come and tell me that what apartheid is doing to us is wrong. I do not need anybody from anywhere to come and tell me that I do not have a house. I do not have it. I need not anybody to come and tell me that the reference, the passbooks, the pass laws, what they are doing to my people. I know what they do. I have seen that. (15:478)

Molefe's answer to the same assumption resonates with his own experience:

The masses of our people have long been part of the freedom struggle. . . . Since the implementation of the policies of apartheid, they have known that they were involved in the struggle against apartheid. I grew up as a child. Once I started talking to other people and seeing what was happening around me, I knew that I was part of the struggle. I belong to a community that was involved in the struggle against apartheid. Therefore, the struggle for freedom.

It is not as though you are talking to people who are not conscious of what is happening to them and you are manipulating them to accept that there is something foreign to them that is called a national liberation struggle. We are talking here about people whose daily life is the life of experience of apartheid, shunted from pillar to post and suffering under the deplorable shortage of houses, no proper facilities in the townships, walking around in winter without a pair of shoes on, going to school with a pair of trousers that is torn at the back and the buttocks sticking out. All those things are the things that people experience, and they have become part of the struggle against apartheid. . . .

When you talk about the black community, you are not talking about people who are like white people, who have lived the rest of their lives as lives of privilege and protection from the government. You are talking about people who have suffered, who have gone through pain of deprivation, who have experienced extreme illiteracy, who have had to work for a pittance.

They had to go through a situation where they could not organize themselves for better wages. A situation that did not exist in the white community.

When we really deal with the situation in the black community, we must understand that we are not dealing with people to
whom suffering is a foreign thing. (13:654–55)

Molefe insists that the power of the UDF derives from the trust
of its supporters, not from decisions taken by its officials.

If the UDF was created in response to the call by Tambo, the
UDF might be a creature of the ANC. In 1984, the ANC claimed credit
for forming the UDF and said it intended to "guide" the UDF by
having its own "underground structures within the UDF."[1] Chaskalson argued that both the order of events and the testimony of a
witness for the prosecution made it more plausible that the ANC
piggybacked on the UDF.

We see ... first, that the ANC, through its political department,
keeps a very close study on newspapers and what is happening
within South Africa. We see that it looks particularly at issues
which seem to have grassroots community support upon which it
can capitalize. And we see that if it believes it can capitalize on
such matters, it would do so, and that really, it goes so far as to
claim credit for demonstrations and possibly even unrest in the
country, even if it may not have initiated the ... protest or ... objections. (25:347)

In 1976, many youths left the carnage that had started in Soweto
over the issue of Afrikaans as the medium of school instruction, and
they sought military training abroad. Many received training from
the ANC and its allies. In the eighties, the ANC claimed credit for a
number of strategic and visible acts of sabotage. From 1979 to 1982,
twenty-two people died in incidents attributed to the ANC.[2]

The body count was about to rise. Tambo warned that the armed
struggle would "develop into quite a war, and the civilian population
will be affected."[3] In May 1983, a car bomb outside the South African
Air Force Headquarters in Pretoria killed nineteen people. South
African forces soon attacked alleged ANC centers in neighboring
countries, killing at least seventy-four people, most unconnected
with the ANC. The government is widely thought by its critics to be
behind the assassinations of prominent ANC officials that soon followed inside and outside South Africa.

While disavowing a policy of violence directed against civilians,
the ANC, based hundreds of miles away from South Africa in Zambia,
admitted that people it had trained might not obey orders.

As part of its response to the "total onslaught," the government tried to present itself as repudiating apartheid. Officials started to reject the word. They promised "reforms." The most lavish reform was a new constitution which offered Coloureds and Indians their own Parliaments.

Molefe rejected the government scenario of reforms as fundamentally flawed in conception:

MOLEFE: It is my belief that apartheid cannot be reformed. It must be ended, and a non-racial order must be established. You cannot hope to co-opt people in an apartheid order because apartheid itself embodies contradictions. It means people cannot live together, they cannot be one, they have got to be separated, they have got to be addressed as racial groups, their treatment must be based on the color of their skin, their education, the trains they travel in, the hotels they must use, and so on. So apartheid must go, and we must have a situation where people are regarded as citizens of the country, and they can live together, they can take any kind of job they want to take, they can attend any school they want to attend . . .

JACOBS: What must take the place of the unreformable structures?

MOLEFE: A non-racial system of government representative of all the people of South Africa, black and white, on the basis of equality, where people are not judged on the basis of their color. (14:695–96)

Molefe rejected the contempt implied in the new constitution:

The attitude of the government has always been that Africans have got a vote in the homelands, and their issue does not warrant any attention except participation in local government.

I remember very well a statement . . . about the possibility of a fourth chamber. [A Member's] attitude was very clear, that there is no place for a black person in the white parliament in this country. The message was loud and clear. Similar statements were made by other people, including the leader of the Nationalist Party in the Transvaal, Dr. de Klerk,[4] and many others. (13:205)

On January 23, 1983, Dr. Allan Boesak (President of the World Alliance of Reformed Churches, who was to become Barend Strydom's preferred target) made a speech opposing "government structures" and called for a united front:

There is ... no reason why the churches, civic associations, trade unions, student organizations, and sports bodies should not unite on this issue, pool our resources, inform people of the fraud that is about to be perpetrated in their name ... [5]

Molefe heard about Boesak's speech:

When that call came, I found it to be a very attractive idea, and I understood it to be similar to the one I myself had made in 1981. It was also a call similar to the one I had read about in the pamphlet by Dr. Neville Alexander. I found it to be quite in keeping with my own views. (13:172)

I made that call myself in 1981, and I had made a similar call in 1980 in Soweto, and Dr. Neville Alexander made a similar call in 1982. Similarly, in 1942, a call was made when the Non-European Unity Movement was formed. In 1936, a similar call was made. (14:423)

In 1981, Molefe had said,

A united front becomes an imperative in our chief endeavors to meet the demands of our time.... The broad front envisaged here is the major challenge of the day, and can be pursued in the following manner: By forming, initially, an ad hoc committee of all social, political, religious and cultural organizations from all sections ... we are thinking of political bodies, sports bodies, churches, teachers organizations, workers, nurses associations, etc.... The ad hoc committee would consult [other organizations] to formulate and adopt similar stances on national issues.... It would create a dynamic system of coordination and communication between the organizations and the masses, and among the organizations themselves, resulting in a mass-based program of action at all times of need. The time has come for all oppressed people of South Africa to address themselves to the objective conditions, the realities of our situation.... Ideological differences should not bar the way for a common program of action. This is very simple indeed. The black people are oppressed collectively as a group.... Noting that we are faced with a powerful and united oppressor, our salvation, equally, lies in our unity. (13:157–59)

The defense quoted AZAPO claims that "The idea of a national united front was hijacked," by Allan Boesak's call. (14:915)

In March 1983, Molefe was invited to join a group establishing a United Democratic Front in the Transvaal.

Those of us who had read about . . . how that new constitution was intended to operate believed that it was going to have
very serious implications for our society. . . . It was dividing the
oppressed people. . . . This new constitution was now saying that
we are accepting the Coloured and Indian communities as part of
the white government structure . . . but the black African people
are not to be part of that. . . . Africans would be alienated com-
pletely from other communities . . .

I believed . . . that the only constitution that could meet the
needs of all the people of this country and . . . give an end to the
polarization and hostilities . . . was . . . based on universal franchise
. . . in which all the people of the country will participate as
equals. (13:177–80)

The new constitution came at the same time as the Koornhof
bills, the Black Local Authorities Bill, Black Communities Bill, and
Orderly Movement and Settlement of Black Persons Bill. Molefe testified:

Taken together [the new constitution and the Koornhof bills]
carried within them the main thrust of the new style apartheid,
the attempted co-optation of certain middle class Coloureds and
Indians, and the enforcement of harsh controls over the African
working class. . . . Apartheid was to be retained, but in a much
more subtle form. (13:201–2)

Opposition to the new constitution among the white electorate
came mainly from the right and led to the formation of a Conservative Party, pledged to resist the germ of racial integration.

By May 1983, opponents of the new constitutional proposals and
the Koornhof bills had formed united fronts in two of South Africa's
four provinces, the Transvaal and Natal, and were discussing a front
in a third area, the Western Cape. By the end of July, they decided to
go national at a launch on August 20, 1983.

During the July meeting, Molefe left for three or four hours to
attend the launch of the Soweto Youth Congress. In his absence, the
UDF National Interim Committee appointed him General Secretary.
He was pleased, and he immediately set to work on logistics and on
winning alliances for the launch.

On the one hand, there was a feeling that protest and united
action could make a difference.

The government was talking about change.... We sought to influence that change to be a better change, much more than the government sought to present ... (14:318)

We are motivated by the assumption that we are dealing with a rational government that is capable of assessing the feelings of the people and responding correctly. (13:357)

On the other hand, activists knew a long and vivid history of what happens to those who protest. Lekota had known Steve Biko, killed in 1977, and Abraham Tiro, killed in 1974. Molefe was a student in Soweto in 1976, and he saw some of his school fellows shot. The day of their second appearance in court, in June 1985, the defendants observed a minute of silence for the recent deaths of Mathew Goniwe and his associates. These deaths were only a few.

The prosecution, pursuing its allegation of treason, insisted that the real initiative for forming the UDF came from the ANC. It pointed to the UDF leaders' frequent references to the ANC's history of struggle for political rights. Lekota, dancing on the edge of the precipice, answered:

[The ANC] was the most representative African organization, and ... the one that did make more efforts than any other ... to raise the issue [of] our political rights with the government ... Without that history, we had no point of reference as to what non-violent methods of struggle had been there. (15:651–52)

Molefe also admitted a continuity of purpose. He said:

The UDF has never sat down to decide and say that it accepts the struggle of the fifties of the ANC as its struggle, but surely the UDF came into existence in the context in which the African people and other communities which do not have the vote in this country had been striving to get that vote. So that the UDF becomes part of the history of resistance against apartheid.... That would include the activities of all other groups right from the eighteenth century. (14:195)

By implication, if the UDF was guilty, all resistance to apartheid was guilty. It was not the connection with the ANC: it was the connection with what the ANC wanted that the government would not permit.

Without disavowing sympathy with the ANC, Lekota insisted on his independence:

No, no. . . . They do not decide for me. I decide for myself
what I want. . . . Of my own, I reflect on things. I read, I think
about them, and I am mature, like anybody else. I do not get told
by somebody that, You must do this, and then you must do that,
and so on, and so on. I have got my own independent mind.
(16:270)

Molefe said:

The perceptions are fundamentally different between the two
communities [white and black]. . . . In the black community generally, the ANC is regarded as a movement that is fighting to free the
oppressed people. . . . In the white community it is regarded as a
terrorist organization. [13:362 (a)]

While insisting that the UDF is an independent organization,
Molefe believed no political settlement could come without ANC
participation:

The ANC was one of the important factors . . . in the politics
of our country. . . . [Given] the measure of support it enjoys within
the black communities, it would be difficult to persuade the black
communities that a settlement . . . is legitimate if we did not involve the African National Congress in the process of reaching
that settlement. (15:665)

During Lekota's testimony, van Dijkhorst questioned this prem-
ise indignantly:

VAN DIJKHORST: So what you are in fact saying is that, with
certain variations . . . the government must hand over control of
the state to the Rivonia trialists [Mandela, Sisulu, and others convicted in 1964 of turning to sabotage, after the banning of the
ANC, and sentenced to life imprisonment. All the Rivonia trialists
have now been released] and Oliver Tambo and others?

LEKOTA: No, not at all. What we are saying is that the government must pull together various groupings . . . including . . . some
of those people who enjoy support within our communities, even
if they are in exile. . . . Our concern is that there must be a way . . .
of resolving the conflict . . . and [we cannot resolve it] if we leave
out a sector that on the face of things enjoys . . . considerable . . .
support. It is important . . . to neutralize the conflict . . . to bring

them into it, because then you can assuage ... you satisfy everybody in the process.

It is not because we have a brief for the African National Congress, but we are concerned about terminating this conflict ...
that seems to be growing within our ... society. It must be termi-
nated ... (15:923)

This distinction between negotiation and a handing over of control did not seem persuasive to van Dijkhorst. Versions of the issue
recur throughout the trial.

The prosecution charged that the UDF was really led by ANC
leaders.

Now I put it to you that a number of the UDF patrons and
leaders ... are persons either serving sentences for ANC activities
or other unlawful activities against the state. Another group had
been members of the ANC or the South African Communist Party.
(16:261)

The three presidents of the UDF, Archie Gumede, Albertina Sisulu, and Oscar Mpetha, had all been members of the ANC.

Molefe answered:

When these people became part of the UDF, the consideration
was not whether they had been members of the ANC or not. They
were elected by majority vote, an open vote, and they were respected people in their own organizations and in their communities. ... We have no right to deprive people participation in the organization simply because at a certain point they had been
members of the ANC. (14:545)

Lekota spoke of the "awe and respect" accorded those who have
suffered in opposing apartheid. Fick had started to go through the
names of UDF patrons in prison:

FICK: Now Frances Baard: I put it to you that she was a member of the ANC Congress as well as a member of the ANC's Wom-
en's League.

LEKOTA: I do not know when. Would it have been before it
was banned? Because when it was banned, I was still a young fellow. I would not have known about that. ... But she is a very
highly respected person within our community ...

FICK: I put it to you that she was also sentenced to five years imprisonment . . .

LEKOTA: I have no knowledge of that. Most probably, if that is the position, it may explain the respect people have for her. Not for the offenses, but for her position as somebody who may have sacrificed a lot for equality of status for black people in this country . . .

A lot of these people are respected within our communities. . . . A lot of people may outrightly say, Look, I do not agree with that, and so on, but they will say, Look, these people have made such sacrifices that it is impossible we can ignore them . . .

If there is somebody who has been to Robben Island, people say . . . "Now you know he has been to Robben Island," and you can see the response of people. It is one of immediate awe and respect. (16:263–64)

The prosecution charged that the UDF promoted support for the ANC by "popularizing of their leaders." They credited the UDF with part of the ANC's recovery from influence lost in the seventies. During the early eighties ANC banners were openly displayed, and ANC leaders were referred to as heroes. The depth of this attitude went beyond the reach of government power, and, in the eyes of the defendants, beyond their own power.

The UDF would not have the nerve to tell the community . . . that Mr. Mandela is not their leader.

I have moved around in that community and see little children playing hopscotch . . . I have listened to kids of twelve, fourteen years playing. . . . We in the past used to say, "In, out, in, out." . . . Now the children have developed a new language . . . they say "Tambo, Mandela." When they are out, they use the name of leaders of homelands. They say "Mopedi" or "Mpephu" to show that you have done the wrong thing.

This shows the perception in the communities from which we come. I would not be able to tell . . . the children that Mr. Tambo is a terrorist. I myself am not convinced that he is a terrorist. If all the people in South Africa were given a vote in this country, and somebody tries to bring change by violent means, I would call that person a terrorist. (14:371)

The prosecution never admitted, and perhaps did not recognize, that Molefe was charging the government with terrorism.

Again and again, the prosecution asked Molefe and Lekota why they had not denounced and dissociated themselves from Mandela. Molefe's answer assumes a relationship between leaders and their communities not accepted by the prosecution. In the prosecution's view of the world, leaders tell their people what to do, and are obeyed. In Molefe's world, the leaders obey their people. They can guide, but they must listen. They do not and cannot take positions alien to those they lead.

We did not choose him. He was chosen by ordinary people from organizations.

Who are we to tell people that Nelson Mandela is not their leader? If the perception of the South African government and the Afrikaner people is that Nelson Mandela is not a leader, that is not the perception in our communities. We cannot go and tell our people that a man who has sacrificed so much is not their leader when they regard him as their leader . . . (14:626)

Molefe's assumptions about leadership seem to baffle van Dijkhorst, who has little political experience and appears to have a general distaste for and distrust of political practice.

Lekota also insisted that the honor given to opponents of apartheid was not a matter of UDF choice, although the UDF shared in according that honor.

The truth must be spoken at some point. . . . The price may have to be paid, for the truth must be spoken. Any man, including Nelson Mandela . . . any organization, including the African National Congress, that is today committed to the struggle against apartheid is a matter of pride to this country. . . . Even amongst the Afrikaners, men such as Beyers Naude have been born.[6] People like Helen Joseph, among white people.[7] Those people are the pride of our country. They are the people who carry the hope of the future of our country, and we must make bold to say that we will rally to them. (15:715–16)

As for Mandela, Lekota speaks of him with special warmth rooted in his years on Robben Island:

As I have understood the man, it was really the desperation and the dark mood that beset our communities after the banning of the African National Congress that pushed him to resort to armed methods of struggle.

He, in my judgment, is a man who is very proud of the fact that in 1952 he was the volunteer in chief in the Defiance Campaign in which nonviolence was emphasized so much, and he has great admiration for the men and women who joined him in the Defiance Campaign in 1952.

He is, I may mention, a lawyer by profession, and he is constantly conscious of doing things in an orderly fashion. Now, I have seen Nelson intervene in hunger strikes, or in disputes between prisoners and the administration, and seeking to create a situation of understanding.

So I am quite convinced in my own mind that were a process of negotiation set in motion, and he was convinced that the government was serious about resolving the problems of our country non-violently, he would do so. (15:684)

Lekota was aware that, in honoring Mandela, he stood with the world; in imprisoning him, the government of South Africa stood alone:

I have sometimes felt that the international community and nations of the world have so honored Nelson that we in our communities would be less than human if we turned our back on a man who is so highly respected for his contribution to democracy in our country. (15:688)

10 Two Worlds in One Country

In speaking about other groups in South Africa, Molefe and Lekota constantly looked to the present political situation and to the future. Although they were speaking in a courtroom on trial for their political beliefs and their lives, they knew that they were also speaking for the UDF to the turbulent world outside the courtroom where their words would be noticed by those who feared the UDF, those who hoped for it, and those who competed with it.

In the trial, Molefe and Lekota wanted to reassure whites and enlist them as allies against apartheid. They wanted to make it clear that their position differed from that of black separatists. Most importantly, they wanted to discard categories of race as ways of assessing and assigning political power and to replace them with descriptions like "favoring democracy in a nonracial state," or "supporting apartheid."

The prosecution seemed unable to imagine a nonracial state. Molefe and Lekota seemed to talk in concepts as bizarre and remote from their reality as Ursula le Guin's imagined polity where males can become female.

Molefe said:

> There is a whole question of having to allay the fears of the white community. . . . We have to convince them that they also have a future in this country, that we are not working toward . . . the so-called black majority government. We are not talking about that. We are talking about a majority government on the understanding that the people of this country come from all sorts of racial groups who, under apartheid, have been divided, and [who] under that new government shall have become a . . . non-racial country under a single government. . . .
>
> We are not calling for a black Prime Minister . . . or a black President. We are simply saying we want a government that is elected by all the people of South Africa, and that guarantees the future of all the people of this country on an individual basis . . .
>
> All we are saying is let us be treated decently as citizens of this country. Let us enjoy the rights that everyone else enjoys in this country. Let us share in the wealth of this country. (13:331)

The prosecution asked whether the UDF would be satisfied by a fourth chamber of Parliament for Africans. Molefe answered:

> We would reject that, and my reasons are as follows. We do not want a chamber that wants to keep the black people confined to 13 percent of the land, and the homelands, and the group areas. We wanted a vote, a meaningful vote, a vote that would allow us to change the laws of the country in such a manner that what South Africa can offer, the wealth of the country, can be shared by all . . .
>
> If I wanted to stand as the prime minister of South Africa, I should be allowed to do so. If I wanted to elect somebody else as the prime minister in the central government, I should be allowed to do so . . .
>
> [Not where a minority] have control over all important matters like finance, defense, foreign ministries, and so on. We wanted

a government where all the people would have access to those important areas of government . . .

The struggle that the UDF is involved in is a struggle for . . . meaningful political rights, political rights that would enable all the parties of this country, [including] the black people of this country who have hitherto not been allowed to determine their own future, to do so as part of the broad society of South Africa. (13:633–34)

He pointed out that many parties would participate in the national convention the UDF called for. When the prosecution said that this call would mean, in fact, a seizure of power by the blacks, he answered:

I do not accept that. . . . We are committed to a non-racial South Africa. Trade unions . . . are led today by some people who are white. We in the UDF have got white people in our executive committees. We elect them. . . . We are not looking for black majority rule. We are looking for a government in which all the people of the country will govern together. It is true that in terms of their ratios . . . the African people are the majority, and . . . it is very likely that once a government is set up, a majority of cabinet ministers might come from the African sector. But whatever government is set up, it is guided by the broad principles agreed upon . . . where people are not regarded as whites, coloureds, Indians, and having special treatment because of the color of their skins. . . . People are treated equally. The law would protect everybody equally, not because of the color of the skin. (13:636)

The prosecution seemed blind to distinctions made continually by Molefe and Lekota between apartheid and whites, between the form of government and those who attain power in it, between the government and the state. In cross-examination Jacobs used the words "government" and "state" as though they mean the same thing. There was a revealing exchange.

MOLEFE: I think there is a difference between the state and the government, although sometimes people use it interchangeably. . . . I think the state is something that transcends party politics. . . . The government that is in power is essentially the government of the Nationalist Party, and the state is something much broader than that, as I understand it, because that [the state] would include the courts and so on, and I do not believe that the courts are part of the Nationalist Party.

JACOBS: But the courts are part of the government, man. Part of the state.

VAN DIJKHORST: Is that official, Mr. Jacobs?

JACOBS: No, I asked him.

VAN DIJKHORST: Is it a question?

MOLEFE: No, no. I do not regard the courts as part of the government. The government is essentially that of the National Party. It is set up to promote the ideology of the National Party, of apartheid. But the courts are more than that. They are part of the state. They transcend party politics. The courts are part of the broad structures that deal with the interests of the entire country, the people of the country, black and white, not the interests of apartheid.

JACOBS: Do you say that the courts are part of the government?

MOLEFE: I do not see them as part of the government. (13:663–64)

The difference between the party in power and the ongoing institutions of public life seems to have been unfamiliar to the prosecution. This distinction is regarded by some as critical to maintaining the independence of the judiciary and the civil service from party political pressure. Some consider it a crucial difference between democratic and totalitarian regimes.

Molefe, a politician who thinks tactically as well as for the long term, sought opportunities to communicate with the white establishment:

The white community in this country is a very important sector. It is a section of the society that is in power, and if an organization is committed to peaceful means of bringing about a change, and it wants genuine change, it wants a change that would include the white community. (13:348)

Addressing the white community was not simple. The state-controlled media, and newspapers curbed by severe censorship do not bridge the worlds.

The white community . . . lives in ignorance as to what is happening in the black areas. . . . We saw our duty as having to remove the cobweb that the state-controlled media was continually putting before the eyes of the white community. We wanted them to gain a proper understanding of the kind of people they are dealing with, the kind of people they are living side by side with in this country. . . . It was very, very crucial for us to move the two communities closer together because finally we must converge in a single South Africa that is non-racial . . .

There has been a very abnormal situation here. We were not able to talk to the officials who rule us in this country, but we are able to talk to foreigners, simply because those who govern in this country do not respect our organizations, but these foreigners [do] respect our organizations. (13:347–50)

So the UDF cultivated relationships with people in the international community who could present its position to the white establishment. Molefe and Lekota established warm friendships with reporters and diplomats, scholars and clerics, politicians and business people in Europe and America as well as in South Africa. Many attended the trial.

They could also be in a position to give their own observations. . . . We believed that the government was particularly sensitive to pressure coming from the western governments. It was likely to listen to what its friends in the western countries were saying. (13:350)

Some whites are already supporters of the UDF. Others are potential allies. Molefe and Lekota consistently assume that whites who understand the experience of blacks will want to renounce apartheid.

Ordinary people must understand that [the government] is not the white people. . . . It is the government that formulates policies, that is really oppressing the people. So that the struggle would be against those policies and the government that implements those policies, not against the ordinary white people. Because if they knew the truth, if they had the opportunity, they would do something better. They would not insist on the policies of apartheid. (13:660)

The UDF has made it clear that it is not opposed to the white people. It is opposed to the policies of apartheid (13:850)

The defense quoted a speech made by Lekota before his arrest:

We are not demanding a black government. No way. We are asking for a government of the people of South Africa. Let me repeat that we are not looking for a black Prime Minister. We are not looking for an African Prime Minister. Experience has taught us that among African people as well, there are rascals and scoundrels.... So, we do not want a Coloured Prime Minister, but also we do not want an Indian Prime Minister. Given that such a Prime Minister should be an African, or white, or Indian, that will just be coincidental. The primary condition for him to lead our country must be that he accepts the humanity of the people of our country, all of them ...

We have confidence in the people of South Africa, black and white ... including the Afrikaners.... Even though Afrikaners may have been foreigners, in terms of arriving here [after the Africans], but together with all ... they have made a contribution side by side with us.

We made a contribution. We mined our country. We built the roads. We built the buildings.... This country, we have shaped what it is today. It was a combined effort of the people of South Africa. Let us claim South Africa for everybody. (15:594–95)

Lekota elaborated on his speech when it was quoted in court. Characteristically, he looks toward the future, and makes statements in the present that address the needs of the future. "You cannot just declare non-racialism; you must build it."[1]

The question of reconciling the people of our country is a very, very sensitive question. It is a primary question for all of us. If we were to demand ... a black Prime Minister ... [that] would leave very many sections of our country uncomfortable. And we ourselves would not be comfortable, because if he had pursued policies which were not in the interest of the majority of our people ... we would have to stand up and say, "No," and he would have to lock us up in jail as well ... (15:594)

Lekota, who grew up in Kroonstad where Afrikaners far outnumber English speakers in the white population, shows particular warmth when talking about Afrikaners. Describing a visit to Rand Afrikaner University, he explained:

I considered that going out to meet academics in an Afrikaans institution, speaking to them, communicating our views on mat-

ters . . . one way of reaching an important section that has access
to very many other people in the Afrikaner community. So that . . .
will help . . . us to be understood in those quarters, and at the
same time, to persuade that section of the community to understand that beneath our various shades of skin color is not hatred
for them, but . . . a search for friendship. That we are committed to
them just as much as we are committed to anybody else. (15:604)

In Lekota's testimony, acceptance of whites as important members of the present and future South Africa becomes vivid through
the way he talks about particular people. When he was asked about
the UDF's support for a campaign against conscription, which affected only whites, he answered:

We in the UDF have been criticized for saying that apartheid
also imposes oppression on white sections of the population. Our
reasoning is that even though whites are privileged under the present order, their lives would be even better without apartheid. Parents would not have to stay behind, worried about whether their
children who are somewhere on the borders . . . will come back
alive or not. Young white families would not be split for long periods of time, when husbands are out and away defending policies
which really generate opposition to themselves.

I will sometimes see when people go to the army . . . at the
stations, at the airports, one sees how loved ones cry tears . . .
when they have to part with their loved ones . . .

Sometimes police come into the townships . . . when there is a
protest . . . and . . . they will have to shoot people. . . . I am sure
they do not want to do it, but what does a man do if either he
does it or goes to jail for six years? . . . It is a difficult situation.
Oppression, apartheid is really a heavy burden for all of us, black
and white. (15:628–29)

Lekota testified to set off the UDF's position as distinct from that
of many blacks who condemn whites, believe only in white hatred,
and contemplate responding in kind. Lekota tries to build a future
free of this heritage of mutual hatred and to demonstrate that it is
not race that separates people in South Africa but apartheid. He cites
examples:

There were people who had made a clear stand against apartheid and who had made a call for a democratic government in our
country, and who had made sacrifices for those aspirations. . . . It is

important for us that we acknowledge this contribution.... Some, like Beyers Naude, have been rejected and ostracized by their own communities. They ... are really the prophets of our time you know, and ... in future those of us who will look back, and generations of the future, will be very proud ... that they had been there, and they have sacrificed so much for the peaceful future of our country ...

When the UDF has been criticized for its non-racial policy of allowing white people to participate with us in the struggle, it has been the names such as those of Beyers Naude and Helen Joseph and other white people who have made contributions ... that we quote as examples to our younger people ...

Given an opportunity, the majority of our white compatriots can be moved to a position where they support a joint and common South Africa for us all.

He raises the principle of reconciliation to an extraordinary pitch in talking about General van den Bergh, retired head of BOSS, the Bureau of State Security, the South African version of the KGB:

There are within sections of our communities ... people whose perception is that every white person does not want to hear anything.... You have got to say, "No, man, not all white people. White people do not hate us really."
But then they say, "But where is the evidence?"
I can only point to Dr. Beyers Naude ... to Helen Joseph ... and to people like those because they are living evidence.... But we are not in a position to say the same for instance when General van den Bergh goes to church, and there are black people there ... and they sing there, and then General van den Bergh gets very angry about this, and he goes into the [news]papers, and he says, "The niggers came into the church and sang there," and so on. ["Die kaffirs het in die kerk gekom en daar gesing."] Then it is also a reality.... We cannot deny that reality is there but ... we swing people round and show them that, "No, this is an exception. He is an old man. He comes from a long time ago.... He thinks that way, but it is because he does not understand why these people are singing, and dancing as they are singing." ...
We have to move people this way because otherwise we are going to allow a situation in which alienation increases.
(15:719–20)

11 Rivals

Unlike the UDF, some other antiapartheid organizations do not see a role for whites in the struggle for a new South Africa. Some leading black intellectuals support AZAPO, a Black Consciousness organization that excludes whites from participation. Some do not believe that whites can be relied on as allies. Some believe that whites, trained to illusions of superiority from birth, continue to operate from assumptions of entitlement, even in political organizations that oppose apartheid. Some believe that the dynamics, when whites and blacks work in the same organization, tend to ensure that whites move into positions of power and leadership and to reduce opportunities for blacks to learn how to operate effectively in these roles. Some have learned to hate.

Both Molefe and Lekota had been members of AZAPO. In 1983, when the UDF was coming into being, AZAPO created its own united front of groups sharing its blacks-only position to oppose a new constitution, the National Forum. Its members included Neville Alexander, whose writings calling for a united front had inspired Molefe, and others who had been political allies and friends. AZAPO and the UDF became extreme rivals.

In the Delmas Trial, alleged AZAPO supporters were among the indicted. They were charged with participating in a conspiracy of AZAPO and the UDF to overthrow the state by violence. The defense argued that, far from conspiring together, AZAPO and the UDF were in deep disagreement, and it cited testimony that AZAPO refused to affiliate with the UDF because such affiliation would have compromised its principles. AZAPO, often using a Marxist framework for its critique, could not ally itself with an organization that had "the daughters and the sons of the bosses in their organization." (25:522)

In 1983, Molefe and Lekota were invited to a commemoration service in honor of Steve Biko. Lekota was to be a speaker.

> Initially . . . the meeting was joint effort between UDF supporters and . . . AZAPO supporters. But when we got to the meeting we . . . were told that AZAPO supporters had pulled out. Well, anyway, the meeting went ahead, and . . . I addressed the meeting, and just as we finished the AZAPO people arrived there in large numbers and the meeting was just thrown in disarray. We . . . were advised to clear out.

So there was a long . . . acrimonious history . . . between
AZAPO and [the] UDF (15:703)

Although clashes between the UDF and AZAPO sometimes
erupted into violence, the UDF and AZAPO occasionally united and
spoke on each other's platforms. The Delmas indictment identified
four of the original twenty-two defendants as members of AZAPO.
Only one admitted membership. The prosecution charged conspiracy between AZAPO and the UDF at a high level. The defendants
insisted that although there had been discussions about cooperation,
these had come to nothing.

The UDF rejected divisions between white and black and rejected divisions supported by government structures like the homelands and the "independent" ethnic "states."

We would accept the fact that there are people who speak
Zulu. . . . We accept the fact that there are people who speak
Sotho. We accept the fact that there are people who would speak
Gujerati. There are people who would speak . . . Hindi. People
who speak Afrikaans, English, Xhosa, Venda . . .
The UDF is opposed to attempts by the government to elevate
the difference in language to nation states. . . . Although those
people use different languages, they can live together harmoniously in one South Africa and must not be divided on the basis of
the language they speak and be given little backyards there as governments . . .
Within the white community, you have people who speak
German. You have people who speak Afrikaans. You have those
who speak English. You have those who speak Italian. You have
those who speak Greek . . . but the government has never sought
to divide those people into little compartments, and confine them
into certain sections of the country, and expect one to have several governments . . .
We are opposed to that kind of division that is imposed on
us. . . . I went to school with Zulu-speaking people. I met with
people speaking Northern Sotho. . . . I have never had any problem, but the government . . . wants to say that we cannot live together because it is important for the government to promote its
policy of apartheid and separate development and says these differences are beyond control . . .
Surely a person who comes from Greece came here with a
culture . . . not necessarily part of the culture of a person who

came from England, or a person who came from Holland, or a person who came from Germany, but one cannot say ... these people could not live together.

Why are they able to live together in the white areas today harmoniously? Why are they able to vote into Parliament whoever they want to choose? Why is it that we are not allowed to do the things they are allowed to do? What species are they made of? How different is that from the species that we ... are made of? ...

It is not a way of encouraging peace. It is a way of encouraging tribal conflicts, ethnic conflicts, and so on. We reject that. (13:637–39)

The UDF had a complex relationship with Zulu Chief Gatsha Mangosuthu Buthelezi. It veered from wooing to contempt and fury. Government-paid Buthelezi has for years taken positions that sometimes ally him with the government—he opposes economic sanctions—and sometimes sets him against it—he opposed the new constitution. He says he was once a friend of Mandela. He was a member of the ANC, but he has since been critical of the ANC and has derided it. He opposes the policy that creates "independent homelands" and has refused "independence" for his own homeland, but, as head of the largest tribal group, he has vested interests in maintaining the government-supported division of tribe from tribe. He attacked the new constitution. "Anyone who has anything between his ears would know that this plan is nothing more than a recipe for violence," but soon after the UDF's formation, he followed the lead of government officials in describing it as a front for the ANC.

Inkatha, a Zulu organization created by Buthelezi, and describing itself as a cultural organization, has opposed the UDF since its founding. On October 29, 1983, five students at the University of Zululand who had criticized Buthelezi were killed, allegedly by members of Inkatha, and many were wounded.

After this outbreak of violence and a whites only referendum approving the new constitution, Buthelezi invited Archie Gumede, President of the UDF in Natal, near Zululand, to address the homeland's legislative assembly. The defense quoted his letter partly to show that even people like Buthelezi opposed the new constitution.

South Africa has just seen whites adopt a new constitution which denationalizes every African in the country ... historically

the most determined expression whites have evidenced to put
blacks in permanent political subjugation ...

The tragic events of the University of Zululand on October
29th have been used by some blacks to sow a seed of black/black
confrontation. I believe that a discussion between yourself and
your executive, and myself and my colleagues is urgently needed.

I am therefore inviting you to address the Kwa-Zulu legislative
assembly ... (13:422)

The UDF answered by approving the call for unity and the rejec-
tion of the new constitution. It declined the invitation to address the
Kwa-Zulu legislative assembly.

... an institution which is created without consultation with
the people, and one which is imposed on the section of the population in total disregard of the people's pronounced and demonstrated opposition. ... The UDF prides itself on its democratic
foundations and workings, and will not risk jeopardizing either. In
the circumstances, association with the Kwa-Zulu legislative assembly has the potential of compromising the democratic projec-
tion and character of this front. ... This is not directed against you
and your colleagues in your personal capacities. ... However ...
for members of an oppressed and coerced community to volun-
tarily man and daily keep institutions of oppression serviced to
grind the defenseless masses under the yoke of oppression is suicidal and untenable. (13:426–27)

The letter brought up other grounds of complaint, including
Buthelezi's description of the UDF as a facade for the ANC and the
exclusion of UDF affiliates from institutions in Zululand.

Feelings ran high. The prosecution at the Delmas Trial cited a
bitter speech at a meeting in Soweto where Molefe was present,
although not as a speaker. Oupa Monareng said:

It is clear and obvious that [homeland leaders, including Bu-
thelezi] are prepared to replace the actual enemy and subject our
people to constant harassment and cruelty. ... [The speaker called
for] drastic action against such government-created bodies, puppets and stooges, predictably Inkatha and all its members throughout the country. ... Let us subject them to constant harassment. ... Let us drive them all from our places of operation and
residence. (14:227–28)

Molefe, citing videotapes of the speech brought in evidence, pointed out that the audience was laughing during much of this speech. Jacobs, the prosecutor, took the opportunity.

JACOBS: **Would you say that the people at that meeting find the killing of people, either by the government or anyone else, as a laughable matter?**

MOLEFE: **No, I think they were laughing at the way he was presenting what he was presenting to them. (14:227)**

Although the people were laughing, Molefe was concerned. He discussed the speech with Frank Chikane, another UDF leader. They agreed to correct the course of the meeting through another speech:

I asked him to make it clear that our . . . struggle was not against individuals . . . not against the members of Inkatha. . . . He must correct that situation, and state clearly that that was not our policy to do that [attack hostel dwellers in Soweto who were members of Inkatha]. (13:487)

In cross-examination, Molefe denied UDF responsibility for Oupa Monareng. He was not a UDF official and had been invited at the last minute, without time to consult with anyone about his speech:

He is not speaking for the UDF . . . and I am satisfied that the people . . . there did not take him seriously, because this meeting took place in 1983. I know of no situation where the people in Soweto attacked members of Inkatha in that period, up until the time of my arrest. (14:229)

Van Dijkhorst asked for evidence that the chairman or somebody else had repudiated Monareng. The defense pointed to the next speech by Tiego Moseneke:

I must say very clearly today that those men and women who are carrying daggers, and bludgeons, and spears [pangas, and kieries, and assegais], who walked into the hostels and murdered our people, those men are pure South Africans, and those people, I say, we should not do away with. Those are our people. Those people have been misled by Gatsha [Buthelezi] and Inkatha for their own purpose. Those people are still our people, and our ranks will always be open to them to come and join us in the fight for a true democracy in this country. . . .

I want to advise our fellow students from University of [Zulu-land] who have very strong feelings against Inkatha . . . fellow men, these people who murdered your fellow men are our fellow men, fellow South Africans. If these people knew the truth, only if they knew the truth, those people would have directed their wrath against Buthelezi . . . because this man . . . is causing very serious divisions between our people. . . . This man serves to reproduce an unjust system . . . we shall destroy the system together with him. (14:231–32)

The prosecution presented Moseneke's speech too as incitement to violent revolution. Molefe answered that words like "destroy" had long been used in political discourse and are not to be taken literally. When the prosecution challenged him on grounds that the speakers were really calling for revolution, he answered:

It is true, my consideration was not the question of revolu-tion, at that stage. I was more concerned with the incitement to violence against members of Inkatha and hostel dwellers . . . I was satisfied that if I say he must tell the people that our struggle is not intended to be a violent struggle against other people, and that those members of Inkatha are as oppressed as other people, that was enough. (14:234)

It was not enough for the prosecution, more concerned about revolution than about the dangerous fault line that separates most UDF supporters, urban and not Zulu, from the Zulu organization.

Molefe's style of action was characteristic—unobtrusive, orga-nizational, managerial. Without criticizing anyone in public, without humiliating anyone, without causing anger and rancor for the future, he had ensured that "a situation would exist" in which the crowd would have an alternative to factional rage.

The prosecution pressed Molefe on why he had not taken the platform himself to repudiate Monareng's speech. Van Dijkhorst was especially interested in this question, and would ask similar ques-tions throughout the trial:

MOLEFE: I just took it [as] wild talk, but I was more concerned with the whole question of attacks on members of Inkatha, and I think that was dealt with. I was satisfied with that . . .

VAN DIJKHORST: Can it be that older people like yourself were afraid to repudiate the youth?

MOLEFE: That was not the reason. (14:234)

The students at the University of Zululand were not to be the last caught up in ongoing violence between supporters of Inkatha and the UDF. Violence between the two groups continued and increased during and after the trial, consuming thousands of lives. Official propaganda focused on "black on black" violence, raising the specter of black savagery, and Idi Amin style atrocities. Although both the UDF and Buthelezi spoke of nonviolence, neither succeeded in breaking the cycle of murders. The toll has been accompanied by frequent allegations of police complicity with Inkatha.

Molefe and Lekota saved some of their most eloquent anger for members of the majority who accept the fundamentally racist structures of apartheid. They see those who agree to work in the system as enabling it to survive longer while it continues to grind the majority. The UDF focused on preventing the co-opting of blacks into collaboration in the new constitution. One who changed from resisting to accepting was Reverend Hendrickse, head of the Labour Party, finding its constituency among Coloureds. He had agreed to run for the Coloured chamber of the new Parliament.

Reverend Hendrickse and his party had been very, very vociferous . . . [about] participation in structures that did not have the power to bring about meaningful change. . . . Reverend Hendrickse himself had been a victim of the South African security legislation. . . . He had been detained [in 1981] with a number of other people . . . for their outspokenness against the policies of apartheid.
To me it was a very disturbing experience to learn that now the same man who had suffered under the very security legislation that has led to so much suffering to so many people, a person who had spoken openly and very vociferously against the new constitution, was now telling the Coloured communities to go into that structure. (13:171)

Councillors in the Black Local Authorities structures, officials of the government established and subsidized homelands, and those who agreed to participate in elections under the new constitution were seen as accomplices in the government policy of "Divide and rule."

Jacobs, for the prosecution, argued the issue of Black Local Authorities with Molefe. Why couldn't the UDF work within and through the system?

JACOBS: One could pressurize the government through the medium of the Black Local Authority. Is that not a more direct way?

MOLEFE: That was tried in the past. It did not work. We know that leaders like Chief Lutuli ... participated in those things ... but they reached the point where they felt they were just toy telephones.... There was nothing they could achieve.... Every time important people participate in the structures ... the government says, "Oh yes, I think now we have got better people. They will work.".... If pressure is put from the outside, the government will be forced to come up with something, and begin to consult on what are the better structures. We are not opposed to the principle of local government, but we do not want to be made to participate in the structures that would turn us into enemies of our own people ...

Let the government send its own officials ... [not] cause division within the black community ...

Everyone ... who went into those councils, even if they [went] there as popular people respected by their communities ... they leave as discredited individuals who are isolated. The community no longer wants to accept them....

JACOBS: Will you be party to discussion under the present constitution [on] how to put up ... administrative bodies in the townships?

MOLEFE: Oh yes, if they are not presented as a substitute for our political rights. (13:682–84)

Molefe and Lekota see the complicity of those working in the system as both politically treacherous and personally ignominious. They accept the common description of such people as "puppets," "toy telephones," and "sellouts." Lekota adds his own note:

There are people ... who, in our communities are regarded as ... defeated, and they have no spirit, and they could not speak the truth. Even when a thing is wrong, they are what you may call "baas, boys." "Ja, baas, ja baas." ["Yes, boss, yes boss."] ... not different from what the old Greeks used to call fools, criminals, and eunuchs. He is a perfect tool of a dictator. He would not exercise his own judgment.... This is a classic puppet. (15:496)

During the months following the launch of the UDF, tensions increased between UDF members and members of AZAPO, Inkatha, and Hendrickse's Labour Party, moving from heckling into scuffling and more fighting. Protest against apartheid also continued to take violent forms. Students stoned the house of a headmaster in Soweto. Bombs exploded in government offices and city streets. Police banned protest meetings, confiscated pamphlets, and detained protesters. At a school boycott demonstration in February, where police fired tear gas at students, a police landrover ran over a student and killed her. At her funeral, mourners sang ANC freedom songs. The growing spirit of resistance and defiance sometimes found targets in blacks seen as accomplices of apartheid. In July 1984, a Councillor in Tumahole, near the Vaal Triangle, was threatened with death if he did not resign. In the outburst of September 3, 1984, the main victims were councillors in BLA structures. In the subsequent violence that spread throughout the country, others identified as sellouts, informers, and enforcers of apartheid were stoned or "necklaced." ("To necklace" is to kill by forcing the victim to wear a tire, filling it with gasoline, and setting it on fire.) The prosecution in the Delmas Trial focused particularly on the events in the Vaal Triangle on September 3, 1984. It charged Molefe and Lekota and twenty others with conspiring to create violence there and throughout the country in order to make the country ungovernable. The indictment concludes with five counts of murder.

Part Four
Fire

12 Tumahole

The government might have allowed the UDF to operate at a relatively low level of harassment if it had remained looking as weak and ineffective as some had originally thought, and if protest in the country had remained at a level that did not require new measures of repression. But the UDF seemed to be getting stronger, it was mobilizing support in rural areas and parts of the country that had never been politicized before, and violence was erupting with increasing frequency as students gathered in school boycotts, tenants gathered to protest rising rents, people facing removal from their homes in terms of the Group Areas Act tried to resist the destruction of their communities, and organizations protesting the manifold intrusions of apartheid united in opposition to the underlying political structures that left the majority without rights.

The prosecution alleged that the UDF had used these protests to foment hatred against the authorities such as the councillors who implemented apartheid at the local level and who often used the powers granted to Black Local Authorities by the white minority government to enrich themselves at the expense of the Africans in the ghetto townships. This hatred, the prosecution alleged, was bound to lead to violence. like the rioting that erupted in Tumahole, south of Johannesburg, in mid-July, 1984. Lekota gave his account of what had happened.

On July 14, he said, he and a union worker riding with him were driving to Johannesburg from Cape Town. They spent Friday night in Bloemfontein, and the next day Lekota fixed the bald tires—they had been stopped by police because their tires were in such poor condition. Kroonstad, where Lekota's mother lived, was on their route. They spent Saturday night there and set off for Johannesburg the following afternoon, a Sunday.

The road took them through a small town called Parys where they saw an unusually large number of riot police cars outside the police station. Curiosity piqued, they drove to the African township nearby, where they saw "a lot of smoke, and things like that," and found the roads blocked with stones. They stopped to ask directions to the home of an acquaintance and "obtained an account of the rent protest that had taken place in the course of the day." Learning that their acquaintance had left the area, they turned back and were stopped at a roadblock. Searching the car, the police saw a lot of documents and called the security police. More than an hour later, security police arrived.

Now it was very cold. Then at some point, I asked that we should go to the police station. . . . And then . . . I was taken into one of the rooms there for interrogation. . . . That did not take long really. . . .

As I was coming back from the interrogation room, as I came into the charge office, there was this young man who came in with two . . . riot police fellows . . . and they were hitting him. . . .

I went back into the charge office, and they went on with the inventory to the end, after which I was asked to sign for it. . . . Of course, whilst we were there, there were still some rumblings and some sounds . . . in the other side of the charge office, between this fellow who had come in and the police. . . . (16:504)

When . . . the inventory was being completed, . . . I looked around the partition. That is when I saw him bleeding. (16:509)

At the point when I saw him for the second time, he was definitely bleeding from the nose. . . . There was a lot of altercation going on between him and the police there . . .

In any event, I was finally given this inventory which I had to sign . . . and then they allowed me to go. (16:504)

When Lekota learned that the young man, Johannes Bonakele Ngalo, one of many detained that day, had died in police custody, he filed a statement with a magistrate.

Monday's press reported Lekota's arrest in Tumahole. On the 19th, when he went to the UDF office in Khotso House, also the headquarters of the South African Council of Churches, he received a call from Bishop Tutu who wanted to see him.

In Bishop Tutu's office he found a councillor from Tumahole, an old man, and his daughter there. Bishop Tutu explained, while the councillor sat there, not saying anything, that the councillor had formed the impression that the UDF, with Lekota's involvement, had been responsible for destroying his business.

I said to him . . . I had just seen his [the councillor's] name in the papers. I did not know him. I had never heard anybody complaining about him . . .

I thought this was quite an important matter. Then I excused myself, and went into Bishop Tutu's secretary's office, and I asked her to . . . call Chief [Molefe] to come down . . .

When I came [back to Bishop Tutu's office] . . . I continued to explain that it was not . . . the policy of the UDF to attack its opponents violently. . . . I also mentioned to him that from the information . . . I had got when I was there, . . . people had had a protest march against the rent . . . and . . . as they were leaving, the police had shot tear gas, and that had started the rioting . . .

I remember Bishop Tutu saying that as far as he understood the position, the UDF was a non-violent organization, but that when people are angry . . . they act irrationally, and that may explain what happened . . . (16:512–13)

Molefe arrived. Bishop Tutu explained the situation to him. Molefe, describing the situation in his testimony, said:

My response . . . was . . . denial that the UDF was involved in the unrest in Tumahole. I said it was not involved, and I went further to state that . . . whilst we are fundamentally opposed to the policy of apartheid, it was not our style to attack the properties of those that we did not agree with. . . .

I recall [the councillor's] . . . bemoaning the fact that he had spent many years working, serving his community . . . as a school principal, as a school inspector, and as a councillor, and he said that all his work had been in vain. The community was not thankful to him for what he was doing.

He went on to say that he had spent many years building his businesses. . . . He said that his wife, almost single-handedly, built the businesses which were destroyed on the day of the march in Tumahole.

Then he said he was very angry with the Development Board. He was no longer going to serve as a councillor. He was going to ask them to compensate him for his losses. Once that was done, he was going to resign . . .

I recall Bishop Tutu ... expressing ... a sense of pity that
black people were fighting among themselves because of government policies. ...

[The councillor] then asked Bishop Tutu if he would issue a
press statement calling on the people of Tumahole to refrain from
attacking his property.... I recall Bishop Tutu ... saying he was
willing to issue that statement but ... if people thought that he
[the councillor] was ... increasing the rentals that they were unable to afford, ... they might still attack him ...

On Friday of that week, I received a telephone call from [the
councillor] informing me that he had resigned.... He wanted the
UDF to issue a statement on his behalf. My response to that was
that the UDF did not think it was a matter that had to be handled
by it [the UDF], and that I would rather make available to him the
telephone numbers of various newspapers which he could contact ... (13:490–93)

Molefe and Lekota did not hear from the councillor again. Lekota thought the matter settled.

For me it was finished ... I never heard from him ... subsequent to that. They were in distress, you see, and they had, as I
understood it, the impression that the UDF was responsible for
their distress, and we had done our best to explain the position of
the UDF, that we were not responsible, and we did not know about
it. (16:517)

Molefe and Lekota did not leave matters at that. Bishop Tutu had
already called for calm, even before the meeting with the councillor
and his daughter.

We were quite upset.... [The councillor's] wife was an elderly
person, and he himself was an elderly person. [We] were upset ...

That same day, quite independent from his visit, [at a meeting
arranged the day before the meeting in Bishop Tutu's office, by an
organization not affiliated to the UDF, the Detainees Parents Support Committee] we ... made it clear that the UDF does not use
violence.... We said people must not burn the people's cars, and
burn their houses, and their shops.... At that meeting where I
spoke, there were also some of the people from Tumahole ... I
also reported to President Archie Gumede, in advance.... Even
our affiliates were there. It was a lunch time meeting. (16:519–20)

The meeting was attended by reporters from the domestic and international press, and by diplomats. Van Dijkhorst asked why Lekota had been invited to speak:

Well, I did not ask them the reason why they asked me, but I think maybe they had also read in the paper that I had been there. (16:520)

In his verdict, van Dijkhorst described Lekota's statement, printed in four newspapers, as "a coup for the liberation struggle." (VD:711)

The prosecution put it to Lekota that he blamed the government for the riot in Tumahole.

LEKOTA: Well you know, we said right from the beginning that the new dispensation would not solve the problems of the communities.... We pointed out [that] ... the BLA's ... tend to push the rents up, and that communities would not be able to afford them.... [Almost all black housing in the townships is state-owned. Rents in Tumahole had risen more than 459.5 percent since 1977. A new rent increase had been announced July 1, 1984.]

FICK: Well, I put it further to you that in the presence of the commercial press and diplomats, you could not have said anything else but that the UDF is not a violent organization.

LEKOTA: ... You know, I really reject that.... It is just despising us. We have got a policy ... that we stand for. I do not know why I should say things just because there are some diplomats around.... They cannot tell us what to do. We decide what we want to do. (16:520–21)

The councillor resigned. By October, three councillors had resigned.

As violence escalated in South Africa, the ex-councillor was threatened with necklacing.

During the Delmas Trial, while he was giving evidence *in camera,* his property was attacked again.

His daughter testified in open court. Although she was a witness for the prosecution, her testimony generally supported Molefe and Lekota. Van Dijkhorst noted that she "seemed tense.... The thought crossed our mind that she had possibly been intimidated as well.

This was, however, never taken up with her by the [prosecution] in cross examination." (VD:712)

Another Tumahole councillor, testified *in camera* that in October or November (when Lekota, Molefe, and many other UDF leaders were in detention), six or seven men wearing balaclavas and sunglasses told him to resign. Some of them wore UDF T-shirts.

Van Dijkhorst's verdict does not ask why people who took such dramatic care to hide their faces wanted to display their shirts' political logos.

13 Petrol Bombs

The prosecution had a different version of what Lekota had done in Tumahole in 1984. On April 29, 1986, a 17-year old schoolgirl testified for the prosecution *in camera* for fear, she said, that she would be killed. She said that Lekota had come to Tumahole in 1984, to address high school students:

FICK: Do you see him in the court today?

IC 10: I don't remember the person so well.

VAN DIJKHORST: Let the row behind all stand first. The row in front can remain seated. Look well. Take your time.

IC 10: Number 3, from this side.

FICK: Accused No. 20. [Lekota] (3894)

She testified that at a meeting of Tumahole students on a Friday—after July 17, 1984—she couldn't remember the month—Lekota showed students how to pour flammable liquid and insert a rag wick into a bottle to make a petrol bomb. She said he told them how to make placards. She added that he was present while the students decided to stone the school the following Monday. That Monday, students did stone the school but did not use petrol bombs.

Lekota, she said, addressed the students again in January 1985 and told them to strengthen the UDF and further the ANC.

The following day Bizos cross-examined her. She had been detained seven times—six times for about three days each, and the seventh from February 17, 1986, until she began to testify, March 29, 1986. For the first five detentions she denied any involvement in student violence. On the sixth, in August 1985, she was detained at

2:00 A.M. and questioned for half the night by seven white men. She denied taking part in violence.

BIZOS: What did they accuse you of?

IC 10: That I was present there. I must tell the truth. If I do not tell the truth, they are going to hit me . . .

BIZOS: And did you deny it?

IC 10: Yes.

BIZOS: Did they believe you?

IC 10: They did not believe me. They continued forcing me to tell the truth.

BIZOS: How were they forcing you to tell the truth?

IC 10: They were asking me questions. When I say I do not know . . . then they would tell me they are going to hit me. Because of my being scared of being hit, I then told them.

BIZOS: We have not reached there, because you told us that you made the statement the third day. During this session on the first night, was it only Mr. van der Merwe who was asking you questions, or were there others asking you questions?

IC 10: The others as well. (3989–3900)

In the morning, she signed a one-page statement.

The second night she was awakened from sleep and taken to be interrogated, this time by the seven white men and two black men. They questioned her for three hours. One of the black men whipped her all over her body with a sjambok, a plastic whip about a meter long. The eight other men present were laughing. She agreed to identify the others in her group.

Then she was taken to another place far away, left alone during the day, and brought back by a black policeman at night. This time she was questioned by four or five policemen. (One was in the court room while IC 10 was testifying.)

On her second night of interrogation she was asked if she knew Lekota.

IC 10: I said, No, I do not know him. He then said to me, they are going to hit me. I must tell the truth. Because of my being scared to be hit, I then said, Yes, I know him.

BIZOS: I want you please to take it . . . for what it is worth from me, that whilst you are in this court, you have the court's protection, and your continued freedom depends on his Lordship, and not on the police.

I wanted to ask you to tell the court honestly, did you in fact know Mr Lekota before you were hit with the sjambok?

IC 10: Yes.

BIZOS: You do not have to look at the police officers. Look at his Lordship.

VAN DIJKHORST: She was not looking at the police officers. (3900)

Some wrangling about where she had looked followed, and then Bizos resumed his cross-examination.

IC 10: When I was hit by the police for the first time is when they said to me I must reveal everything about this that I know. On the 17th [February 1986], when they took me into custody, they said if I do not want to give evidence about this, I will go to jail for a long time. (3908)

On the third night, she signed a hand-written statement. Bizos questioned her about when she had made the statement about Lekota:

His Lordship here, and the learned assessors, and Mr. Lekota, and we did not hear . . . about what you say Mr. Lekota did and said until after your February 1986 detention. (3911)

In that detention, IC 10 was arrested at about 4:00 A.M. by a Mr. Nel and a black policeman. Her parents asked the policeman why, but he said "he does not know a thing about what is happening. The whites did not say anything to them. (3912–13). She was taken to Delmas.

BIZOS: Was a statement taken from you?

IC 10: The statement is the one I have made before . . .

VAN DIJKHORST: Was reference made to your statement?

IC 10: I was asked whether I still remember the contents of the statement, on which I said, I do not remember anything. (3913–14)

She was read a typed statement she had not signed, kept in solitary confinement with nothing to read, given the typed statement to read again the day before testifying, and told that if she was a prosecution witness she would not go to jail.

She had seen the man who told her this in the court; Bizos had noticed that she looked frightened.

In court, she agreed to identify the person who had read the typed statement. The following day, when cross-examination resumed, she did identify him. She pointed to Jacobs, leading counsel for the prosecution.

BIZOS: Is he the person who interviewed you on 17 February 1986?

IC 10: Yes.

BIZOS: Is he the person who showed you the typed statement?

IC 10: Yes.

BIZOS: Is he the person to whom you said that you did not remember anything about what was in the statement?

IC 10: Yes.

BIZOS: Is he the person who told you that you must give evidence of what is typed in the statement and nothing else?

IC 10: Yes.

BIZOS: Is he the person to whom you said that you had been assaulted, but that he did not ask you any further questions as to when, where, and by whom you were assaulted?

IC 10: Yes.

BIZOS: Is he the person who said that you would go to jail for a long time if you did not give evidence in accordance with what was contained in the typed statement that he showed you?

IC 10: Yes. (3925)

She then testified that she had not known Lekota in 1984 and had not recognized him in photographs shown to her in 1985.

IC 10: In fact, what happened is, yesterday just before I came into the courtroom here, it was explained to me, and Mr. Lekota was described to me as to how he looks like, and the description was as follows—that he does not have one tooth in front.

VAN DIJKHORST: And what else?

IC 10: That was all that was explained to me.

VAN DIJKHORST: I see. And on that description you identified him in court. . . . How did you see that the front tooth of Accused No. 20 is missing? I have been in court for a long time, and I have not noticed it.

IC 10: When I came in here, I looked at them and noticed that Mr. Lekota was smiling. From where I stood, I could see that he does not have one front tooth.

VAN DIJKHORST: Is that the only one who has got one tooth missing?

IC 10: Yes, he is the one without the front tooth.

BIZOS: My Lord, it is clearly visible from where I am standing.

VAN DIJKHORST: Yes, it is now clearly visible to me also, but only when he smiles. Was there anything to smile about yesterday when the witness came into court?

BIZOS: Far be it for me to comment on the credibility of the state witness at this stage. (3928–29)

Van Dijkhorst wanted to stop the cross-examination because, "as far as Accused No. 20 is concerned, the witness says it is a total fabrication." (3929)

Bizos wanted to continue, claiming that IC 10's testimony about other matters too was fabricated, and that the way her testimony had been obtained suggested that the evidence of other witnesses was also fabricated. When van Dijkhorst allowed the cross-examination to continue, she agreed that the rest of her testimony about other defendants was also not true.

After this part of the trial, the defendants nicknamed Bizos "Power of the Elephant," for the way he had crushed the perjured testimony.

14 We Might Just Push You

The tense commemoration of June 16 in Regina Mundi and the violence in Tumahole were part of a wave of rising protest and increasing repression throughout the country. Eight days after the violence in Tumahole, violence broke out in Worcester, near Cape Town. A few days later, violence marked the first election meeting of the Coloured Labour Party in Cape Town. The UDF tried to place an advertisement in a widely read Afrikaans paper stating that the UDF was nonviolent, but the paper refused to print it. At an anti-election meeting, Boesak again said that his resistance to the government was based on his commitment to nonviolent democracy. In an interview later, he said he knew he was "sticking his neck out" because people in South Africa increasingly believed violence the only way to achieve change.

Van Dijkhorst said of this interview:

> This attitude is strange. One does not expect a man of the cloth to regard it as sticking his neck out to say he is for non-violent reform. One seeks in vain an outright condemnation of violence. (VD:421)

To Molefe and Lekota it was clear that violence was bound to increase and become more dangerous. To them, the cause of the violence was apartheid, and the solution, dismantling apartheid. To the government, the cause was protest, and the solution, stopping resistance. More police, more roadblocks, more banned meetings, more detention, more surveillance. Soldiers would bring, if not peace, law and order.

Many conflicts began around schools. The third UDF official in the Delmas Trial, Moses (Moss) Chikane, had attended the funeral of a girl who died after a police Land Rover drove over her at a demonstration in February 1984. He had participated in negotiations to have students go back to school in the Transvaal. In April, he had issued a statement that the UDF would pull out of any negotiations where violence was used. Boycotts continued and, in July, schools were closed. They would remain closed until October.

Lekota's speeches toward the end of July 1984, quoted in the trial, reflect a heightened sense of urgency as August 22 and 28, the dates of the first Coloured and Indian elections under the new constitution, drew near.

> We are not using armed methods of resistance today. Under the banner of the United Democratic Front, we are arguing that we can persuade, we can mobilize opposition in resistance.... We understand very well what pushed our people to the point [of violence], and today ... we are reminding the masses of our people that if the Nats are allowed to continue with the ... legislation ... they are proposing today, they can only deepen the scale of racial and violent conflict in the country, in the disaster that will engulf all of us. (VD:373)

He called on all to refuse to go to the polls. Addressing a meeting attended by many Indians, he asked:

Are you turning your back on Mahatma Gandhi? Are you turning your back on Lutuli?. . . . I have made my choice. The price may be heavy. (VD:376)

Van Dijkhorst would judge that this warning of the cost of choosing "can only be understood if it means that the UDF is no longer solely committed to protest politics, but will take action which . . . might involve violence." (VD:377)

At another meeting, Lekota spoke about history, saying that the UDF was "not claiming South Africa for any particular section of the population . . . not fighting Afrikaners but the particular system of government they have."

Leaders of the ANC created the Spear of the Nation [Mkhonto we Sizwe, the armed force of the African National Congress]. Mandela said, "This is the spear of the world." He said, "Our forefathers fought with spears," and he said, "This spear, we will call the Spear of the Nation, because our forefathers fought the Boers [farmers, meaning Afrikaners. Now pejorative]. We will remind the Boers that the war that will be fought is not new. . . . That is why we chose December 16 [a major holiday in South Africa, commemorating the 1838 defeat of the Zulu army in the Battle of Blood River by Afrikaners trekking into the interior] as the big day of the Spear of the Nation." (14:563)

It was a difficult decision to make, for our people had no arms. They were not trained in the art of warfare. But we had to take the decision, that either we are going to submit and die the slave of apartheid, or we are going to die fighting and resisting, and so we took on the decision that we were going to fight back . . .

I have found them [Mandela and other prisoners on Robben Island] unbroken. They remain to me a symbol that we, as the people, in spite of many years of humiliation, of being downtrodden, of being despised and humiliated, that we too are people that too can stand, and have produced. . . . We are equal to all others . . .

The decision of '61 [to take up arms] was not taken seriously by many, especially by the government of the country. Today they are taking it much more seriously. Today they understand very well . . . the changes that happen to South Africa which make it necessary for them to defend the border from the Atlantic up to the Indian Ocean, which confronts them with the might of our own Mkhonto [Spear].

Botha is making a big noise like a skinny dog. You read in the papers that the UDF comes from the ANC. We have no connection with the ANC. We know nothing of politics. What we don't want is the apartheid we see with our own eyes. . . .

How many lives did Smith [ex-Prime Minister of Rhodesia, now Zimbabwe, who used the police and armed forces to retain white minority rule] combined with Vorster [Prime Minister of South Africa during Smith's resistance], how many lives did they sacrifice before Smith [came] to his senses, before he was brought to the point where he is sitting now, peacefully . . .

These monkeys here at home want to do the same thing. . . . We are saying, that nonsense must be stopped. . . . Our obligation stretches toward . . . mobilizing even . . . the Afrikaners themselves, to open their eyes to the gravity of the situation . . . Many are refusing to go into the armed forces. Some are [enduring] long years in gaol for refusing to fight an unjust war. Our white compatriots are doing that . . .

We must intensify our mobilization, and we must inform our people that they must not vote on the 22nd and 28th, because we want peace in our country. But you see, we can only have peace if there is justice. . . . Let everybody participate in the government. Let everybody have houses. Let everybody have education. There is nothing to fight about. We will have peace.

As long as you have one monkey sitting there, he takes everything for himself. . . . There is danger . . . in this type of thing, hiding the fire from all of us who made a contribution,[1] and while you are not contributing, we might just push you into the fire to burn . . .

We are very serious about that. Now, we do not want to do that. We are still, now, persuading, "Look, don't force us into a position where we have to push you into the fire. But . . . you are covering the fire, and we are sitting cold . . .

"We will have no alternative, in other words, we are dying, we have to push you into the fire." (14:575–76)

The prosecution focused particularly on Lekota's phrase "our own Mkhonto" to prove that the UDF supported the strategy of armed struggle. Both Molefe and Lekota argued that "our own

Mkhonto" meant only that the organization was created by people resisting apartheid.

Van Dijkhorst would judge that "Violence is throughout accepted by the speakers as a justifiable alternative, and even as the only option for some people. . . . This meeting should be assessed against the back-drop of the violence in Tumahole." (VD:390)

August opened with rioting in Thabong, the ghetto near Welkom, south of Johannesburg. The same day, Lekota spoke again about the violence rising throughout the country. He compared the government to the Nazis and said it was preparing a slaughter of the African people:

> This afternoon Welkom was on fire, schools have closed down, shops are burning, our people are saying, "We will not take this." This morning they announced in Middleburg that the whole community council resigned because the people said, "You are introducing rents which are unacceptable to us." That is the rising tide of resistance of the people . . .
>
> [He compared the tree of freedom to a prickly pear that multiplies when suppressed, and called on the world to know that the government's program was unacceptable.] Because . . . if that doesn't happen, the scale of dissatisfaction must lead to a deepening amount of armed conflict. The country is already at war today. Durban is burning. Bloemfontein is burning. Johannesburg is burning. Today we are uncertain . . . whether we will come out alive. . . . We don't want that situation to deepen. That is why we are saying, "This constitution must be stopped, and it must be stopped now. So our alternative is a call for a national convention." (VD:393–94)

He said the UDF had confidence that the people would not choose bloodshed, that they would sit down and work things out. He said the UDF did not want to see fighting—no one goes into a fight and comes out without scars. "His speech concluded with a call not to vote." (VD:394)

In his verdict, van Dijkhorst said:

> Nowhere is there clear-cut condemnation of violence—whatever its origin. In fact, there is a justification of violence by the so-called oppressed because, according to the speakers, the government is structurally violent. (VD:396)

In his eyes, the UDF tried to satisfy moderates, who would support nonviolence, and militants, not averse to violence, at the same time:

Statements by office-bearers, and especially speeches, were ambivalent, and could be interpreted by the starry-eyed idealists as advocating nonviolent means of opposition, and by the hard-bitten young radicals as support for violent action. At times, however, even a dyed-in-the-wool blindfolded liberal could have felt with a stick that revolutionary action was propagated. (VD:222)

On August 2, a crippled child was killed at Welkom. The student affiliate of the UDF, the Congress of South African Students, invited Lekota to speak at the funeral on August 11. With many other gatherings forbidden, the funerals of victims of violence often became occasions for mourning the reasons for their death, and therefore occasions of political protest.

Lekota found a police roadblock at the entrance to the township. Lekota's car was searched and, as soon as the security police identified him, they called a more senior officer, a Mr. Hugo, who took Lekota to the police station, searched the car, took all the papers in it, made an inventory, gave Lekota a receipt, and allowed him to go to the funeral.

When Lekota arrived, people were already moving to the graveyard.

So I went on with the cortege to the graveyard, and after the funeral rites were carried out, I was given the opportunity of saying a few words to the mourners. There were no loudspeakers of course, so I had to stand on one of the graves and speak from there, and then afterwards the grave was filled and we had to come back.

All the time, the police were standing, taking positions up around the graveyard, just observing the proceedings . . .

As we were going back to the township, I noticed that . . . ahead of us were some of the police vehicles . . . I noticed them shooting teargas. I cannot say what had really happened. . . . People ran away into the side streets. (15:755)

Mr. Hugo testified that it must have been what was said at the funeral that led to trouble. Answering this charge, Lekota said:

Speaking for myself, I deny that. In fact, the whole spirit of
that funeral was not of the nature that would suggest trouble.
There were a lot of elderly people there. The taxi association . . .
was actually transporting everybody there. I found it to be a very
orderly funeral. This is why I was actually surprised when the
teargas was shot when people were going back. I do not know
what had happened there, but it came as a surprise to me.
(15:756)

Police and students had been facing off at Daveyton, another
township near Johannesburg. On the 14th, a student was shot and
seriously wounded.

On the same day, Molefe called on churches to hold services to
mark the climax of the campaign against the new constitution, saying
that the UDF saw the reform as the surest way to violent confrontation. He called for a selfless contribution "to avert the bloodbath that
this new constitution will cause." (VD:235)

In his verdict, van Dijkhorst viewed the new constitution as a
good thing and Molefe's warning as a sign of his guilt:

At this time, the constitution was a *fait accompli.* It, in fact,
broadens the electoral base by including the Indians and Coloureds. It did not deprive Africans of something they had had.
The main force working against the constitution was the UDF.
To say that the constitution would cause a bloodbath somehow
implicates the UDF. (VD:235)

On the 16th, a bomb exploded in the police headquarters of a
town near Johannesburg. The explosion would soon become the
topic of a song.

On the 19th, the UDF commemorated its first year with rallies
in several parts of the country.

On the 20th, children in Sharpeville, in the Vaal Triangle. over-
turned a bus.

On the 21st, a year and a day after the exultant launch at Mitchell's Plain, police detained more than thirty-five UDF and affiliate
leaders throughout the country. Lekota was among them. The police
could not find Molefe. They arrested AZAPO leaders during the next
few days and weeks.

On the 22nd, Coloureds voted for the first time under the new
constitution. In most constituencies, fewer than ten percent of eli-

gible voters went to the polls. On the 28th, Indians voted. Again, polls of less than ten percent in many constituencies discredited the new constitution.

On the 29th, the student shot at Daveyton died. The police shot three other children. Also on the 29th, at a meeting in the Vaal Triangle, where councillors had declared a raise in rents, a councillor was routed from a hostile meeting and his house was attacked.

The most recent rent increases in the ghettos of the Vaal Triangle were authorized by a Council elected under the BLA's but opposed by the UDF. The Council exemplified the reasons the UDF objected to such bodies. It had little power in its own right, and it had virtually no strategies to raise revenues except raising rents and fees for the people forced by apartheid to live under its jurisdiction. Within three years, it had raised rents more than 459 percent. It exercised the little power it had with ostentatious corruption. It awarded liquor licenses and other privileges to its own members, families, and henchmen who became noticeably wealthy. It accepted bribes and raised its own pay. In July, the BLA passed new rent increases in secret and "leaked" them to the public after it appeared too late to contest them.

On September 2, roadblocks appeared in Boipatong, a Vaal Triangle township. Motorists were attacked on a highway near Bophalong, a neighboring township; and in Sharpeville another councillor's house was attacked.

The next day, a Monday, opened with rent protest marches in several Vaal Triangle townships. During one march, Caesar Motjeane, another councillor, was stoned to death. The indictment held organizers of the march responsible. The deputy mayor of Sharpeville was hacked to death. A large contingent of police in armored vehicles and a helicopter intercepted the march. They were commanded by Colonel Viljoen (the officer in charge in Soweto in 1976). The police fired rubber bullets at short range. High school students stoned buses, police vehicles, private cars, and attacked houses and police buildings with petrol bombs. Beer halls and liquor stores were set on fire.

On the same day, the Cabinet installed P.W. Botha as acting State President under the new constitution, and a bomb exploded in offices of the Ministry of Internal affairs.

Sixty-six people died in the first week of violence in September 1984, and rioting spread throughout the country.

During the days and weeks that followed, funerals, conflict with the police, and more funerals brought the country into a period resembling civil war.

The indictment alleged that Molefe and Lekota had planned to create situations in which such violence and deaths would occur.

Molefe made himself scarce without actually going underground and continued his work for the UDF. On October 2, he was detained and kept in prison without charges until December 10, 1984.

15 Ramakgula's Door

The events in the Vaal Triangle brought Molefe and Lekota into the same prison and court as a handful of the people they wanted to set free. The testimony of those defendants illustrates vividly the conditions of everyday life that had pushed them into political life.

Among the defendants prosecuted because they lived in or were supposed to be connected with the Vaal, one was a stock controller in a furniture store, one worked as an agent for a dry cleaning factory, another sold picture frames, two were electricians, two sold insurance. One was a university student, several worked as researchers, trainers, and field workers for social service, trade unions, and churches, one sold wood and poultry, one owned a small restaurant. The restaurant owner had participated in civic life as secretary of a ratepayers association in one of the few areas where blacks had been granted freehold rights, but he had reached the conclusion that nothing could be achieved through such structures. The trainer testified that his father had served in local government until he became disillusioned. A councillor had invited the trainer to become a councillor as a way to become "a man of status," but he declined. Most defendants were breadwinners in their families, several had children, one is gay. They seem a fair cross-section of the men who live in the black ghettos of South Africa.

The youngest defendant, Gcinumuzi Petrus Malindi had his own story about the pass laws. His parents did not have legal permission to live in Evaton, where he grew up. He recalled a pass raid:

We had gone to play outside. On our return to our home, I found my parents just at the doorway leaving with the police . . .

What hurt me most, I understood my father to be saying to
the police that he is not the head or the father of the family which
lives there, but he is just there as a visitor [who could have been
there legally]. At that stage, my mother was busy protesting,
speaking loud, saying that they must leave this person, referring to
my father as a stranger. The stranger is just visiting here. "The
owner of the of the house," namely the head of this family—I am
referring to my father—"has not yet come, so they must leave this
stranger alone."

On my arrival there, the police asked me who this person
was, pointing at my father, on which I said, "I do not know this
person." They asked me if he is not my father. I said, "No. He is
not." (10:733–44)

At this point in giving his testimony, Malindi stood, unable to
speak, tears rolling down his cheeks.

Malindi was convicted of terrorism and sentenced to five years.
Six others convicted of terrorism were given suspended sentences
and restrictive conditions of bail. Malindi was sent to Robben Island
because he had been convicted earlier for political activism and had
not learned "to desist from such conduct." (VD:28:948)

The story of another defendant illustrates with the clarity of a
fable how it is impossible for blacks to live untouched by apartheid.
In this case, apartheid shows itself in an impenetrably indifferent
bureaucracy exercising the daily banal evil named by Hannah Ar-
endt.

Ramakgula got into the treason trial because of his door.

A child of parents so poor they sent him to his uncle on a farm
where he worked as a herd boy, he had never been to school. In
night classes, he had learned to write his name and read a few words
in Sotho. He does not speak English or Afrikaans. He worked as an
auto electrician for a transportation company and would help
friends fix their cars in exchange for a shared beer.

In 1973, Ramakgula married and applied for a house to rent. In
1977, he was assigned a house and paid four months' rent for the
right to move into it. When he entered, he found that "even walls to
that house are cracked," there were holes in the floor, and the outside door was rotted beyond repair. He complained to the authorities. They did nothing. He complained again. They did nothing. He
sent his wife to complain. They did nothing. He complained again.

In 1978, his elected town councillor promised to talk to the town manager, but "there was no progress at all." In 1981, he told a superintendent about the door and learned that the Board no longer paid for repairs. They said, "'Look here, there is no law that there was ... now. That old law doesn't exist any more, that is, the law to repair the house. You have to pay for any repair that is to be done.'" He protested that he had started renting the house in 1977. "Then they said to me, 'There is no such law which still exists.'"

So he bought a new door. He was earning R30 a week (about $12.50), so buying the door, which cost R78, was a major project. He paid installments every week for about four months. But the financial effort was more than he could manage, and in 1983, he fell into arrears with the rent. The Administration Board decided to attach some property. In the middle of winter, they "came there and removed that door and said I was owing rent."

With the Administration Board in Sebokeng, [a town in the Vaal Triangle] if you are owing one month in arrears, by the time you go and pay, after they have been to your place, then you have to pay for the other month in advance. So what I did was, I went to my employer and asked for a loan to go and pay that rental.

He asked for the door and was told it was not stored at the Administration Board offices. The Superintendent looked in a book and gave him an address in his own street.

RAMAKGULA: I went to that house and found the door there. I found it without the locks. I took the door from that house to my place, that is, to my house, I put it back on the wall, on the frame, fitted it on. But I did not have the locks. I had to go and buy other locks.

BIZOS: It was your door that had been stored in this woman's house?

RAMAKGULA: Yes. My door, which I paid money for. Which money, in fact, was supposed to have been paid in for the rental. Which rental caused them to come and take this very door. In fact, that is the door I am talking about, which is mine.

No one could ever tell Ramakgula what had happened to the locks.

A few months later there was an election, and one of the councillors who knew him because of his door asked for Ramakgula's vote [in the BLA elections criticized by the UDF]. Ramakgula did not vote.

Soon after, returning from a visit to his brother's house, he passed a meeting in a church nearby and went in. People were singing hymns, and several speakers addressed those present. One, a former councillor, described how, in winter, councillors would keep blankets meant for pensioners and, in summer, distribute them just before the elections. Someone spoke in English, which Ramakgula did not understand. Another person spoke about education. Ramakgula, never having attended school, could not assess what he said.

At this meeting, people decided to form the Vaal Civic Association which would later become a UDF affiliate. Bizos questioned Ramakgula:

BIZOS: **Now the accusation against you, Mr. Ramakgula, is that you helped and voted for this association as part of an unlawful agreement with the African National Congress, the South African Communist Party, and the UDF to overthrow the South African government.**

RAMAKGULA: No, that is not correct.

BIZOS: **What, before this case started, did you know about the ANC?**

RAMAKGULA: I do not know, what is that.

He attended a few meetings and told his area representative about his door and about a toilet tank. She said they must unite to speak with one voice.

Soon, another problem arose. In 1983 and 1984, the troubles in black schools endemic since 1976 included allegations about stolen papers, corruption in grading, secret quotas of those allowed to pass, excessive corporal punishment, sexual harassment, and friction over school boycotts. At the beginning of 1984, the local high school refused to admit any student who had failed the previous year. This ruling affected Ramakgula's adopted son and two of his uncle's children. A speaker at the VCA advised joint action. A group of parents and students should go together to talk with the school principal.

We explained to him that our problem was that if children are being chased away from school, and they are now going to be in the township for the rest of the day, they will end up being hooli-

gans or turned into *tsotsis* [gangsters], and then later they will not
have anything to do in life . . .
You can teach them outside in the sun there.

The school agreed to readmit 300 students.
Ramakgula had discovered the power of joint action.
The area committee that had organized the petition to the
school became an area committee of the VCA. Ramakgula acted as
its treasurer.
He marched in the front row of the rent protest on September
3, 1984. He was detained in October 1984. In 1987, he was released
on bail. During the reading of the verdict, he, Malindi, and six others
released on bail were imprisoned again. He was convicted for terrorism and sentenced to five years. His sentence was suspended on
condition he take no part in public life.

16 Black Christmas

South African law forbids description of what happens in prison, so
the trial says almost nothing about the detention period between
August 21, for Lekota, October 2, for Molefe, and December 10, 1984,
when they were released. Toward the end of the trial, Lekota broke
this law that shrouds prison life in a letter to a friend that gives a
glimpse of one aspect of that life:

Hi . . . ,
You commented in the course of today that you would not
like to be my guard seeing as you would forever be a victim of my
dribbling maneuvers. Although I chuckled lightly at the time—
yes, because the remark was as profound as it was a sincere
tease!—later on it kept coming back to my mind. And I find that
even now it keeps intruding upon my consciousness to the extent
of disrupting my reading. So now I have put my books away,
drawn my dictionary and Roget's *Thesaurus* near to myself. Let us
share views on this question for what it is worth. For us in the
thick of the struggle for freedom in this country, the relationship
between captor and captive is a significant aspect of our lives. In
the case of blacks . . . it permeates life both inside institutions
such as police stations and prisons and, under apartheid (that is,

legislated racial discrimination), in the larger concentration camp
that is our society.

I remember very well the first occasion my attention was focused on this intriguing matter. It was around the (S.A.) spring of
1976 in this very prison. The late Pitman who was one of our defence advocates had lent one of the accused Hugh Lewin's then
recently published book "Bandiet." When my turn came to read it,
I did so with utmost interest and concentration. Then suddenly
Hugh started dealing with survival in captivity. It was the first and
last time I read the book but I can still recall him writing that
prison is a very powerful and grinding institution. It was not
to be confronted. You have to cheat prison, or words to that effect.

I realized that in two or three months time I would start my
own maiden prison stint. It was with a view to prepare myself for
the ordeal that I read that section of the book. Over the years
since then I have grown to dislike the expression—'cheat
prison'—which Hugh employed. But my own experience has convinced me of the correctness of what he intended to communicate. Perhaps the difference in expression between Hugh and me
derives from the fact that he was a product of S. Africa's white
community whereas I am that of the black community. When one
comes into prison from the white community a phenomenal process of adjustment is necessary. A citizen with rights that have always been acknowledged, honored and respected is suddenly deprived of these. The insecurity that accompanies the trauma is
perhaps not within my full grasp.

On the other hand, black communities have wallowed for so
long under the security of political rightlessness and economic
deprivation that imprisonment only aggravates an existing condition. It is not something new, only the degree of insecurity and
deprivation. So where something new happened to Hugh on imprisonment, with me an existing state of affairs was only aggra-
vated.

And very strangely that aggravation of insecurity through imprisonment actually becomes a reversal of the insecurity of life in
larger society. Whereas in everyday life, out of prison, Africans
cannot tell the course their fate might or might not take, once
sentenced to a prison term, they know with a certain confidence
what tomorrow and the day after tomorrow will bring. This is or-

dinarily missing in 'normal' life in the police-infested and security-forces-encircled townships.

But in spite of all this, prison is ultimate captivity even for the rightless black South Africans. An attempt at a frontal assault on that institution is suicidal in almost all cases. One has to find a way of going around it and dexterously negotiating survival without losing oneself to the enemy camp in the process.

It was with the senior fighters in the island that the initial comment of Hugh was both translated into practice and expanded for me and the other younger prisoners. Fighters with many years of struggle to survive under white domination—a domination that was keenly kept alive and felt on Robben Island since every single warder [guard] is a white person there—systematically passed onto us their accumulated experience. An experience which when thoroughly broken down consisted of political belief, an adaptation of that to daily life, and an ability to improvise in impossible situations.

To start with, those of us who shoulder the burden of the liberation struggle in South Africa trace the roots of that struggle to the turn of the present century. To the founding conferences of the African, Indian and Coloured Congresses to put it broadly. Those of our forebears who initiated the movement were inspired primarily by the urge to unite the people of our country into one nation. No one can doubt this if such personalities as Mahatma Gandhi, . . . are taken into account.

From this generation of freedom-fighters we have inherited the ongoing task of sowing reconciliation among the people of our country. Every day we try to win our people to the friendship of the movement. Help strangers (even prison guards) overcome their suspicions and fears of the movement. Often we have to endure abuse at the beginning but soon enough we climb on top of the situation. There are many of course who do not share our ideological position. They too follow their own path, often with disastrous results. Many end up on our side—the faith of our forefathers conquers everything and continues to live in and through us. That is our ideological position and it says simply: TO WIN ALL S. AFRICANS TO ONE NATION! That is the task of the movement and everyone of our members and activists move from day to day with it in front of them.

In breaking down this ideology to daily life we always tried to proceed from where our guards' understanding was: As they

would have been harangued with the diatribe of us being enemies
of S. Africa (by which is really meant white domination and the
National Party) we started by being always courteous to them:

"More, meneer!" ["Good morning, sir!"]

'What?' the chap wonders, 'A terrorist that speaks my holy language? Is courteous and friendly? But these people are supposed
to be the onslaught, etc., etc.?' Those questions led to doubts and
soon enough genuine questions about what wrong we had done.
What could we say? What *wrong* had we done indeed? Even we
could not tell.

Many of those who looked after us ended up with troubled
consciences and very significant unanswered questions—not
about us but about those who had assigned them to guard us and
the system that they had to defend. Yes, our task was simply to
turn them round so that they could look at the government and
its apartheid policies. In most cases we did not even have to suggest to them as to what questions to ask? What parts to scrutinize?
and which side to take? Human beings, however lowly or less educated they may be, have their own value systems, intelligence and
a conscience to go with. In their own humble ways they can dis-
criminate between right and wrong when the two are contrasted
one against the other. That has been the discovery of many of us
in the liberation struggle of this country. We know that in the end
so many of the people of our country shall have discovered the
fallaciousness of the pronouncements of our present apartheid rulers that they will dispense with them.

This knowledge has been acquired in the very heat of our life
and death struggle for freedom. In solitary confinement accompanied by torture and other abuses, dramatic things—tales which
will only be told after freedom day and many of which will sound
like fables—happen as a result of this practice. They are carried
out by people who have been 'cheated' but individuals who have
been won over, convinced by the genuineness of our activists in
the field that our movement is the friend of the people of South
Africa. It is not true that we take people for a ride as the government is wont to suggest. We respect the people of this country
too much to make them fools. We love them too much to make of
them cannon-fodder for the repressive apartheid machine. Any
such action on our part can only alienate the majority of the
people of the country from the liberation movement. And that
would surely be reactionary . . .

What I have tried to communicate here is simply that the relationship between us and the employees of the state is not essentially and should not be treated as one of hostility even though it appears so formally. Many of these people do not serve there primarily because they believe in the correctness of apartheid. This is certainly so for blacks and to a lesser extent with whites, particularly those of Afrikaner extraction. In the main they accept the job for want of anything better to do or because they genuinely believe that it is a service to the country. The conflict and contradictions of the situation usually impose themselves in the process. Our freedom-fighters and activists are, therefore, obliged to help them resolve these questions in such a way that they are not alienated from the movement. We have also been trying our best. How far we have succeeded in making friends for the movement will be for those who will follow to judge and say.

Outside, the period after August 21 and the detention of major UDF leaders was a time of turmoil marked by the first elections to the Indian and Coloured houses of the tricameral parliament, the explosion of violence in the Vaal Triangle, and the rapid spread of violence to other areas. A judge in Pietermaritzburg ruled invalid the detention order applying to seven leaders detained August 21 and they were released September 10, but detainees in other jurisdictions, including Lekota, remained in prison. The Minister of Law and Order issued redetention orders for the seven who had been released.

Several UDF leaders reopened the issue of relations with diplomats from countries that seemed to support apartheid, including Britain, the United States, and Israel. They decided to turn to some members of the diplomatic community for help. On September 13, six of the seven men who had been released and were soon to be redetained sought refuge in the British consulate in Durban. One was Archie Gumede, a president of the UDF. The six sought legal representation from Zak Yacoob, who would be one of the Delmas Trial defense team and one of the 911 cited in the indictment as co-conspirators.

In October 2, Molefe was detained. A few days later, Bishop Tutu, a patron of the UDF, was awarded the Nobel Peace Prize.

While Lekota, and then Molefe, were in prison, violence and deaths were continuing in the Vaal Triangle and other parts of the country. On October 23, seven thousand police and troops cordoned off the town of Sebokeng and other towns in the Vaal. They searched all 19,500 houses and arrested 350 people, many of them younger than eighteen. The following week they searched vehicles in Sharpeville and other Vaal towns. The Minister of Law and Order said, "As far as we're concerned it's war, plain and simple." The South African Defense Force would remain in the townships around Johannesburg for many months and would be deployed in other areas as resistance and violence continued. Resistance to conscription, virtually nonexistent a few years previously, increased as the army was more frequently used to repress protest.

On November 5 and 6, for the first time, labor unions supported a large work stoppage protesting apartheid and recent government action. Unions with primarily black membership have been allowed only since the beginning of the eighties when the business community needed them to negotiate about rising labor unrest (and partly in response to international pressure). For their first few years the unions tried to keep labor and political issues separate. They declined association with the UDF when it was first launched to maintain this strategy. But after the army occupation of Sebokeng, many unions allied themselves with the UDF. Charges in the Delmas trial included allegations that the UDF had been actively involved in the stayaway (during which Molefe and Lekota were in prison).

The strikes of November 5 and 6 led to mass firings and evictions of fired workers from urban areas. The Federation of South African Trade Unions initiated a boycott of Christmas shopping, saying blacks had nothing to celebrate. The Black Christmas, a consumer boycott, was taken up throughout the country in 1984 and supported by the UDF. Consumer boycotts in 1984 would prove "a potentially powerful pressure on government through pressure on local business."[1] They gave business people reasons to put pressure on the government to listen to the demands being made by the UDF and its affiliates. The prosecution charged that the UDF had supported coercion to achieve the success of the Black Christmas in 1984. Molefe answered:

The purpose of that campaign, as I understood it, was an appeal for calm during the period of Christmas, to demonstrate to the government that the people were not happy with what had happened in the Vaal Triangle, and it was an appeal for solidarity with the families of people who had died, and those who had been in detention. ... It ... appealed to ... residents not to be in a

festive mood during the Christmas period, not to indulge in luxu-
rious things ... buying a lot of food, throwing parties ... because
the nation was mourning ... (13:230–31)

In November, in the United States, prominent people began to
stage sit-ins at the South African Embassy.

A report for the Roman Catholic Southern African Bishops Conference estimated those killed since August at 150, and it accused
police of "totally uncontrolled use of firearms." Archbishop Hurley
said a state of war now existed between police and the people.

The prisons and judicial system were choked. The government
had to release detainees, some even after charges had been filed
against them. It quickly mounted a case against people alleged to be
directly involved in violence. It also started to look for high-profile
persons whose cases would demonstrate the futility and viciousness
of opposing the government. The UDF and trade unions began to
look like good targets for indictments.

On December 10, Molefe and Lekota were released without
being charged. Six other leading antiapartheid campaigners were
charged with treason. Some had been in prison with Molefe and
Lekota.

Lekota went back to work:

There was nothing wrong I had done. I carried on. (15:599)

That was how he saw it. Van Dijkhorst would present another
point of view—that by raising day-to-day issues and continuing in
existence after the referendum, and after the first Colored and Indian elections under the new constitution, the UDF deceived its supporters:

**As we have seen, the front changed its tactics. What had been
a movement for protest against proposed legislation became a
force which challenged the state itself. (VD:48)**

One of Lekota's first tasks was to rush to Durban to talk with the
people in the British consulate there. Three leaders had left the consulate. The three activists who remained as refugees in the consulate
emerged on December 12. Two were arrested immediately and
charged with high treason.

The detentions made UDF work much more difficult. "There
was general chaos, really," Lekota said, and then described one effect
of the detentions:

Within the communities, when there is an organization, and leadership figures, . . . they are able to maintain a certain amount of discipline, and to give direction. . . . When leadership figures get arrested . . . it becomes very difficult to find replacements. . . . People are . . . afraid that if they assume those positions, they may themselves be detained. . . . Then the community has nobody, no point of reference. . . . The detention of leadership figures creates a . . . free for all. . . . So . . . communities are thrown in confusion . . . and then quite often, . . . irresponsible elements . . . jump onto the wagon and then start their own thing. . . . It really takes time . . . to build new and responsible leadership figures who can . . . contain the situation. (15:600−601)

Molefe had also gone back to work. One of his first actions quoted in the trial was an appeal for nonviolence. He appealed to UDF members and affiliates not to victimize people who ignored the call for a Black Christmas:

We want to assure the people that nothing will happen to them. In fact, we will call upon our people to exercise a high level of dignity by not using force to persuade people to observe the Black Christmas . . .
People who have already made preparations for Christmas, such as cultural and family gatherings, should at least observe a moment of silence for ten minutes. . . . (13:231−32)

Violence before the Black Christmas was a foretaste of things to come.

17 In the World's Eyes

1985 opened with a heightened sense of danger. The repression needed to enforce government control in the townships had been extreme and not entirely successful. The government had not been able to act in total obscurity The media had pushed the struggle for human and political rights in South Africa to the headlines in South Africa and throughout the world, and calls for international ostracism that would have economic and political effects were becoming significant. The violence beginning September 3, 1984, the army occupation of ghetto townships in October, the strikes, school boycotts and retaliatory firings of November, the widespread detentions of children as well as adults—at least 1,110 by December 12[1]—the celebrity demonstrations in the United States beginning late November 1984, and the activists seeking refuge in the British embassy were all attracting the cameras of international news services. The government confiscated journalists' film,[2] seized cassettes for evidence of treason by UDF officials,[3] and refused admission to a CBS team headed by black newsman Ed Bradley[4] who was preparing to cover the visit to South Africa of Senator Edward Kennedy in early January.

The turmoil of events was bringing Molefe and Lekota into greater prominence as spokesmen for the majority. The new interest in South Africa gave Molefe and Lekota opportunities to create relationships with media people, diplomats, and members of the international community who could take messages from the voteless majority to the ruling minority. The events now drawing them into contact with shapers of opinion at home and abroad became the foundation of several friendships that sustained them during the trial.

In this atmosphere of heightened domestic and international attention, 1985 opened with much work to be done. The usual operational difficulties of running the organization on a shoestring were increased by interruptions and backlogs. Lekota's description of the situation, during an exchange about documents in the trial, gives a picture of an office swamped by paperwork:

When the police officers got there . . . they would have found a filing cabinet . . . but they would also have found several boxes of documents lying around the office, some of which were publications from other organizations. Others, miscellaneous papers. . . . As to the period after we had been detained. . . . there had been times when, for one week somebody is in the office, then that person gets detained, and somebody comes to . . . help them, and that person for some reason or other has to go. It is a very chaotic situation. When we came out in December, 1984, we also found the situation very chaotic. . . . Sometimes the mail arrives . . . on one day, and there are several piles of documents. . . . There may not be time to go through all of them that day. . . . What one simply does, is to put it aside and hope you will get some time to look at them. And then maybe one would rush out to attend to other issues, and then tomorrow another pile comes with other documents. So somehow the piling up process takes place on its own, at its own momentum. (16:625–26)

In spite of this chaotic atmosphere, the national secretariat of the UDF met in early January. One of its decisions was that the UDF must intervene in the persisting schools crisis. Moses Chikane, Transvaal secretary of the UDF, spent considerable time acting as peacemaker and urging students to return to school with a Congress of South African Students official. Molefe sent a memo asking for proposals for action to Bishop Tutu, Archbishop Hurley, Dr. Boesak, the South African Council of Churches, the South African Catholic Bishops Conference, trade unions, and others.

There was general confusion, as students did not know whether to go back to school or not; ... whilst some students had gone back to school, many [were] still out on boycott. (14:790)

Some of the demands that [students] were making, were really demands that could be met, like an end to corporal punishment, an end to sexual assault on students by teachers. That was a matter that could be handled administratively within schools and the Department [of Education]. ...

The [UDF] intention was to get the students back to school, and to get the DET to address those problems that it could address. ... We wanted to demonstrate to the ... Department of Education and Training, that the issue of education was not a matter of little hotheads in schools. It was a matter that the community as a whole, and important personalities in that community and organizations, took very seriously, and they wanted to resolve it. (14:794)

The students had achieved some results. In some schools they were allowed to have Student Representative Councils. In some, corporal punishment was forbidden. Molefe had written, "The students are on the threshold of victory, and this ... should not be allowed to slip out of our hands."

To the UDF, it seemed clear that, if the student demands were not met, boycotts would continue and there would probably be more violence.

There were specific demands they were making which we ourselves said ... were justifiable and the surest way of normalizing the situation in schools. ... If this situation continues [unresolved], it may well result in violence at a larger scale. We want

them to go back. . . . We . . . know that if they are not at schools . . .
the police would want to get them back by force . . . (14:795)

The prosecution presented Molefe's memo as evidence that the
UDF wanted violence to continue. Molefe answered:

No . . . that is why we involved people like Bishop Tutu,
Bishop Hurley, people who are known to be . . . committed to
non-violence. . . . The point one must make here is that students
are not just children who can be told, "Go back to school," and
they do that. They have got their own views, and if they decided
otherwise, one cannot just overlook their views. (14:794–95)

Once again, this view of how the UDF exercised power, by listening and coordinating, rather than by giving orders, seems to have
met with incomprehension. The prosecution soon changed the subject and, alleging that the UDF did nothing to curb the violence at
schools, said, "This is on par with the case of the person who came
from Tumahole to ask your assistance . . . that the UDF did not assist
him. . . . Why did you not refer him back to Bishop Tutu?" To which
Molefe explained again that the councillor from Tumahole had
Bishop Tutu's telephone number. Then Jacobs, the prosecution lawyer, presented an indignant portrait of Bishop Tutu:

Was a churchman not willing to help this poor man under
these circumstances [by issuing an appeal to the press on his be-
half]? (14:797)

The prosecution's habit of switching from topic to topic and of
circling back to old topics, repeating questions, and adding new details, contributes to a sense of getting nowhere in a hall of mirrors,
of nightmare and morass that made the trial itself a punishment and
a prison.

When the prosecution cross-examined Lekota, it reopened the
issue of the UDF role in the schools. Lekota reiterated points made
by Molefe.

The most important thing is not just students going back . . .
but that they will stay in school. (16:471)

He quoted a document he had written in early 1985:

Our fear is that many young lives will . . . be lost in running
street battles in which armed police and soldiers will confront unarmed and defenseless pupils in the townships. (16:472)

The prosecution construed this fear as an encouragement to the students to maintain the boycott and as an encouragement to violence.

Senator Edward Kennedy arrived in South Africa January 5, as the guest of Bishop Tutu and Allen Boesak. His brother Robert had visited South Africa in 1967. His tumultuous visit was marked by hostile and embarrassing demonstrations by AZAPO supporters who saw him exploiting South Africa for his presidential ambitions, and by cold uncooperativeness from the government. The UDF was divided. The National Executive Committee was willing to assist him, but a number of regional affiliates were not. As on the issue of the referendum, the National Executive did not take a position that required everyone to "toe the line." Kennedy met Molefe and Lekota, who came to believe that he, and some Americans represented by him, understood and cared.

On January 23, William Kratshi, an executive member of the UDF in a small town in the Eastern Cape, was shot at allegedly point-blank range. The prosecution challenged Lekota on his press statement about the killing. Lekota described what he had heard.

LEKOTA: The police had come to his house, and they wanted to go with him to the police station. They asked him to go with them. He was helping a little child there [his five-year-old son[5]] because he had just been released from prison and his wife was working and he was looking after this child. So, I am told, he asked them for permission to get somebody to look after the child. I do not know exactly what happened there, but they shot him in the house . . .

FICK: Seeing that you had no knowledge about what had happened, why he was shot, why do you call it a brutal shooting?

LEKOTA: . . . I cannot think of any other adjective that I could attach to it . . .

FICK: Did the man attack the police?

LEKOTA: No. There has not been any suggestion by the police then, and at any time as far as I know, that he attacked the police.

FICK: The third paragraph—"His shooting shows that . . . the state was frustrated by its inability to control growing resistance, especially the UDF. It will eliminate its opponents in this fashion." Again, seeing that you had no knowledge about what happened in the house, on what basis do you call this the elimination of a man?

LEKOTA: Yes, but the man was eliminated. He was shot and killed in his house, and there was never any allegation that he had a weapon or anything. . . .

I do not know of any reason why, if a man was sitting in his house with a little child because his wife had gone to earn some money for the family, and he had just come out of jail . . . why they had shot and killed him. . . .

VAN DIJKHORST: Was there a postmortem on this man?

LEKOTA: I think, up to the point of our arrest [April 23, three months later] there had not been any. . . .

FICK: I put it to you that you issued this press release . . . with the intent to anger the people, to incite them against the police . . .

LEKOTA: No, that is not so. In fact, if we look at the last paragraph . . . , it says, "We shall insist on [our right] to defend our last possession, that is, the right to oppose apartheid." Where does it say we must now hate the police? That is not true. It was never the purpose of this statement. (16:480–82)

On January 31, Botha offered to release Mandela on condition he renounced violence. Mandela had previously refused conditional release. The press asked Lekota for UDF comment. He said:

We cannot see him making a pledge of that nature. A pledge like this one would mean that Mandela should distance himself from the ANC and his entire political struggle to date . . .

Only the unconditional release of political prisoners and the dismantling of apartheid structures will bring about stability and lasting peace in this country. (VD:259)

The prosecution questioned Lekota on why the UDF had commented to the press. Lekota answered that there was considerable speculation about what Mandela would say. The legal play at this point in the trial shows some of the political forces underlying the law. Lekota took the opportunity to imply a political lesson on the futility of trying to repress opinion. Van Dijkhorst revealed that he was not aware of some holes prised through the armor of censorship. He interrupted Bizos with questions that suggest surprise and, perhaps, dismay. Bizos, veteran of innumerable legal battles against apartheid, knew to a hair's breadth where legislation and regulation met a limit.

LEKOTA: Perhaps one of the reasons people were coming to get opinions [from] all the other people including ourselves, because they could not actually get to him . . .

FICK: Yes, but why did you not refer the press to his wife?

LEKOTA: I understood that they would also have consulted the family to find out what they have to say. . . . They may, perhaps, not have published Mrs. Mandela's response because she was banned herself at the time . . .

VAN DIJKHORST: I was wondering about this answer. . . . Was that permissible in law? Was there not a prison regulation, or a prison act or something, that says you cannot quote prisoners?

LEKOTA: As we understood it, the family, which handled the matter, had done it through their lawyers, and they were satisfied that the matter was perfectly legal . . .

BIZOS: It is limited to the circumstances of the offence for which he was imprisoned, and also to the conditions of his detention in jail.

VAN DIJKHORST: So one may not quote him at all, or you may not refer to him?

BIZOS: No, you can refer to him and you can quote him, but it must not be in connection with the . . .

VAN DIJKHORST: You can quote him about sports if he is being convicted of violence?

BIZOS: Or something. . . . He cannot make statements that "I am innocent," or "I was wrongly convicted," or . . . but you can quote the evidence in his trial. You cannot quote . . .

VAN DIJKHORST: But that [Mandela's answer to the offer of conditional release] was public. So, that you can, in any event, quote.

BIZOS: Yes.

VAN DIJKHORST: But can one sort of have a running debate between somebody who is in prison, through the media, with somebody who is outside?

BIZOS: Provided it is not in that narrow ambit.

VAN DIJKHORST: Say it is on theological grounds?

BIZOS: No, there is nothing to prevent that. There may, of course, there may be prison regulations.

VAN DIJKHORST: There may be access problems?

BIZOS: Access problems. If it is a legal [lawyer's] visit, then your lips are tied. If it is a family visit, it is supervised. So, those may be the problems. (16:580–83)

Van Dijkhorst's verdict criticized the UDF statement:

One would have expected the UDF, if it stood for non-violence, to urge Mandela to renounce violence and join the UDF. (VD:259)

The UDF had called for a rally on February 10, 1985 to celebrate the award of the Nobel Peace Prize to Bishop Tutu.

Winnie Mandela invited Molefe and Lekota to her home. She scolded them for implying any doubt that Mandela would refuse conditional freedom, and she asked that Mandela's reply be read at the rally.

Mandela's daughter, Zindzi, read his answer. "He wanted the reply to be read directly to his people. It was the first time in a quarter of a century that he had been able to communicate with them, albeit through a third party."[6]

Mandela offered to renounce violence if the government renounced violence. He refused conditional freedom, pointing out that, outside prison, the ANC was banned, he would be subject to the pass laws, and his wife would still be banished to live in a small town in the Orange Free state. He said, "I am not a violent man," and that, in the fifties, he and others had repeatedly asked the government for discussions to find a solution for the country and had been ignored. "It was only when all other forms of resistance were no longer open to us that we turned to armed struggle."[7]

The prosecution alleged that Lekota influenced Mandela.

FICK: You made it impossible for Mr. Mandela to say anything else . . . after this press statement of yours.

LEKOTA: How did I make it impossible?

FICK: You decided for Mr. Mandela what he should say . . .

LEKOTA: I think Nelson Mandela would feel very insulted if it were ever to be said that his response to the State President's offer was dictated to him by myself or the UDF. This statement here does not say he must reject it. . . . It says we had doubts about it. . . . Why? . . . Because as it stands, it suggests that he must distance himself from the ANC, . . . and . . . because of his very deep commitment to the ANC, we cannot see him making a pledge of that nature ...

VAN DIJKHORST: Why should he distance himself from his entire political struggle to date? Was it not merely required that he distance himself from the violent part of his political struggle to date?

LEKOTA: Well ... as we understood the position, first of all, Nelson's commitment is, one, the elimination of apartheid; two, that over the years that they had campaigned, the government had ... made it impossible for them to continue the campaign nonviolently. (16:582–83)

FICK: But why did you call for his unconditional release if he is a man committed to violence?

LEKOTA: I have said here, if the government releases these people and opens a process of negotiation, ... if it opened up ... a search for a constitutional settlement ... I am convinced ... that they will not choose violence. ... They will seek a peaceful settlement. I have said it over and over again, in meetings in private and in public. (16:589)

The UDF distributed copies of Mandela's speech, which had been widely reported in the press.

18 Lekota's Weekend

By February 1985, the temper of the government was sorely tried. It felt surrounded by a press more ready to show pictures of police tearing down hovels made of plastic sheeting and fruit boxes in Crossroads than to accept the words of apartheid apparatchiks. It had been humiliated by the UDF fugitives in the British embassy, the continuing celebrity demonstrations against South Africa in the United States and Kennedy's visit, the glorification of an impertinent Anglican bishop who was not even entitled to vote, and now Mandela's public relations coup. It was time to crack down.

The day after the rally where Mandela's statement was read, police killed a seventeen-year-old student near Kroonstad during demonstrations there that led to vandalism and arson. Two days later, police used whips on students who were commemorating the death of a schoolgirl run over a year previously by a police Land Rover. The Minister of African affairs promised to speed removals from Cross-roads, and violence erupted when people gathered to protest.

When Botha had offered to free Mandela if he renounced vio-lence, Helen Suzman, a veteran and for many years sole opponent of apartheid in Parliament asked, Would Botha grant freedom to any political prisoner who renounced violence? Botha said he would, and, on February 17, four PAC members who had served more than twenty years on Robben Island were released. Eighteen other pris-oners accepted this offer, including one convicted with Mandela in the Rivonia Trial.

Botha's gesture did not stem criticism or turn back support for sanctions. The government needed to discredit resistance.

At this moment, when the government was poised to act, Lekota attended the funeral of the student killed in Kroonstad the previous week. The prosecution alleged that he encouraged people to ignore regulations governing funerals, that the UDF provoked the police to violence and provoked further violence after another funeral in Kroonstad on February 21.

The UDF had no affiliates in the Orange Free State province, but Lekota accepted an invitation from a Kroonstad friend, Dennis Bloem, who suggested that he attend the funeral on Monday, Febru-ary 18th. Lekota drove to his home town with Patrick Lephunya and went directly to the home of the deceased.

LEKOTA: Both Lephunya and I were wearing UDF T-shirts. Mine was . . . yellow. . . . Patrick Lephunya had a white T-shirt.

We found a lot of people already there, . . . almost ready to go off to the graveyard. . . . There had been time restrictions placed on the funeral proceedings, and even the route of the cortege to the graveyard had been indicated. So, after a short prayer and some hymn singing, the funeral cortege started off to the grave-yard.

VAN DIJKHORST: Were they not in a church?

LEKOTA: No, we were at the home of the deceased.

VAN DIJKHORST: Was there a service there?

LEKOTA: There was a service. Just a prayer, I think, and a hymn. It was just a short service . . .

One of the conditions was that the coffin should not be car-ried by people walking on the street. . . . It had to be in the hearse

or ... in a vehicle.... The people used the family van [truck]. It does not have a canopy behind, it is just an open one. They had people standing in the van, and they were carrying ... the coffin, but standing in the van.... The route had been defined in such a way that we just had to move on the periphery of ... the locations [ghettos] ...

We followed the cortege in the UDF car. I had Patrick Lephunya ... and several other people, and one blind young man [as passengers].... We proceeded to the graveyard without any incidents, and the police, of course, were keeping watch ... right through, even as we were marching there. And when we got to the graveyard, the police took a position ... northwest of where we were, but inside the graveyard ... about 150 to 200 meters away ...

We had a prayer service by the Reverend Mosia. We then had a sermon by the Reverend Mamabolo. I then addressed the mourners, and then we began to fill the grave. Whilst that was going on, ... to avoid overstepping the time limits, both Dennis Bloem and I asked the main body of the people there to begin to move back and go ... to the home of the deceased. But we ... retained a small group, [about] ... twenty people, to finish off the task of filling up the grave. And in fact the main body of mourners ... took our instructions and moved away.

It was whilst we were ... busy filling the grave that the police fired teargas at us. As far as I was concerned, we were still within the time limits, and I did not hear if the police had given instructions that we must go away from there. But, on the other hand, they ... could not have known what our purpose was because we did not have a loudspeaker. So when we were speaking to the people, it would not have been audible to them, ... what we had said the people must do, and what must not happen.

In any event, they did fire the teargas, and ... we had to retreat into the trees that surrounded the graveyard, and I had to take this blind young fellow, because he was one of my passengers he had been waiting for me, and I had to take him and run away from there.

We retreated into the nearby trees, waiting for the teargas to clear off.... After the clearing of the teargas, we returned to the cars, and I did not wait any more for the filling up of the grave. I just took my passengers into the car.

There was also the old man ... it must have been the grandfather of the deceased, who had collapsed because he had been

overcome by teargas. And then somebody took the old man with
[by] the car to the hospital . . .

I got into the car and drove away with my passengers, back to
the home of the deceased.

Except for that incident, there was no act of violence of any
kind. . . . There were no stones thrown by anybody, in particular,
not by the main body of the people that we were with, and those
who had remained behind. (15:742–45)

When I returned to the home of the deceased, . . . we parked
the car and washed our hands. This is ceremonially done at funerals, and we stood just outside the gate, next to our car, waiting for
the main body of mourners who we had by-passed on the way,
who were still coming. . . . People had to come and wash their
hands and then have refreshments.

Whilst we were standing there, Dennis Bloem had arrived . . .
and several of the others . . . so we were just chatting, standing
there in our T-shirts.

Then one of the police vehicles, one of these hippos,[1] came
down the street. It seemed to be doing just normal duties to
check that there is nothing untoward. But when it was just left of
us, it stopped suddenly there, and then two police officers jumped
out, and one of them said, "Here are the other two with T-shirts."
["Hier is die ander twee met T-hemde."] There were more of us
with [T-shirts], because Pat had a white T-shirt, but they seemed to
be interested in the yellow T-shirts, because they took me, . . . in a
yellow T-shirt, and they also took Dennis Bloem, . . . in a yellow
T-shirt. Then they took us into the hippo, but they left Lephunya
there.[2]

They took us to the police station, and at the police station I
found, or rather, we found, a number of police officers in the yard.
Several . . . were actually security [political] police . . . I had met
before. . . . The issue that was raised . . . with me was that I had . . .
been served with a subpoena to appear at the magistrate's court in
Johannesburg [for] the inquest into the death of Ngalo in Parys.[3] I
was arrested in 1984, before . . . the inquest. . . . So when the date
came, I was in detention . . . and the police wanted an explanation,
why I had not honored that subpoena. I then explained that . . . it
was impossible for me to go there unless the police took me . . .

I was then separated from Dennis Bloem . . . I was taken to
another office . . . and it transpired later on that the police were
preparing a new subpoena for me . . . (15:746–47)

When the prosecution said that Lekota was at the funeral in Kroonstad on February 21 where rioting broke out, and a mourner was killed, Lekota allowed himself to express some indignation.

Bizos: [The prosecution witness] says, not only did he see you there, but he ascribes acts of violence to you.

Lekota: Well, I cannot explain why these reports have been made to create the impression before this court that if I am not teaching people to make petrol bombs then I am teaching people to throw stones around.

I am not a very important member [of the UDF], but I have standing in my community. I carry a lot of responsibility, and I am conscious of the responsibility I carry on my shoulders. . . . I am just not in the line of people who would go around picking up stones in the streets and throwing them around.

In a place like Kroonstad, where I am so well known, for me to do an act of that nature, to start with, would just destroy the standing of our organization, because people would see me, people know me, and if I act in a manner of that nature, I actually negate the task for which the United Democratic Front has elected me, to present it as it is. I would be misrepresenting my organization.

I must say quite firmly that there are a number of things that have happened in the course of these proceedings that have left me absolutely hurt. The fact that at times little children are encouraged to come and mislead the court about my behavior at a time when I am faced with five counts of murder, when I could face untold consequences. The suggestion that I go around the country teaching people how to make petrol bombs, literally that I am an anarchist, that is what it amounts to.

Not my family, not any of the people who are responsible for the position that I occupy in the United Democratic Front would have a bit of respect for me. . . . And for me to go into Kroonstad, an area where we do not have affiliates, it is important that my organization must be seen for what it is . . .

I think there has been a very wrong approach to some of the people who were in positions of trust. They have misused it. The state has got law enforcement officers. There is no need why, for instance, counsel for the state, men who are supposed to uphold the law of the country, should encourage people to come and lie.

Van Dijkhorst: On what basis do you say this?

LEKOTA: I say this on the basis of sworn evidence which we had at Delmas from one of the witnesses [who confessed that she had given false testimony about Lekota[4]].

VAN DIJKHORST: Well, it still depends on whether that evidence is accepted. (15:750–51)

It was a clear warning, but van Dijkhorst's verdict seems remarkable:

The funeral ... took place on 18 February 1985. In the crowd UDF ... T-shirts were worn. There was a banner, "We are not fighting to bury our heroes" ... The Amandla [Power] sign was given. Freedom songs were sung. The police were taunted.

This funeral was organized by UDF activist Denis Victor Bloem and attended by accused No. 20 and Patrick Lephunya of the UDF. Accused No. 20 was the main speaker. He spoke at the house of the deceased, and also at the grave. Restrictions laid down by the magistrate were blatantly ignored.

Some defense witnesses testified that in his speech, Accused No. 20 spoke out against violence. It is not clear whether he limited his objection to indiscriminate violence. It is not necessary to determine this issue as these witnesses were so untrustworthy that no finding at all can be made on the contents of No. 20's speech. (VD:639)

He found "no proof of UDF involvement leading to the riots." (VD:643)

19 In Hiding

The funeral in Kroonstad was to be the last event where Lekota would give advance notice that he would appear in public. He testified:

After coming back from Kroonstad ... on the night between the 18th and 19th, in the early hours ... of 19 February, police ... there was a swoop on the homes of very many UDF activists and officials, and a number of our people were arrested.

When Accused No. 19 [Molefe] and I got to the offices of the UDF ... we were driving in two separate cars. I had parked my car and was reading a newspaper in the car. ... He came up after he

had parked his car. I then said he must go to the office, and "I will
be coming later." Then almost a minute later, he came back, running, and he told me there were police in the office . . . and they
were searching the office.

I said to him, "The last time, I was the first one to be arrested.
You go there, and find out what is going on. If anybody gets arrested, you get arrested first this time." So he left his bag with me,
and he went. . . . But apparently, halfway, he decided to phone our
lawyers and tell them that police were in our office. . . . He discovered that people had been arrested in other parts. . . . He came
back to say that. "Things are bad. People have been arrested, and I
am getting arrested."

. . . From that day onward, I did not appear in public. I did not
address any public meeting or attend any public gathering. . . . I
had just come out from a long period of detention . . . and I was
not keen to return to it again. (15:745–46)

Thirteen antiapartheid activists, including several members of
the UDF national executive, were detained February 19 in a country-
wide sweep. Six of them would be charged with treason.

Protest and repression continued. By March 21, the twenty-fifth
anniversary of Sharpeville, more than ten thousand people had been
detained.[1] On that anniversary, police, unaware of the significance of
the date, opened fire without warning on mourners following a funeral in Langa in the Eastern Cape. The initial official toll was eighteen. By June 11, official numbers would rise to forty-seven killed,
thirty-five of them shot in the back. Resentment and anger at the
police and others seen as collaborators erupted into stone-throwing
at police, councillors, and alleged informers, and police killings of
black demonstrators rose to about one a day. Army personnel were
believed to be involved as well.

Lekota came and went, "still staying out of the public eye."
(15:606) On April 5, 1985, the National General Council of the UDF
approved a statement on the events shaking the country:

There is still time for the racist minority regime to consult
with the authentic leaders of the people, with the sole objective
of making the necessary arrangements for the speedy and effective dismantling of the apartheid state and the transfer of power to
the people. The precondition for the achievement of peace in this
country is the removal of the evil apartheid system. That is why
we say that our struggle for liberation is a struggle for peace. Not

one more drop of blood need be shed, not one more family need
live in misery and starve, no man or woman need go without
work, not one more family need go without shelter if these conditions are met . . . .

The state and its agents are engaged in the wholesale letting
of blood in the townships. Billions of rands are spent maintaining
apartheid subsidies . . .

We pledge to organize the masses of our people to effectively
challenge the apartheid state by frustrating its efforts, preventing
its advance, forcing its retreat, and if possible, to cut off all its lines
of retreat (26:457, 26:462, VD:281)

The prosecution took these words as an obvious threat that the
UDF would provoke violence until its demands were met. During
the final oral defense argument, the statement appeared crucial in
van Dijkhorst's thinking. Chaskalson was arguing that, although strident, the document was a warning, not a threat:

CHASKALSON: To warn people that violence will continue if
you do not change is not proof of a policy of violence. It is not
only Prime Ministers and State Presidents who can talk about fu-
tures "too ghastly to contemplate," [2] or the need to "adapt or die." [3]
There are other people who can also see the dangers and issue the
warnings, and the issuing of a warning, or the pointing to the dangers of continuing with a policy which is bringing forth so much
conflict, if that is what you feel, well then, to remain silent is a
crime. If you are a political leader of your country, if you want to
participate in the politics of your country, to remain silent in that
situation is actually appalling. (26:461)

Van Dijkhorst interrupted Chaskalson to ask with apparent passion, as though he had been wrestling in his mind with the possibility that the defendants were really, as they claimed, men of peace:
"But then, why, why had they not spoken out against the violence of
others?"

VAN DIJKHORST: Where is there a statement in this statement
by the UDF National General Council which deplores the violence
which gripped our country at the time? Not only the violence of
the SADF [South African Defense Force] or police, as it is alleged,
but the violence of the hooligans in the townships. . . . Why
merely blame the police for the blood letting, or whatever is mentioned here . . .

But nobody could have perceived it to be the situation, that it is solely the state that is responsible for everything. Is that your contention, that anybody in his right senses could have perceived it that way?

CHASKALSON: I think that people in their right senses could have perceived the state to be primarily responsible for that situation. Perceptions are very different. Depending upon where you are and who you are, one does perceive things differently.

But again, your lordship may feel that this is a very one-sided, strident unfair statement, that is your lordship's ...

VAN DIJKHORST: I am not concerned with fair or unfair. That is not the point. The point is that the UDF stands for nonviolence. It issues a statement at a time when the whole country is in turmoil. In that statement, there is no mention at all that the UDF deplores the violence in which our country is gripped, and then on page two of this statement, the UDF pledges itself to organize the masses of our people to effectively challenge the apartheid state by frustrating its efforts, preventing its advance, forcing its retreat, and if possible cut off all lines of retreat. Now in the circumstances, what does it mean? ...

Is there not a situation in which ... one would expect a responsible body to state clearly and unequivocally, "we are nonviolent, and the methods we intend employing are nonviolent" and is this not the situation where that would have been expected? And it is sadly lacking?

CHASKALSON: But how can your lordship take the next step, and say, "Because you did not say that, therefore your goal is to overthrow the state by violence?"

VAN DIJKHORST: I have not got to the next step yet. I am merely interpreting the document, and making a couple of remarks on it that have been troubling me all along on this document.

CHASKALSON: Yes. Well again, that was not really an argument that was put up in the "Betoog" [the prosecution summation]."

VAN DIJKHORST: Yes, but I hope I have the liberty to put a couple of personal problems also to you.

CHASKALSON: No, all I am saying, my lord, is that if your lordship puts a personal problem to me, I would like to look at the evidence ... (26:462–64)

If van Dijkhorst were asking because he felt these questions personally, Chaskalson, careful, lawyerly, and suspicious on his clients' behalf, was not the one to ask. He promised to return to the issue but, for the moment, interpreted the document to answer the points made by the prosecution, not by van Dijkhorst.

During his passionate appeal for help, van Dijkhorst did not glance at those who might have been able to answer, the defendants in the dock.

In the verdict, van Dijkhorst described the UDF statement as "audacious," and "an unequivocal declaration of war on the state." (VD:281–82)

Still working as publicity secretary, Lekota emerged from hiding to tell the UDF's national conference that mass demonstrations would be held across South Africa if a New Zealand rugby tour went ahead. A few days later, he issued another public statement that the protests were to be nonviolent:

There had been a lot of spontaneous undisciplined action that had been taking place in some of our townships, and it was important that our organizations ... move into the situation ... so that when people have got a protest or ... complaint, there must be clearly disciplined action taken.... First of all, the complaints of the people must be clearly stated so that the government can hear what the complaint is.

... There were a lot of unruly elements, people who belonged to no organizations and who were doing just as they pleased, and it was important to undercut that kind of thing. There must be clear, publicly acknowledged organizations that the people would respond to, and not respond to any Tom, Dick and Harry [who] said he was a leader.... People are not then exposed to anarchy, [when] people lose their lives unnecessarily. (15:608–609)

A few days later, the Attorney General of the Transvaal announced that another group of detainees would soon be charged with treason.

Botha, making concessions to world opinion, promised to abolish a law prohibiting sexual contact between people of different races and to allow a few Africans to own land in South Africa. On April 19, in Parliament, he attacked the UDF as an extension of the ANC and the South African Communist Party, bent on destroying South Africa. On hearing the allegation, Molefe asked Lekota to immediately prepare a statement. It was quoted in the trial:

In the past, the UDF has stated that it had no formal or informal link with the ANC other than the historical fact that both organizations were of South African origin and were opposed to apartheid. . . . It is irrelevant whether the UDF and the ANC called for a national convention. What matters is whether that situation can bring about a democratic and nonracial constitution for this country in a reasonably peaceful fashion, or whether Mr. Botha would allow his army and police to shoot and kill black children for the preservation of apartheid. Mr. Botha has conceded that real grievances existed which created unrest among black people. The UDF has asserted that this, his new dispensation, fails to solve those problems. It is a lie that the UDF is intent on precipitating a revolution. We are determined to see real change rather than such massacres as at Uitenhague. Nor could the UDF be blamed for the deteriorating economic situation. (14:903)

Molefe's youngest child, Albertina, was born during this period in which he was keeping out of the limelight. Both Lekota and Chikane also had children born a few weeks later. Although being more open meant danger, the UDF officials decided that their absence from the office was giving the wrong impression. They returned to work in the office after April 19.

A newspaper, describing Lekota as a "gentle giant," reported that he had come out of hiding because the UDF's work was suffering, not because he thought the danger was over:

As the UDF operated on a nonviolent level, it was important for its leaders to be seen acting legally. (15:610)

Once again, they chose to show in present action the future they wish to create.

On April 23, police arrested Molefe, Lekota, and Moses Chikane. On June 11, twenty-two defendants, including Molefe and Lekota, other UDF officials and activists in affiliated organizations, and Black Consciousness and AZAPO activists from the Vaal Triangle and Soweto appeared in court on charges of treason, terrorism, subversion, and murder.

Part Five
In the Jaws of the Crocodile

20 The Trial

Between September 1984 and March 21, 1985, the official toll of violence throughout South Africa was 217 killed, 700 injured, and 10,000 arrested. One of those killed was white. The toll rose rapidly after the massacre of March 21. In early May, mobs started to "necklace" (with burning tires) suspected "sellouts" and informers. Among prisoners held in detention the number of "falls," "suicides," and other sudden deaths escalated. In a few weeks, troops were sent to occupy more African townships.

Although many in the government would gladly have banned the UDF in 1985, some believed it more politic to rely on treason trials to keep leaders out of action and discredit their cause. The actual trials would thwart this strategy. The collapse of the Pietermaritzburg trial would discredit the government, and the Delmas Trial would give the defendants a platform, opportunities to extend their network, and protection from death squads.

In the courtroom, Molefe and Lekota continued to work for the UDF. The police watched what they were doing and noted who came. The defendants believed that visitors forced their captors to observe what they described to U.S. Ambassador Edward Perkins as "the necessary decorum."

On July 21, 1985, South Africa imposed a State of Emergency that placed wide powers in the hands of the military and police. By December, more than 7,000 had been detained, about a third of them minors. Some mob violence was directed against alleged informers and sellouts in black townships. New police, quickly enlisted and trained, were soon nicknamed "instant constables," by analogy with instant coffee.

The economy, strained by a long and severe drought and a falling gold price, was threatened now by a climate of investment discouraged by arson and murder and by a sense of the ineffectiveness of mere might to impose order. White confidence in the inevitability and righteousness of the existing order was eroding, and white unity was splitting. Botha swung from belligerent righteousness to concessions. Among a few whites, growing feelings of impotence led to increasing support for the Conservative Party, to the right of the National Party, and still further right, for the yet more extreme Afrikaner Resistance Movement (AWB), which tapped into an old sense of alliance with the Nazis. AWB salutes resembled the Nazi Heil, and AWB flags flew three-legged swastikas.

But some whites, acknowledging that the majority must be heard, wanted to talk with the ANC. Few saw full political equality as either desirable or inevitable.

On August 1, four days before the Pietermaritzburg treason trial was due to begin, Victoria Mxenge, one of the defense lawyers, was murdered outside her home. Her husband, Griffiths Mxenge, had been murdered four years before. Like the deaths of Goniwe and his companions, her death was widely believed to be the work of police or extremists known to the police. [A death row prisoner confessed in 1989 that he had been part of a death squad that killed Griffiths Mxenge. Other allegations about police death squads soon followed.]

In the Delmas trial, the first of many appeals for bail was heard September 3.

International condemnation of South Africa was taking practical form in sanctions. Business leaders seemed especially aware of the effect of the continuing turmoil on international opinion and the economy. A delegation set off to talk to leaders of the ANC in Lusaka. They seemed amazed that the horned ANC monster painted by government propaganda dissolved at human contact.

This high-profile visit was soon followed by a delegation from the Progressive Federal Party, largely supported by business interests. A group of Afrikaner churchmen planned to go in October, but their passports were withdrawn and they were warned that their visit would amount to provocation against public authority. A growing number within the country believed that the end of intransigent white minority rule must come in their own generation.

When Molefe testified in August 1987, two years after these visits to the ANC, Jacobs challenged him with UDF responsibility for white defection:

JACOBS: And I put it to you that another achievement claimed by the UDF since its launch in 1983, is that it has sowed doubts in the minds of many whites about the ability of the state to resolve the present crisis, and to acknowledge the inevitability of majority rule and the importance of the ANC. . . .

MOLEFE: I do not know about that. But it is true that an increasing number of people have begun to accept that the policies of apartheid are unworkable. . . . An increasing number of people, professionals, businessmen and so on, have begun to argue that the government must negotiate, must begin to lay the basis for talks with the ANC . . . Several trips that people have taken to talk to the ANC in Lusaka . . . but I cannot say that it is to the credit of the UDF (14:830)

Jacobs changed the subject.

In October 1985, van Dijkhorst refused bail to the Delmas defendants. In November, the prosecution added another charge to the indictment: "furthering the aims of the ANC." The defense would point out that the defendants were charged with crimes treated as innocent in others. It pointed to slogans like "Amandla!" (Whose is the power? Answered "Awethu." It is ours.) and to statements used by Buthelezi, other homeland leaders, AZAPO members, and members of the opposition. It did not say that no business leader who went to Lusaka was charged with furthering the aims of a banned organization.

In the Pietermaritzburg treason trial, the judge, breaking with South African tradition, chose two blacks as assessors, one a retired African magistrate, the other a practicing Indian attorney. An "expert witness" on revolutionary theory and practice made a dismal showing, and videotape evidence proved unreliable. On December 8, authorities dropped charges against the twelve UDF and affiliated officials. Four union leaders remained on trial until June 23, when charges against them too were dropped.

On December 23, 1985, two days before Christmas, during busy shopping hours, a bomb exploded in a shopping mall in Amanzimtoti, a holiday resort. A baby, an eight-year-old boy, a girl, and two women were killed. Forty-nine people were injured. All the dead and most of the hurt were white. It was the most devastating of more than forty terrorist attacks since August 1984.

On December 27, the police arrested Andrew Zondo, a nineteen-year-old who confessed to placing a limpet mine in a trash can outside a fast food restaurant. The contrite Zondo said he had never intended to kill anyone. He said he had planned to call a warning before the bomb exploded, but his plan failed because all the Post

Office pay phones were busy during the few minutes between his setting the mine and leaving the scene.

Zondo had received military training from the ANC and had been assigned to avenge the deaths of nine ANC members in a South African raid on Lesotho, a few days before. He knew he had disobeyed the ANC policy of avoiding civilian deaths. The government media played the story to elicit terror, revulsion, and condemnation of the ANC.

It was a new nadir, but the father of the eight-year-old victim said, "The government must talk to the ANC."

In early 1986, South Africa, which had been sending troops into Angola, to defend apartheid on distant frontiers, became more open about its attacks.

In March 1986, President Botha rescinded the State of Emergency, in April he promised to abolish the pass laws, and in July he did. One of the most oppressive apartheid laws was gone. But a new State of Emergency was imposed on June 12. It would not be lifted during the trial or appeal.

In the trial itself, there was a change from the procedural maneuvres of 1985. In January 1986 the prosecution started to lead witnesses. Some proved an embarrassment. A key witness from the Vaal, Reverend Lord McCamel, was greeted by the defendants as a friend. His testimony supported their versions of events. A pilot describing the lay of the land in the Vaal Triangle misplaced key landmarks. At the end of April, IC 10, who had testified that Lekota taught students how to make petrol bombs, recanted and pointed to Jacobs as knowing that her perjured testimony was coerced. Brigadier Viljoen, in command of the police who opened fire in the Vaal, was contradicted by a video that showed him taking no measures to control police who were whipping and beating apparently peaceful mourners.

The prosecution called 152 witnesses, almost all members of the police force. Almost all the others testified *in camera,* not seen by observers, not quoted by name. This practice of semisecret trial is justified in South Africa as protection for witnesses from retribution, although the identity of witnesses is usually known in their community. *In camera* witnesses may actually feel the protective—or threatening—power of the justice system more vividly than the opinion of their community.

An American observer in early 1986 reports that Jacobs complained of the difficulty for a prosecutor of getting witnesses to testify when they saw so many black faces in the dock and the gallery and began to think of "getting the necklace." When the observer suggested that defense counsel might be equally frustrated if they felt the defendants were giving testimony purely to end long, solitary detention, Jacobs inferred that the American was biased in favor of the defense.

Three *in camera* witnesses in the Delmas Trial testified that they were members of the ANC and the UDF. Two of the same witnesses testified against the remaining four defendants in the Pietermaritzburg trial too, and in other trials. Some observers described witnesses like these as itinerant witness in virtually any case where the prosecution thought it useful to have inside testimony about the ANC.

Four key prosecution witnesses were either brought from detention to testify or had been detained and gave evidence after detention. One witness admitted under cross-examination that during a week he had spent in detention, in October 1984, he had been assaulted by at least three senior police officers during interrogation. He described the week as "a nightmare that will be with me for the rest of my life." In detention another time, he had frequently contemplated suicide.

BIZOS: Did you ever agree with the ANC to overthrow the state, you personally?

IN CAMERA 8: No, not at all, not with the ANC.

BIZOS: Did you ever know of any agreement between AZAPO and the ANC . . . to overthrow the state?

IC 8: No, I know nothing about that.

BIZOS: You know nothing about it. Did you feel that, whilst you were in detention, that you were responsible for any of the deaths of any of the councillors that were killed?

IC 8: What occurred to me while I was in detention, in fact, which is one of the reasons which cause me to think about killing myself, is that this government will not look deep into the whole thing. They will just accept it on face value that we, the people who had a lot to say, are the people who caused, by having a lot to say, that the councillors be killed; and therefore I felt it would be wise to kill myself. (26:108–109)

He had been in detention and interrogated for four months. He was still afraid of his interrogators while giving evidence in court.

IC 8 had served as an *in camera* prosecution in another case arising from the violence in the Vaal. In that case he and other witnesses for the prosecution were described by Justice Pieter van der Walt as "strangers to the truth." (26:153)[1]

Another witness for the prosecution, Rina Mokoena, had such a hard time during her detention that when asked whether she had made her first statement during summer or winter, she answered "No, during that time it was bad with me. I know nothing." She heard voices and believed in premonitions, contradicted herself, and admitted such confusion that she could not sort out what she had testified. In court she seemed to feel such terror that the defense asked the investigating officer to leave before she was cross-examined.

The prosecution closed its case October 22, 1986.

The trial's length drove it off the front pages and, for long periods, from public attention, except for unusual events. The youngest of the Vaal defendants was married in court in June 1986. Van Dijkhorst vacated the judge's bench so that the bridal couple could have the place of honor in the courtroom. At the end of November, three of the defendants, including the young groom, were dropped from the indictment.

The defense began its case on January 21, 1987, and Joubert won the bottle of whiskey van Dijkhorst had bet on his certainty that the defense would not call the defendants to testify. On March 10, 1987, van Dijkhorst insisted that Dr. Willem Joubert favored the defendants, was "unable to act as assessor," and must recuse himself. He did not allow Joubert to answer these charges.

On March 30, 1987, the defense asked van Dijkhorst and Krugel, the other assessor, to recuse themselves because they were not neutral. Van Dijkhorst answered with a sixteen-page statement criticizing Joubert. Then Joubert signed a report about van Dijkhorst's early comments that the case was an answer to a "total onslaught" and about van Dijkhorst's bet that the witnesses would not testify in their own behalf. Without reading it, van Dijkhorst ruled this report inadmissible and forbade any reference to its contents. He threatened to charge Chaskalson with contempt. The defense withdrew its application for recusal and the case continued.

The charges were so voluminous that the defense divided the case roughly into different areas of responsibility: the UDF officials generally to Chaskalson, the Vaal to Bizos, and the charges connected with violence in thirty-one other parts of the country to Karel Tip, Gilbert Marcus, and Zak Yacoob.

In mid-1987, ten defendants from the Vaal were released on bail. By the end of the trial, the only three still in prison were the three UDF officials.

In August, Molefe took the stand for twenty-one days; in September, Lekota took the stand for fourteen.

The prosecution summed up in early August 1988, and the defense began its final arguments a few days later.

Chaskalson began his summation with the indictment, "because the indictment defines the parameters of the case, and that is important, because the state has frequently in its argument gone outside those parameters, and indeed, it has on occasion lost sight of the allegations which it made and to which the accused pleaded." (25:282)

In the early maneuvers, the defense had tried to have the case divided into several trials. Having twenty-two defendants from different organizations and with vastly different degrees of political involvement complicated the case immensely for each one. Van Dijkhorst refused. In his summation, Chaskalson attributed the length of the trial, so wearisome to van Dijkhorst, in part to this jointure of all the cases. Chaskalson complained, "We have just a conglomerate," and he protested that the defendants needed specifics "because they cannot be expected to defend themselves, as it were, against a generalized allegation." (25:325)

What is it meant to be we are dealing with? What evidence must now be totally excluded from the reckoning because it is not evidence admissible against the accused on any basis? How does one even begin to deal with that? Part of the problems of this case comes from this attempt to roll up into one conspiracy people who really did not belong together, and to be able to join them together, the state has rolled them up into this one single ongoing conspiracy, saying everything is admissible against all of you, every act done by every person is evidence against all of you, and to try and catch everyone in the net it put them down together in this way. (25:292–93)

In November 1986, van Dijkhorst had ruled that there was a link:

In my view ... a pattern emerges. In those areas where damage and disturbance conforming to the pattern ... occurred, or where there is an active UDF presence, shown by its officials or its pamphlets or its affiliates or active supporters or by its own admission, I am not prepared to find that no link has been shown to

exist between the damage and the UDF, and through the latter, with the accused, or some of them. (157:7632–33)

To support its loosely defined charges, the prosecution produced masses of documents and parts of documents: 14,425 pages in all. Chaskalson described many as inadmissible under either common or statutory law and some as "neither admissible nor relevant." (26:364)

The prosecution also submitted forty-two videotapes of meetings in evidence. Bizos pointed out that some of the videotapes were Westerns.

At one point, when Chaskalson complained of the unfocused character of the charges and the evidence, the tension between the defense team and the judge rose to the surface.

CHASKALSON: Any document which contains any reference to any term really which we have in this case is produced. It is put in. Any evidence of any acts of unrest anywhere in the country at any time is put in, and it is all put into a pot and stirred and put into the oven, and out pops a conviction, with no attempt to disaggregate what has gone in.

VAN DIJKHORST: Do you think it is so easy? (25:400)

This exchange harked back to their bitter exchange about whether van Dijkhorst should recuse himself. Van Dijkhorst resented deeply any suggestion that he was unable to divorce his judicial stance from his political opinions.

Van Dijkhorst was even more irritable with Bizos. In his argument, Bizos called the testimony of several *in camera* witnesses into question. One, Mahlatsi, had made two conflicting statements under oath. After making the second, he was told he could be a witness and was given a luxury radio. When Bizos commented that the state did not make the conflicting statements available to the defense, van Dijkhorst sounded tested almost beyond endurance.

VAN DIJKHORST: But now, what do I do with it [a reference]? I know there is an appellate division authority on this, but do I, do—having said that, what do I do with it?

BIZOS: You put your lordship pen right through Mahlatsi's evidence.

VAN DIJKHORST: Why? Because the state did not do its duty?

BIZOS: Yes, because an accused is entitled to a fair trial. (26:162)

Bizos continued with his argument against the credibility of the witness. The next time he offered a reference, van Dijkhorst sounded both resigned and dismissive.

VAN DIJKHORST: If you want to give a reference, give it and it will be in the typed summary, and if I want to look it up, I can look it up. (26:163–64)

In his summation, Chaskalson argued that there was no substance to prosecution charges of violence:

The cornerstone of the prosecution's case against the accused persons in this trial is the allegation that they planned and began to implement a scheme to overthrow the state by violence. The prosecution led no direct evidence of any planning of such a scheme, but it argues that such a scheme must have been contemplated, because the UDF made demands to which it knew the government would not submit. (25:273)

The demands are these: first, for a true democracy; secondly, for all South Africans to participate in the government of the country; thirdly, for a single, nonracial, unfragmented South Africa; and fourthly, for an end to group areas, and all forms of oppression and exploitation. (25:276)

Now the state has called not a single witness to suggest that there was amongst the people associated with [the UDF] or among the communities with which it was working, that there was a perception that the UDF was a violent organization. Nobody has come to this court to say that although the UDF was preaching nonviolence, we did not believe that, we knew it to be a violent organization. Nobody has said that. That is the argument for the state, but where is the evidence for that? If that was indeed the perception of the policy of the UDF, if that was what the people thought about the UDF, why couldn't we have had evidence to say that its policy was understood in this way? People who had adhered to it? Affiliates who knew that when they adhered to it? . . . None of that has been produced. (25:482)

The state is saying, Well, though you said this to your own supporters, though you publicly project this image, though you never mention violence in your documents, though we produce no witness to confirm our case by direct evidence, somewhere there were people plotting violence. (25:511)

Citing the Universal Declaration of Human Rights, which South Africa has not signed, he argued that the defendants had exercised a fundamental human right to protest, a right that must be respected, lest those who are silenced turn to violence as a last resort. He argued that it was better for those in power to hear objections to their policies than to be taken aback.

Outside the courtroom, the continuing unrest in the country and wars in Angola, Namibia, and, in spite of official denials, Mozambique were proving costly in a time of deepening recession, and when South African forces suffered defeat in Angola, South Africa withdrew. Negotiations for South African withdrawal from Namibia started to sound more real than ever before. Pressure to release Mandela continued, contacts with the ANC continued, and the electorate seemed increasingly pulled between those determined to fight for minority rule to the bitter end and those who wanted the struggle to end and allow a new South Africa to emerge.

The bitter-enders represented a force still strong in the country, especially in the police and military. A group calling itself the White Wolves started to take credit for bombings and assassinations. Many believed the police were implicated in these activities and that they were supported at the highest level of government. During the final weeks of the trial, Khotso House (where the defendants on bail parked a van that drove them to court) and the headquarters of the South African Catholic Bishops Conference were bombed.

Van Dijkhorst appeared to be in misery. Imprisoned on the bench, he shifted from one buttock to another, leaned forward, leaned back, leaned his head on his fingertips. He occasionally made puns, but they were rarely received with amusement.

In the third week of defense argument, van Dijkhorst refused to hear more. After protest, he extended the time for oral argument a few days and agreed to read further written argument submitted before a deadline.

The night before he read the verdict, a caller claiming to be head of the White Wolves threatened to kill the Prime Minister if he released Mandela.

21 History and Legitimacy

While Barend Strydom's targets were bleeding in the streets of Pretoria on the morning of November 15, 1988, Kees van Dijkhorst, wearing the red robe of a judge, ascended the bench and sat facing the nineteen defendants. They were flanked by lawyers, press, dignitaries of church and state, legal observers, relatives of the defendants, and policemen armed with automatic weapons. On van Dijkhorst's left, robed in black, sat Krugel, the remaining assessor.

There was no jury. Van Dijkhorst alone would decide guilt or innocence.

Many in the courtroom considered the day historic. Van Dijkhorst's verdict would legitimate or condemn the methods of the UDF. His verdict could mean freedom, death, or prison for its leaders. It would define the boundaries of lawful protest against apartheid. It would be heard by the international community pressuring South Africa for change. It would be considered by the State's President. His verdict would be heard and studied by the legal community in which he had learned, taught, and become a judge.

Some thunder had been stolen from the occasion by succeeding states of emergency imposed every year since 1985 to resist the "total onslaught." The states of emergency, superseding the rule of law in many cases, made his verdict less necessary and less powerful. In November 1988, most UDF leaders were in prison, or banned and forbidden access to their supporters in person or through the media. Several had died in police custody and through vigilante action. A proclamation in February 1988 had forbidden the UDF and sixteen other organizations to act politically. Censorship, and a few notable deaths among those who defied it,[1] had stilled the international uproar about apartheid that had shaken South Africa during the period of the UDF's creation and accession to opposition leadership.

The verdict would set van Dijkhorst free for a longed-for sabbatical.

He began to read:

> This has been a trying case for all concerned in it. . . . It commenced on 16 October, 1985. Thus far we have had 437 days in court, stretched over a period of 37 months. 278 witnesses testified. The record consists of 459 volumes and runs to 27,194 pages. We had as exhibits 1,556 documents consisting of 14,425 pages, 42 video and audio tapes, 5 rolls of film, and numerous photographs and maps. (VD:2)

Van Dijkhorst's verdict would add 1,521 pages to the record. He would spend four court days reading it and submit the rest in writing.

He confessed to exasperation at "the repetitiveness, tediousness and protractedness" of the process. He said he had tried to approach the problem "with patience and discernment," even when tried "almost to the point of exhaustion!" (VD:5).

He criticized the prosecution, gently, for the wide indictment and the large number of accused. He described the "quest for justice" as following "a route so tortuous that it seems never-ending, and is costly beyond endurance to both the state and accused." (VD:2) He did not say that it had been his decisions that kept all the accused joined in one trial.

The defendants, and particularly Molefe and Lekota, seemed cheerful and unwearied. The private doubts, grief, and anger expressed in the letter Lekota had just written in the holding cell below the courtroom were put aside for a characteristic wide smile. The defendants, aware of how people would read their demeanor, acknowledged friends and supporters in the gallery, and comported themselves like free men going about the most important business of their lives.

By the end of the Delmas Trial, some saw already that power was slipping out of the hands of those the prosecution spoke for. Visitors crowded around Molefe and Lekota during breaks. When van Dijkhorst returned, they left. In the courtroom, as in the country, power was passing to the leaders of the majority. But for the verdict van Dijkhorst had an audience. He spoke like one with authority, and he seemed unaware that he had not read the signs of the times.

Noting his weariness, he recommended improved trial procedure.

Before focusing on the specific case, he turned to the historical context in which it must be understood, almost as though agreeing with Lekota:

If the present South African situation is to be understood, properly understood, it must been seen against the backdrop of the history of our country, so that the past helps to explain the present. In the same spirit, if we are to go forward, it will be the present correctly understood, that will guide our steps forward. (15:650)

The history each knows, and how each knows it, differs significantly from the other's. The first thing van Dijkhorst's notes in his history, is racial and ethnic differences:

The exceptionally complex character of its population has been the dominating factor in the history of South Africa. It has seen wars of blacks against blacks, whites against blacks, and whites against whites. (VD:16)

After race, van Dijkhorst, man of the law, sees history through laws:

In 1910 the whites owned most of the land and capital and did most of the skilled work. They were attempting to heal the wounds of the South African War [the Boer War] and little attention was given to the political rights of the black[2] majority . . .

The British Parliament gave the vote to all whites, and to some blacks. . . . The African National Congress was founded by blacks to further their political aims by peaceful protest and petitions. They made no significant headway.

In 1913 the Natives Land Act established scheduled native areas . . . The scheduled native areas were small [approximately 13 percent] in proportion to the total area of the Union of South Africa . . . (VD:17)

He continues in a recitation of laws passed by a government in which no named person is responsible for any act. Laws are passed. They "establish," "decree," "create," and "deal with". . . . The laws he described restricted the vote, land ownership, freedom of movement, and employment. [He would have considered as biased words like "deprive," "humiliate," or "coerce".] The record suggests that he rejected any suggestion that his own point of view could be limited by his own experience, education, and membership in the establishment.

In van Dijkhorst's history of South Africa, there is no need to ask who passes laws, or why. Laws are static and certain, received rather than made, and not historically limited like other things made by human beings.

In 1936, the Representation of Natives Act placed the names of [most] blacks who were entitled to vote on a separate roll . . . (VD:18)

As the verdict continues, the style itself shapes what can be seen and what is never seen. Events come into the world irresistibly, like acts of God, weather, and disasters. No one knows why specific things happen at one time rather than another.

Lekota's history is full of purpose and of people. The laws affect people and they act in response to the laws, and to the people who make the laws. Lekota gives the people names. He knows how they made the laws or sought to change them. He knows who teaches history and how they teach it. He says what history means to him personally, and to other people. He says how he uses history. He says what contribution he wants to make to future history. Although Lekota is a voracious reader of history, he talks as though he knows it primarily through voices and gestures, and most of all, through the lives of people who demonstrate their convictions by their actions. He describes the history he knows as secret—it is not taught in schools, many of its heroes are unknown to written history, many are banned or condemned to prison.

He learned much of this secret history "on the knees" of Mandela and other leaders during his term on Robben Island. Describing the period of 1910 to 1948, the same period van Dijkhorst presented only through laws, Lekota says:

I learnt about how our people had for so long been denied political rights, how even some of those political rights that African people had enjoyed before the turn of the century in the Cape had been systematically taken away from them.

I learnt from them about how, time and time again, reputed leaders of my people, some of them church men, others teachers, some builders, some chiefs, others paramount chiefs, had from time to time stated and re-stated the plea of the African people that they may be included in a South African state. I got to know from them about how . . . so many . . . had taken trips abroad, going for months on end on ships, after every household or village had taken out 2/6—the money they used that time was pounds and so on, and every family gave something, two-and-six [two shillings and six pence] . . . so that they could go to Britain and state to Britain that the political direction of South Africa was taking, was one that excluded the African people, and that they wanted our people to be included in it.

I learnt from them about the long constitutional struggle that was waged from 1912 [founding date of the African National Congress, known at that time as the South African Native National Congress] to 1949 . . .

Indeed I heard from them about how in the course of the Second World War, many of my own people contributed in the struggle against Nazism and Fascism, with the hope that when all was said and done, African people would be afforded a place in the South African sun. They had come to naught. Our people had only been afforded bicycles and the overcoats that they wore as they served in Egypt and other countries. (15:459–60)

In van Dijkhorst's history, it is not clear why black resistance changed after 1948.

After 1948 the ANC Youth League became more radical and militant. Its aim was to liberate Blacks from White domination by strikes, boycotts, civil disobedience, and refusal to cooperate. There were several mass protest demonstrations. (VD:21)

Lekota's history, where events, like a living organism, give life to new events, proposes a clear sequence.

That constitutional struggle, I understood, lasted 39 years, coming up to 1949, when the Youth League moved to a more radical and militant program of action. Not armed, but radical and militant in the sense of the sacrifices imposed upon my people. It was out of the 1949 Program of Action that African people took a decision that now, the Nationalist Party had come to power in 1948 and it was introducing its policies of apartheid, African people would have to stand up and make clear their position on this policy.

That led directly to the defiance campaign [of 1952] at the head of which was Nelson Mandela himself. He was the Volunteer in Chief. And I am told about how he travelled from city to city and town to town. He urged our people to make known their objections to the laws of apartheid and not to do so by way of using violence. He said they must defy those laws. He said they must defy, that they must not use violence, even if they were assaulted. He said. Even if you are assaulted, you must not—that was the Volunteer In Chief of 1952.

I learnt from them that in spite of those efforts, in spite of that determination to appeal to the better judgment of our white compatriots, those sacrifices, those efforts resulted in naught.

I learnt from them, therefore, that increasingly as our people made pleas for a democratic share in the country, so proportionately did the rulers of our country tighten the noose, and systematically stripped African people of whatever rights they may have

had, denied them an opportunity to continue to contribute on an
equal footing to the development and government of our country.

I heard about how in 1953, Professor Z. K. Matthews[3] raised
the question to the African people that perhaps it is appropriate
that we must now say what future South Africa we want. Perhaps
that might disabuse our White compatriots [of] all their fears that
our nationalism is a nationalism that is selfish and thus seeks to
destroy them. And that indeed, as a result of that plea, our people
came together at a big meeting at Kliptown in 1955, and there
drew up the Freedom Charter, in which they stated publicly—
even at the expense of sections of the African community—that
South Africa belongs to all of her people, Black and White.

That [statement] earned those men, and others who were
with them, contempt from certain sections of our community, but
they made it clear that they were not prepared to retreat on the
only principle that could guarantee our country its future.

And I also learnt, sadly, that the year following that declaration, 156 leaders of our people who had made that noble statement found themselves arrested and charged for treason.
(15:459–62)

Van Dijkhorst does not mention that treason trial in his history.

Initiated by the ANC, a Congress of the People was convened
in 1955 in Kliptown. This congress adopted a Freedom Charter
which claims equal rights for all, and that South Africa belongs to
all its inhabitants.

In 1959, the Pan African Congress was founded . . . (VD:22)

The Treason Trial of 1956–61, was South Africa's longest trial
before the Delmas Trial. Some of the 156 defendants were arrested
in the middle of the night. The defendants included Albert Lutuli,
Nelson Mandela, Oliver Tambo, Z. K. Matthews, and other major antiapartheid leaders. They were accused of "a country-wide conspiracy" inspired by international communism to overthrow the state by
violence. "Not since the burning of the Reichstag in Berlin in 1933—
with the notable exception of the special trials in Nuremburg—has
a trial attracted such international attention."[4] During the trial, the
State withdrew charges against many of the accused, and only
twenty-eight were left by the time the trial ended "suddenly on
March 29, 1961 . . . the three judges were unanimous in finding the
. . . accused not guilty."[5]

Chaskalson had cited the Adams trial extensively in his summation.

Van Dijkhorst did not forget the 1956–61 Treason Trial. He did not see it as part of South Africa's history. It was a legal precedent he would reject as an unsuitable model for his own decision—the country in 1956 had been at peace, whereas during the life of the UDF it had been, he said, at war.

The omission of the Adams trial from van Dijkhorst's history reveals how the history important to Lekota has come to be a "secret" history. It is omitted when those in power construct history.

In omitting what he did not want to see and did not want others to see, van Dijkhorst implicitly denied its existence. Under the guise of fair-minded objectivity, he spoke for a government that had repeatedly silenced the voices of those who challenged its version of reality and its claim to have the one only true version. Although he would resent and reject any explicit injunction to find the defendants guilty, he did not stand outside the field of contest.

The absence of human agency in his history lets him evade recognizing personal bias and responsibility.

1960 saw extensive mass protests by Blacks against the pass laws, which, on March 21, 1960, led to violent confrontation with the police and a tragic loss of life at Sharpeville ... (VD:22) [At Sharpeville protests against the pass laws, police killed sixty-nine people and wounded hundreds. One of the wounded was the father of a childhood friend of one of the Delmas defendants, Oupa Hlomuka. Hlomuka remembered terrified women calling him and his friends away from play on March 30, 1960.]

To van Dijkhorst, it seems obvious that "the protests ... led to violent confrontation." By implication, if there had been no protests, there would have been no violence. A similar structure underlies van Dijkhorst's verdict on the Delmas defendants. Contemporary photographs show the crowd at Sharpeville unarmed and peaceful when the police opened fire. Van Dijkhorst does not admit any suggestion that the police panicked or were in any way at fault. The question simply does not arise.

As van Dijkhorst's history approaches contemporary events, he appears fair and neutral again:

The control of White Urban Local Authorities over their own Black townships was abolished in 1972. Blacks had no say in the administration of their affairs at a local level. (VD:22)

Unexpectedly, revealingly, his chronicle leaps from the seventies to the eighties:

The late 70's saw a gradual movement away from this autocratic rule. Community Councils were replaced by Town Councils created by the Black Local Authorities Act, 1982. (VD:24)

This leap lands van Dijkhorst directly in the case: the UDF had vigorously opposed this bill, one of three known together as the Koornhof bills. Van Dijkhorst takes a step back. He cannot pass over the most important events of the seventies in total silence.

Meanwhile, on 16 June 1976, Soweto erupted in riots. . . . Led by the Soweto Students Representative Council, protest marches, riots, strikes, and general vandalism abounded. General unrest prevailed in South Africa for a long time. A large section of the Black youth was politicized, and Black education became a burning issue. A large number of people died tragically, and, like Sharpeville in 1960, Soweto 1976 had repercussions which still reverberate.(VD:24)

His characterization of the events of 1976 is like that of Sharpeville. No one is responsible. Although in 1976, according to van Dijkhorst, the students started it all. We are not even aware that the government played a role. It is not present. It is innocent.

Van Dijkhorst's version of what happened in 1976 is revealed even more clearly later in the verdict:

The lessons of 1976 had been well learnt by scholars. It is that what one cannot get redressed by the stifled bureaucracy of the Department of Education and Training in years of representations can be changed within three weeks of school boycotts and rioting. (VD:184)

The anniversary of the outbreak of violence in which more than 900 people died, June 16, has become a day of commemoration in South Africa. During the Delmas Trial, Lekota and the prosecution differed sharply about the events of Soweto, 1976. During cross-examination, Fick asked:

FICK: Why do you, the UDF, call them "our martyrs"?

LEKOTA: Because these people come from our communities, and these people died in the struggle against apartheid. When the government was trying to impose a medium of instruction on them they did not agree with, and then they were shot for that . . .

FICK: Mr. Lekota, I put it to you that no one in 1976, during the uprising, was shot simply because they were opposed to Afrikaans as a medium in the school.

LEKOTA: What were they shot for, if I may ask? . . . Those students were protesting against the imposition of Afrikaans as a medium of instruction, and they were . . . moving toward Orlando stadium. The police came there, and it was in the course of that that the police shot them. All the accounts in our communities, and people who were there, [say] that those children had only their fountain pens and their books. They were going to protest, and they were shot.

FICK: For no reason whatsoever, peacefully marching?

LEKOTA: I was not on the scene, but I am giving the account as it is understood and accepted in my community, and I accept it also.

FICK: Well, I put it to you, that is the account propagated by the UDF.

LEKOTA: No, no. This is what I am now saying to the court . . . I was in this court here, I was on trial here when I got newspapers, and I got reports from other people who came from there. Those children were shot there. They did not have weapons. They did not have any other thing. (16:232–33)[6]

Almost immediately after this exchange with Fick, Lekota's difference with him on what had happened in 1976 led to a direct challenge.

LEKOTA: We have not transgressed your laws, but we will not acquiesce in the oppression of our people. Never.

FICK: Why do you say, Mr. Lekota, it is "your" laws?

LEKOTA: You represent the, you represent the government which has pursued these policies. I am not referring to you in your personal capacity. I have nothing against you, Mr. Fick. But I must say to the court here, now, how we feel about these things, and how I myself feel about it. We want our rights, and we want to enjoy equality of status with all the people of South Africa.

Many years ago, our forefathers staked a claim for us on the South African heritage. What we are doing today is merely to press that stake. And what we are saying is that our white compatriots have a right and a share also, to share life with us. We will not ac-

cept a status . . . inferior to any man, whatever his color may be.
(16:234)

The court adjourned for lunch.

This silence of the court may display a theory that the judiciary
is, or should be, independent of politics. A judge's duty is to apply
the laws, not to make them. Making laws is the work of Parliament.
The judge's aloofness from politics is essential to fairness and the
independence of the judiciary.

In this conception of the judge's role, there is no room for con-
sidering the legitimacy of specific laws and no bill of rights or constitution that legitimates appeal from particular laws by reference to
other principles.

Van Dijkhorst's approach in the Delmas Trial seems generally to
hold to this vision of an independent, aloof judiciary. Assuming neutrality and fairness in himself, his image of the judge's role required
concentrated focusing on only the letter of the law, not the context
in which laws come to be what they are.

That view, and his distaste for the untidy aspects of politics, may
have meant that van Dijkhorst, busy with the trial, had lost touch with
the country and did not recognize how it had been changing. A difference between van Dijkhorst's tone in the verdict and in the sentencing several weeks later, when he had heard reactions to it, suggests that he was taken aback by criticism.

Omitting other events such as the end of white rule in Angola,
Mozambique, and Zimbabwe—neighboring countries that had
shielded South Africa from the rest of Africa—changes that had provoked Lekota to celebration and led to his first term in prison, van
Dijkhorst comes to the new constitution:

In 1982 the President's Council proposed a new constitution
for an Executive State President and for three legislative assem-
blies, one each for Whites, Coloureds, and Indians. . . . Blacks were
not catered for.

On 2 November 1983, the White electorate expressed overwhelming support for the new constitution. . . .

The constitutional amendments still left Blacks out in the
cold.

The period 1982 to 1984 saw the proposals of the Koornhof
bills. Two were passed. One was withdrawn because of great opposition. . . . (VD:25–27)

At this point, van Dijkhorst departs from dry listing to express an opinion, to take issue with the defendants.

The term Koornhof bills was by some speakers used without having a clear picture of what they meant. (VD:29)

Obviously, in van Dijkhorst's mind the defendants did not understand the law: if they had understood it, they would not have opposed it. He continued:

The constitutional proposals gave rise to a tide of anger in the black community....

The UDF and its affiliated organizations campaigned for a boycott of elections, intending to demonstrate that blacks rejected this form of local government.... A low poll in these elections was claimed as a victory for the UDF ...

The Coloured and Indians elections ... were held amidst feverish political activity on the part of the UDF.

Just prior to these elections, on 21 August 1984, the UDF leadership was detained ...

It is against this background that the state's case is to be viewed. The indictment can be divided into two sections. One deals with the UDF and its aims generally, and the alleged effects of its actions countrywide. The other pertains to the effect of the UDF's actions in the Vaal Triangle and the activities of its affiliates and other groups active in that area. This division amounts to two separate cases held together by the spider's web of an alleged conspiracy. (VD:29)

For some, van Dijkhorst's history, its omissions, its overt support of government claims that the reforms of the early 1980s were improvements on the past, and its criticism of those who rejected the Koornhof bills presented a central dilemma of the case. For the trial to seem legitimate at all, it must seem to resolve conflicts through a fair legal process. Could a judge appointed by the apartheid government offer any precedent for resolving the conflicts of the country through law? Or had the whole expensive exercise been merely a charade with a verdict predictable before the case began?

This was not an issue in van Dijkhorst's eyes. He declared the center of the case to be "the spider's web of an alleged conspiracy."

Lekota had repeatedly challenged this view of the trial. For him, the center of the case was the law's legitimacy. In his version of history, the laws, unlike weather, are made in a political process, by

people with names. These people are responsible, to be admired or
rejected, argued against, negotiated with, known. The people laws
affect are also to be known. To Lekota, reserving to a minority the
power to make laws was a central question of the trial. Who makes
the laws defines their legitimacy. He had testified:

> Every law that had been passed had always been decided for
> us by white people. The new dispensation, as was then being
> given to us in 1983, was similar. We had not been consulted. We
> had not been asked what we want. We had not been invited to
> become part of the process. And that—the fact that we had not
> been part of the formulation of the model—which is actually the
> cause of the failures of so many of the other models that had been
> brought forward before—was not being cured. It was not being
> gotten rid of. As long as the government was not involving us in
> the process of evolving a model that was supposed to cater for us,
> it was not solving the problem . . .
> All that we are asking for is that if there has to be a correction
> of the situation in our country, we must participate in the process
> of correcting it . . .
> Our complaint is that the manner in which it is being done
> does not take into account our dearest aspirations. We want to be
> there. We want to take the decision. Not by ourselves exclusively
> but together, as countrymen, to sit down and decide the constitu-
> tion of our country.
> That is what we wanted, and the new dispensation failed to
> do this. It was not a new problem to us. In 1960, . . . Professor Z.K.
> Matthew told [Afrikaner churchmen] "If you want to decide the
> future of the Africans, consult with them." Those men then said to
> Professor Matthews, "But we have consulted your leaders." And he
> said . . . "You choose the leaders you want to consult. . . . Let us,
> the African people, let us, the black communities, decide who will
> speak for us." (15:476)

He rejected representatives chosen by the government rather
than by the people they represented:

> There will always be a lot of men who are black like I am,
> even blacker than I am, who will . . . do anything just to please the
> government. . . . But that is not the truth, and if it is not the truth,
> it will not satisfy us. . . . Not because we want to be mischievous,
> but apartheid has meant a lot of suffering.

It means a lot of suffering for our people. We have gone
through the grinding wheel, and we go through it every day. We
have an obligation to our compatriots. Whether they are in the
prisons or in the courts. Let us go up to you and say, "It is no
longer possible for us to bear it." (15:476–77)

Van Dijkhorst intervened after this passage of testimony to say,
"I think we must now get back to the subject."

He never admitted "the subject" to be the question of who
makes the laws and who decides what to include in history. Lekota
insisted on it:

The question of proper representation, of participation in the
government of our country . . . is a matter that concerns our very
survival. . . . It is too pressing a matter for us to toy with. . . . We
have families, we are parents, we have ambitions which we cannot
achieve because of apartheid. We know that when we stand up
and we say that apartheid is unacceptable . . . for us the consequences are serious. It could mean many months of imprisonment. It could mean many months of detention without trial.

When we say to the government, "Apartheid is unacceptable
to us," when we say that we do not support its structures, the consequences for us and our families are killing, to say the least. . . .
We could go to jail. We have done so. For the last two years we
have been in jail. We have not seen our families. We have not seen
our children. We knew that these things would happen. (15:535)

Lekota's views about "this system of South African law," and his
tendency to see people as responsible for their relationship to the
law, led to challenges in the courtroom. The day after confronting
Fick on the issue of "your laws" and "our martyrs," Lekota confronted
Fick again. The prosecutor had been naming, one by one, the many
leaders and patrons of the UDF who had been imprisoned, or
banned.

LEKOTA: What is significant about that for the UDF? . . . Why
should I know about this? . . . The fact that he was banned does
not make him a criminal or [a member of the] ANC. . . . He was
never arrested and convicted for any crime . . . I do not see anything wrong here and in fact, the government has banned lots of
people before, we know, and no reasons were given why they
were banned.

To be banned is just a thing that the administrator has just decided to do. It is like myself getting detained in 1984, and staying

in jail for three or four months, and then coming out, for having committed no crime. It is just arbitrary.

It is part of the policies that we are against, now, apartheid. That is what we are complaining about.

When we express our opposition to apartheid, you get banned. When you express your opposition to apartheid, you get locked up . . . when you have not committed any crime. That is what happens. . . . Some organizations were banned for no reason given, for no crime people had committed and were convicted [of].

I said this yesterday here—I do not have anything against you, Mr. Prosecutor, but I have something against the policies that you are supposed to defend here. I have something against that. (16:287)

Fick continued as though he had not heard the challenge.

Commenting on the "political nature of the trial," van Dijkhorst ignored the issues of legitimacy and who makes history. He did address the defense claim that denied that the defendants stood on trial and at risk simply for challenging the policies of apartheid:

It should be remembered that ideas cannot be snuffed out by closing a prison door and that the courtroom is not the forum for a political debate. . . . (VD:12)

Then, ignoring most of the laws he had just described, he spoke of South Africa as though it has no "secret" history known to those in prison, no police torture, a free press, a rule of law, habeas corpus, and few like Barend Strydom in the police or military:

This case is not about the freedom of speech or the right to disseminate ideas or about freedom of association. These rights are part of our common law and exist unless they are curtailed by statute and then only to the extent specified. (VD:12)

The case, he said, was about treason.

22 The Verdict

Lekota describes the holding chamber under the courtroom as celebrated because Mandela and many other political prisoners have "been forced to wait here" before ascending to the courtroom or,

after sessions, for the prison vehicles that will take them to their
cells. "The wall is marked all over" with graffiti. Inscribed on those
whitewashed, grimy walls are dates and names and words like "freedom," "choice," "future." They claim a legitimacy that challenges the
legitimacy of the court above and the prison around. Some graffiti
address themselves to the world and reveal a history and profile of
the struggle. Some catch Lekota's eye to quote. He reads them to a
friend: "Lutuli says, 'The road to freedom is via the Cross.'" "Mandela
says, 'No easy walk to freedom.'" Later yet, "There comes a time in
the life of every nation where there remains only two choices, to
submit or fight, and that time has come to South Africa. We shall not
submit. We have no choice but to hit them with all means we have
in our power in defense of our people, or freedom, and our future."
Some graffiti are signed by whites who have died for a nonracial
future. Among the African names are the signatures of Afrikaners and
English-speaking whites arrested in December 1984 who had exposed South African undercover operations contravening treaties
with bordering countries: "Hannekom, Trish; Hannekom Derek;
Hunter, Roland."

On the morning of the verdict, November 15, 1988, surrounded
by these testimonies of "the struggle," the other prisoners sharing
breakfast with members of the defense team, and the police in an
adjoining room, Lekota was taking time to write a letter. As he and
Molefe had done throughout the trial, he was keeping alive bonds
created and sustained during the years of UDF activism. He wrote
about the recent election in the United States, sent greetings to
friends and asked after their health, and, only after establishing that
caring tone, mentioned his own waiting for the verdict and his concern that, giving all his years to the struggle, he had neglected his
family. Within a sentence, he turned away from doubt to the indignation at injustice that has required his political activism and led him
to prison. "African life remains extremely cheap in this country."
Within a few hours he would hear how Barend Strydom had been
putting those words to red proof in the bloody streets near the court.

Above the holding chamber, in the courtroom decorated with
arches and pilasters, armed police, reporters, political leaders, legal,
diplomatic, and religious figures, and the families of the defendants
waited for the proceedings to begin. In an ironic echo of the founding rally, "White people were there. Coloured people were there.
Africans. Indians." All of them came together for that historic event.
This time, the friends and supporters of the defendants and the UDF

were not relaxed and happy, as they had been five years before at Mitchell's Plain. Although all other defendants in recent treason trials had been acquitted, in this court the judge might find them guilty and might impose long sentences. He might impose death.

Before van Dijkhorst entered to ascend the bench to read his long interpretation of what he had heard and seen, an Anglican priest and former Archbishop of Southern Africa sympathetic to the UDF led those present in prayer. The gesture confirmed what had been clear from the earliest days of the trial, when Geoffrey Moselane, an Anglican priest and one of the defendants from the Vaal, was in the habit of leading the court in prayer before each session. The issues of this trial, as of the country, were seen by many as spiritual and moral, as well as legal and political. The defendants articulated and stood for meaning in the lives of many present and in the country. Of necessity, the words of the verdict would stand for more than a temporary moment in the constantly renewed interpretation and recreation of law, the flux of political power, in the pressure of history pushing the dammed up desires of those who had been denied against the strained gates of minority rule.

Although the state allegedly threatened by the UDF had asserted its power to detain, arrest, charge, and try those who opposed it, and although it claimed power to legitimize a verdict and penalties even to death, that claim to legitimacy was now on trial. Van Dijkhorst would have to persuade the world that his decisions were lawful. If possible, that they were just.

In the streets outside, red was flowing. To some, the actions of Barend Strydom that day and the actions of Kees van Dijkhorst had nothing in common. To others, they were different expressions of the same view, that in South Africa blacks do not have the same rights as whites. And if they protest and struggle, and whites, in nightmare terror that others will do to them as they have done, choose to defend their own rights and privileges with the only instruments of power they know how to use, blacks may not have rights even to life. To some, the verdict in the courtroom that day would show the strength of the alternative instruments of political power Molefe and Lekota use and teach.

All stood as van Dijkhorst, robed in red, took his seat in the high bench. He was flanked on one side by an assessor in black. No one sat on his right. This asymmetry of the court, visible to all, made its own comment on the proceedings. It testified to deep divisions in the Afrikaner establishment. In the bench, a member of a secret society sworn to uphold Afrikanerdom and a judge seeking to defend the country from a total onslaught at home and abroad. Banished, as if in disgrace, a lawyer and professor faulted for wanting to find a way for those in power and those in the dock to create the future of the country together.

Van Dijkhorst in his red robe addressed those at a lower level— the lawyers gowned in black, the defendants in the long carved dock dressed in civilian clothes like free men—Lekota wearing a yellow, black, and red UDF button, the press up front, ready to deliver its own judgment on these events, the dignitaries seated on rows of chipped wooden benches without backs, the armed police in their sky-blue uniforms observing those in prison and those who had come to observe from their stations at the dock, by the bench, along the walls, and at every door. Van Dijkhorst began to read. He complained of the length of the trial and suggested procedural rules to limit the length of cross-examination. He gave his version of South Africa's history. He started to describe the UDF.

Dismissive indifference seems to underlie much of the prosecution's case, as though it was confident that broad brush-strokes would do. Van Dijkhorst would understand the big picture, and, although crucial details connecting the specific charges to the big picture might not bear scrutiny, the cumulative effect would damn the defendants. Van Dijkhorst said:

> **The defense sought to isolate each piece of evidence the state adduced, and (often unsuccessfully) sought to give it a possible innocent interpretation. This approach is not, in itself, incorrect provided that it does not lead to a distorted picture. (VD:115)**

The big picture was the violence racking the country. To van Dijkhorst it was obviously caused by people resisting apartheid. The tone of the verdict suggest no doubt. The defendants resisted apartheid and often spoke passionately against it. Therefore the defendants caused the violence. Although his personal questions to Chaskalson suggest anguish, the verdict presents a world without doubt, defiantly presenting views van Dijkhorst knew would contradict many who heard him.

Van Dijkhorst's assumptions and pattern of reasoning appear clearly when he describes a memorial service at Turfloop, June 16 1985 (by which time all the defendants were in prison). He describes the massed students as a mob and gives an account of riotous behavior that ends with a revealing sequence of sentences:

The police had to use tear-gas and bird shot. In the process, Shadrack Mafokane was shot dead. He was a scholar who had no business on the campus. Four students were injured. (VD:632–33)

The pattern is as clear in his comment on the UDF's campaign against the BLAs. Although a government commission investigating Black Local Authorities had found bribery, graft, nepotism, self-dealing, intimidation, abuse of office, and other widespread corruption, he describes the UDF's charges as propaganda, not founded in experience:

> The attack of the UDF and its affiliates upon the Black Local Authorities was ad hominem. The councillors were vilified in extreme language, generalizations about dishonesty were made, and they were called traitors and oppressors of the people. A climate of universal rejection of the councillors and of hatred against them was fostered. (VD:175)

Therefore, those who foresaw and warned that anger at the councillors and frustration at not being able to get rid of them was bound to lead to violence were guilty of fomenting violence. Because they expressed anger at the system and those who collaborated with it, they were guilty when collaborators were killed. If they called for reconciliation, they were lying. If they used nonviolent methods, they were duplicitous. They must have foreseen that nonviolence leads to violence. Those who have no guns force those who have guns to shoot. Those who die are guilty of disturbing the peace.

Describing school boycotts that disrupted black education "for the latter half of 1984 and often the best part of 1985" (during most of which time Molefe, Lekota, and other defendants were in prison), van Dijkhorst said that, had it not been for student movements affiliated with the UDF and the UDF, "one would have wondered what all the fuss was about." (VD:190) He condemned "the UDF's manipulation of the youth for its own ends." He sounds indignant:

> The boycotts brought the youth on the streets, and it was inevitable that riotous conduct and clashes with the police would ensue. Deaths of rioters led to political funerals followed by further rioting. All this mobilized and politicized the youth and others still further, to the advancement of the liberation struggle. (VD:190)

Van Dijkhorst was certain that the UDF leaders were responsible for much of the turmoil of the mid-eighties. Unfortunately, the prosecution had not been able to prove the case. Van Dijkhorst tried to deal with the difficulty by abandoning the need to prove in detail that violence was planned or instigated by the defendants:

> The UDF did not express itself openly in favor of the boycotts. Yet indirectly it did. It wholeheartedly supported the struggle of the scholars of which the schools boycott was a major component, and it never clearly, publicly expressed disapproval of it. (VD:210)

He frequently points out that the UDF—unlike van Dijkhorst himself—did not rebuke supporters in public as he would have wanted them to do. "Should [a] speaker overstep the mark, one would expect him to be rapped over the knuckles and voted out of office. Affiliated organizations which flout the principles of the UDF could expect to be reprimanded . . ." (VD:220)

He accepts the premises of the prosecution, stated nakedly when Jacobs cross-examined Molefe:

> JACOBS: Mr. Molefe, is it correct that you in the UDF realize that if the government is not prepared to agree to a national convention, and if the UDF keeps up organizing, mobilizing, and politicizing the people to take active action, that it must lead to some violence?
>
> MOLEFE: We do not look at it that way. We have not seen it that way.
>
> JACOBS: Have you never said so? Have you never seen it that way?
>
> MOLEFE: We have never said that the people we are organizing will go on [to] violence. All we are saying is that you cannot perpetually deny people a vote in the country of their birth . . . (14:335)

At times van Dijkhorst gives political advice. Had it followed his leadership, the UDF would have castigated its supporters, tried to solve local issues piecemeal and locally, and—what? It is not clear what kind of political action against apartheid van Dijkhorst would consider lawful. He cited legal rulings that only protest in Parliament is legal, although the central issue of the case protests that the majority has not voice in Parliament.

At times, the records suggest that what he objects to most is the passion of political activists.

We do not think that one can read into Exhibit C.14 [about whether to boycott the Indian and Coloured elections] a call for violent action. Rather the opposite. Violence would give the detractors and enemies of the UDF a reason to disrupt its work. The unbridled language used, however, indicates total animosity towards the state, and advocates its disorganization. (VD:227)

Supporters of the UDF said that if UDF had spoken with neither passion nor effect, he might have found it lawful.

The big picture painted by van Dijkhorst presents a "total onslaught"—widespread rioting, looting, arson, and murder instigated by a known terrorist movement, the ANC, which, in his imagery, has wormed its way into the leadership of the UDF. Blacks, he concedes, have some legitimate grievances, but the government, he says, has acknowledged past mistakes and is reforming apartheid by extending the vote to Indians and Coloureds. Black grievances do not warrant the kind of fuss that turns into boycotts and then into riots where the police are forced to shoot, and police and soldiers get unfairly blamed. The UDF, he believes, will not be satisfied by anything less than black control. What decency and order has been established in South Africa, he implies, will be destroyed.

He does not share the faith expressed by Molefe and Lekota that reasonable people can find ways to deal with their history and create a new society more just than the old. He seems to have no mental image of change achieved through persuasion, alliances, lobbying, and negotiation rather than through confrontation and violence. This, although, in the trial and negotiations about when to hear arguments for leave to appeal, he could strike a reasonable tone about daily decisions and set dates to achieve results desired by all parties. Throughout the trial, his skill at courteous negotiation with colleagues in the law seemed fragile, prone to break down under stress, even with the prosecution, and more seriously in the disagreement with Chaskalson about the assessor and in his impatience with Bizos.

Van Dijkhorst's picture of the country and the UDF foreshadowed his verdict. So did his ruling that bail granted reluctantly during the course of the trial should be withdrawn for eight defendants. He explained that the state had proved no direct violence done or planned by the defendants, but the essence of treason is not violence but hostile intent. His tone was clear, and friends of the defendants listened in gloom and distress. Still, when the time came, three days after he started reading the verdict, and he said, "Accused No. 16, No.

29, No. 20, and No. 21 are found guilty of treason," (VD:1011) observers gasped.

Political leaders, patrons of the UDF, leaders acquitted in previous treason trials, expressed dismay, anger, and grief. Some wept.
Archbishop Tutu said he was shattered by the decision and especially
by the unexpected guilty verdict for Tom Manthata, whom he had
sent to work in the Transvaal.

Molefe and Lekota were about to be silenced, their history joining the "secret path" Lekota learned during his first prison term on
Robben Island.

Awaiting sentences that could have included death, they continued to attend to friends and supporters they had created during their
years of public leadership. Among the many letters they sent, was
one to the Ambassador from the United States, Edward J. Perkins:

> We can no longer delay the writing of this note to you. As you
> are aware, when we next return to court, it will only be to hear
> evidence in mitigation of sentences. Soon thereafter, sentences
> will be passed. Then there will no longer be proper opportunity
> to communicate with those who stood by us throughout the dura-
> tion of the trial.
>
> We are writing to convey our final gratitude to you and your
> staff for all the warmth, deep concern, and general sympathy you
> showed us and our families during these past three and a half
> years of trial. The presence of all of you ... providing us with a
> measure of reassurance. We always felt then that your presence
> would somewhat force our captors to observe the necessary de-
> corum ...
>
> But above all, your company during the brief and boisterous
> adjournments gave us a sense of belonging and of community.
> Your kind words immensely fortified us, for we realized from them
> that the world beyond the borders of our country is filled with
> millions of people who understand the agony of our lives under
> apartheid. Our faith in humankind was therefore greatly strength-
> ened.[1]

The phrase "final gratitude" may betray what Lekota would not
say to friends. In the letter he had written the morning of the verdict,
he wrote:

> The sudden death of my brother has impressed upon my mind
> just how quickly people can cease to be. I am beginning to under-
> stand the transience of human existence.

But in public, he smiled and showed only confidence. On hearing the verdict, before going down to the prison holding chamber, he said, "We don't apologize for our stand," and promised, "We will correct things in this country. It will come right. It will come." Then he and his comrades went down the prison stairway. For a while longer they must remain cut off from family and friends, imprisoned with those who go through the fire.

23 Shouting at the Crocodile

Inside the courtroom, van Dijkhorst could assert his verdict and make it law. Outside, others judged his verdict. At home and abroad, it was widely criticized by both press and diplomatic rebukes. Some criticism argued general principles. The verdict departed from Western legal standards to an extraordinary degree in ruling that political activity considered normal in most other countries was treason. Among those who knew Molefe and Lekota, the verdict seemed preposterous and vindictive.

In the midst of the outcry, the Prime Minister, P. W. Botha, commuted the death sentences of six prisoners who had been condemned to hang for sharing a common purpose in the murder of a councillor in Sharpeville during the violence in the Vaal. At the same time, he commuted death sentences for two whites. He promised that Mandela, in treatment for tuberculosis, would not be returned to prison. It turned out that he actually meant that Mandela would be sent to a more comfortable prison.

The defense presented arguments in mitigation and called on a new figure to speak on behalf of the defendants, Enos Mabuza, a traditional leader in one of the "homelands." Turning against the supporters of apartheid who had created his role to foster disunity among the majority, he expressed his solidarity. He testified, as the defendants had, that the ANC was widely accepted as a legitimate organization representing the views of the majority in South Africa.

Observers report van Dijkhorst profoundly perturbed to find someone he expected to testify against the UDF speaking for the defendants like a friend. Had he been paying attention to politics, he would have foreseen what Mabuza would say. Defying his paymasters, Mabuza had visited the ANC in Lusaka. When he returned to South Africa, he spoke favorably about them. Because of his position as chief of the tiny "homeland" of KaNgwane, Mabuza's trip had been widely reported. But van Dijkhorst disdained politics and seems to have been unaware of what he would hear from Mabuza. He seemed unable to conceive of laws as embedded in political legitimacy or to imagine how quickly the solid ground of legitimacy he assumed for his own point of view would erode.

A few days later, on December 8, 1988, he sentenced those he had found guilty.

Preparing themselves to hear their sentences, the defendants discussed whether to shout "Amandla" ["power"] before or after hearing van Dijkhorst. Lekota, the experienced prisoner, quoted an African proverb, "Do not shout at the crocodile until you have finished crossing over the river."

Van Dijkhorst again started with the big picture. He said that the march and stayaway in the Vaal, "with the aim to contribute to violence and to encourage others . . . is a serious misdeed. This was not done during a period of tranquility . . . but against the background of a history of violence stretching as far back as 1976 and earlier. The action was taken and proceeded with when the Vaal was exploding." (VD:948) Saying that he would rather err on the side of lenience, he gave suspended sentences to all the prisoners from the Vaal except Malindi. Those with suspended sentences had to obey restrictions that cut them off from public and political life.

Sentencing Tom Manthata, of the South African Council of Churches, he said there had been strong "character evidence led by the defense. The witnesses clearly know only one side of his character." (VD:953) He gave Manthata a "lenient" sentence of 6 years.

He called Molefe, Lekota, and Chikane part of the UDF's "conspiratorial core . . ."

[They were guilty of] fomenting a revolutionary climate. . . . Violence was an intended, necessary and inevitable component of such action by the masses. . . . [Their plan] was executed over a prolonged period, with devastating effects. Though not all unrest and unrest-related damage can be ascribed to the UDF and some of its affiliates, the UDF has a lot to answer for.

The defense led evidence of a number of prominent figures in the political, educational, and literary fields that they saw nothing wrong with the UDF. When regard is had to the limited perspective of some of them and the bias of others, it was a futile exercise. I must repeat here what we said in the judgment, namely that

there must be many members and supporters of the UDF, especially those on the periphery, that would not have become aware of the course that the UDF took. There must be many more, woven in the cocoon of their political outlook, who closed their eyes to the fact that this course was leading to revolt. . . .
  I accept that in order to work out, through negotiation, a peaceful coexistence of all people in South Africa, a credible leadership is needed. I accept that the UDF was seen by many to have an important role in that process. I fully appreciate that the demise of the UDF may leave a void which may take a number of years to fill. It may well be that this will slow down the process of reform. . . . For these consequences, however, the UDF has itself to blame. . . . It chose the path of violence instead of moderation. Thereby it did South Africa a disservice. (28:954)

He acknowledged that his judgment had been severely criticized:

In our sharply divided society which is a cauldron of conflicting forces from which the amalgam of our future is to be forged, the courts are in an invidious position . . . When the community itself is divided, any sentence . . . will by some be seen as far too lenient, and by others as far to severe. (28:955)
  None of the accused has been found guilty of executing or planning direct violence . . .
  I hold the view that these accused, especially accused No. 19 [Molefe], can in future play a constructive role in the political scene provided they, by word and deed, foreswear the violent option, and act within the law. (28:955)

He sentenced Lekota to twelve years in prison, Molefe and Moss Chikane to ten. The prisoners were taken aback by the suspended sentences for all the Vaal defendants except Malindi and by van Dijkhorst's insistence that the sentences were especially lenient. Their "Amandla," sounded somewhat straggly, and Bizos was weeping as they were led away.
  The defense filed for leave to appeal. They cited the dismissal of Joubert and the prejudice of the judge. They were weary and saddened. During the application to appeal, the small respect and collegiality between defense and prosecution evaporated to nothing. When Jacobs, for the prosecution, described Chaskalson as acting in bad faith, Chaskalson, without formal epithets about "my learned friend," answered:

Mr. Jacobs has accused me of acting in bad faith and unprofes-
sionally in seeking to have a point reserved for argument by the
appellate division. Since I have no particular respect for his views
in regard to my professional responsibility, I do not really care
what he says about them. Your Lordship knows that . . . Bar Councils have ruled that it is the duty of counsel to do what we want to
do in this case, and I choose to take my advice there rather than
from Mr. Jacobs. Having said that, I choose to say no more about
that. (29:206)

Chaskalson went on to the business of scheduling. Van Dijkhorst
worked with him in a tone that sounds businesslike and willing to
accommodate to Chaskalson's confessed exhaustion and need for a
vacation and van Dijkhorst's long longed-for sabbatical. Then, like
men who can collaborate, they are done.

Van Dijkhorst granted leave to appeal on the matter of the assessor. "It is high time that this ghost which has haunted this trial be
finally laid to rest." (VD: Judgment on leave to appeal, 6) He rejected
several arguments having to do with his prejudice and conduct of
the case as "frivolous or absurd," and he refused to record them. He
described yet other grounds as hopeless. In South African law, the
Appellate Division may still hear an appeal even when the judge who
heard the case does not grant leave to appeal.

During the months that followed, the country was tried by another year of political turbulence. Toward the end of January, P.W.
Botha suffered a stroke and, in a publicly bitter contest for power,
resigned his offices to F.W. de Klerk. The weeks preceding another
election under the constitution the UDF had contested were marked
by passive resistance campaigns organized by the Mass Democratic
Movement, an organization looking remarkably like the UDF under
another name. Passive resistance was met by massive violence. Police
dogs attacked people picnicking on a beach reserved for whites, and
water cannon sprayed purple dye on demonstrators near the Houses
of Parliament. In response, placards appeared punning on the opening words of the ANC's Freedom Charter: "The purple shall govern."
On election day, a strike immobilized much of the country. On election night, while the television cameras of the world were trained
on South Africa, rampaging police killed a baby, a pregnant fifteen-
year-old girl, and more than twenty other people. It seemed to be
the mid-eighties all over again.

But this time, the protective silence of the State of Emergency
shielding the police was broken by an officer who denounced fellow

police as "wild dogs." Denials were met by a grim Archbishop Tutu
on TV showing the relatives of victims. A day later, TV cameras followed Tutu into his cathedral near the Parliament. It had been des-
ecrated by police. He reconsecrated it and called for a peaceful
march to mourn and protest the deaths on election day.

De Klerk seemed to change overnight. Taking instructions from
Tutu and others speaking for the majority, he told the police to keep
away from the march in Cape Town. There was no trouble. ANC banners were displayed, but the government behaved as though nothing
untoward had happened. At a march in the university town of Grahamstown next day, police gave marchers flowers.

In the weeks that followed, many political activists were detained and restricted. At the same time, large antiapartheid marches
were allowed throughout the country, and the government promised
to release Mandela's fellow prisoners and a PAC leader who had
spent more than twenty years on Robben Island. In mid-October, at
a mass rally to celebrate the release of Walter Sisulu and others originally imprisoned with him, ANC and Communist insignia were displayed by thousands. Even skeptics began to believe that changes in
the country might be more than cosmetic.

From his prison, once the house of a warder, Mandela was issuing invitations to political leaders of the generations following his.
Molefe and Lekota were among those he summoned. Outside their
prisons, the country was turning away from the image of the total
onslaught, to be resisted by any means, to another vision, of negotiating how to live together.

In September, the five-judge Appellate Division agreed to hear
the Delmas appeal. The court had a new Chief Justice, Michael M.
Corbett, who allowed the defense to separate its argument into various grounds of appeal and to argue one before the Christmas break
in 1989. On November 27, 1989, little more than a year after the
verdict, the defense made its case that in dismissing Joubert as assessor van Dijkhorst had acted improperly.

On December 15, 1989 the Appeal Court voided van Dijkhorst's
verdict on the technical ground the defense had chosen. Underlying
the technical decision lay a judgment that van Dijkhorst had over-
stepped a judge's power. Only the prosecution or defense, not the
judge, has the right to demand that an assessor or judge retire from
a case because of prejudice. The ruling also said that both van Dijkhorst and Joubert had said things during their dispute that they
might later have regretted. Between the carefully worded legal lines,
the ruling read as a harsh rebuke to van Dijkhorst.

Ambassador Ronald MacLean of Canada sent a telex to the defendants, Chaskalson, and the newswires calling the ruling "the best Christmas present imaginable."[1] Archbishop Tutu, in a crowd waiting for the ferry from Robben Island that would bring the released prisoners, said, "Now justice has been vindicated." Lekota, speaking to the press again, said it had been "a privilege" to serve in the struggle for freedom.

No one had officially told the Delmas Five that they would be set free. Malindi, listening to a rock music station, heard the announcer reading among the day's newspaper headlines that the Delmas appeal ruling was due that day. A warder asked Molefe to settle his account for supplies like toothpaste that day instead of at the end of the month, as was the usual practice. Molefe found the warder's explanations unsatisfactory until he looked at the new account book and saw in it only accounts for the Delmas Five. At one o'clock, Lekota was watching a tennis rally that was about to decide a crucial point. Other prisoners were listening to the official news. One called out, "Delmas is free," and Lekota never found out who won the tennis point.

Prisoners poured into the highest security section where Molefe and Lekota were kept, hoisted the Delmas defendants on their shoulders, and carried them around the courtyard. The warders, guns idle in their hands, waited for the singing and cheering crowd to calm down.

The prison ferry took the Delmas Five to a jetty some distance from the one where their supporters were waiting. Although the welcome was marred in Cape Town, a large crowd, chanting their praises, had gathered at the Johannesburg airport by the time the Delmas Five landed. On the front page of the *New York Times* the next day, Molefe, carried on high by a supporter, smiles and holds his right hand clenched in the UDF gesture of victory.

Pik Botha, the Foreign Minister, was due to arrive home the same evening, and mercenaries were flying in from the Comoros where another South African effort to buy or bully allies had collapsed. Eventually, the police started to beat the crowd and set dogs on supporters of the Delmas Five. They arrested Allan Boesak briefly.

The association of Lawyers for Human Rights called on the government to say how much it had spent "on this abortive prosecution which took years of blundering incompetence to achieve nothing but red faces."[2] More costly than the money wasted, the time lost, during which Molefe and Lekota could not make the contribution even van Dijkhorst saw as significant—at least in the case of Molefe—may have cost the country violence and bloodshed that make future reconciliation more difficult.

But the trial may have saved their lives. On Robben Island, Molefe learned that he and Lekota had been targeted by death squads. In 1984 their would-be assassins acted too slowly. By the time they were released from detention in December 1984, the time was not opportune. Because of Tutu's Nobel Prize and Kennedy's visit, the world press was focusing on South Africa. When the reporters left and other UDF leaders were arrested and charged with treason in late February 1985, the time was opportune again, but Molefe and Lekota had donned the uniforms of delivery men and servants to go out in public and had become "invisible." When the UDF leaders decided to go back to the office openly, the death squads went on alert again. The arrest and imprisonment of the UDF leaders may well have protected their lives.

The trial also gave them a forum and a base, in the courtroom. During their time on the stand, they had an opportunity to say what they believed and what they had done.

During the trial, Lekota answered a charge that the UDF advocated violence, because it called on people to be willing to sacrifice.

FICK: Now I put it to you, the reference is made to the 1976 Soweto uprisings . . . to incite the people to violence, and to make it clear to the people what the nature of the struggle is, violent struggle, that they must be prepared to die fighting.

LEKOTA: No. I deny that. . . . If we take an example of a man like Martin Luther King Junior, who is well known for his non-violent stance in the world, and second only perhaps to Mahatma Gandhi, we find [in his speeches] . . . that he would die for freedom.

One of my favorite quotations from Martin Luther King's words is . . . where . . . he said that there are things so dear, some things so precious, that they are worth dying for. And if a man does not discover something he is [willing] to die for, he is not fit to live. When he made that statement, he was not suggesting that he was going to use violence, but . . . that he was prepared to live for the ideal, whatever the consequences may be for himself.

Indeed, in my reading of the Dialogues of Socrates in ancient Greek history one will find . . .

VAN DIJKHORST: Did you read it in the original?

LEKOTA: Not in Greek but in English. Where he makes the point that . . . a man who is worth being called a man does not worry about how long he is going to live, but whether what he was doing is right. . . . (16:663–64)

Lekota came back to these readings later the same day when Fick repeated the same charge:

Just this morning I was quoting . . . Martin Luther King and other people who said similar things but who were not men of violence. Chief Lutuli himself has said that. But we know quite well that he was never a man of violence. He went into his grave without ever raising his hand against anybody.

I myself have said that I am prepared to give my life for this and that, but I have never . . . used violence against anybody, nor do I intend to do so. (16:733)

The words he had read became his own life. Like Gandhi and King, Lekota and Molefe saw the political strength of the ideals and strategies they had followed. Their premier patron, Mandela, walked out of prison less than two months after their release. (The Conservative Party promptly filed charges of treason against him). Like Socrates, Lutuli, Mandela and other heroes of the tradition they draw on, Molefe and Lekota contribute to the future. The principles they enunciated during the Delmas Trial will inspire and teach others who "would show the light."

Notes

1 Introduction

1. I usually avoid the racial categories used by the apartheid system, although it causes some inconvenience and it goes against the grain of habit. Most of us think in terms of a world where "white" and "black" give information succinctly. We recognize that "Jew," "WASP," and more pejorative classifications also give quick information, but we usually avoid these. In South Africa, where part of the struggle of Molefe and Lekota is to create new categories, to show that some whites are friends of the majority and some blacks are supporters of apartheid, the critical difference is not race but where people stand. I want to avoid the habit of mind exploited by apartheid.

In the United States, when I talk about the trial, many ask as a first or second question, "Are they black?" The people who ask do not know yet that in South Africa today apartheid is enforced by blacks as well as by whites. They do not know that the government has created people in all communities with vested interests in maintaining apartheid. The discussion of "group rights," the new code for apartheid, shows that thinking in these categories maintains the systematic privilege of the few by refusing the many ordinary daily rights people in the United States call inalienable.

Where I do use racial categories, as in this paragraph, I do so quoting directly or implicitly.

2. *Weekly Mail,* May 19, 1989.

3. Ibid., May 26, 1989.

4. *New York Times,* November 19, 1988.

5. Monica Wilson and Leonard Thompson, eds., *The Oxford History of South Africa,* 2 vols. (Oxford: Oxford University Press, 1969), 1:428.

6. *New York Times,* November 19, 1988.

7. *Pacific News Service,* November 1988.

3 "Terror" Lekota

1. Quoted in Millard Arnold, *Biko* (New York: Vintage, 1979), xx.

2. Ibid., xxii–xxiii.

3. An 1815 rebellion of Afrikaner frontiersmen against British rule. It was provoked by the use of Coloured troops to apprehend a white man charged with abusing a Coloured servant. Several rebels were hanged. Their story became a rallying point for trekkers into the interior who preferred the spartan life of frontier exploration and settlement to foreign rule, especially rules that enforced equality before the law of black and white, master and servant. Lekota often refers to Slagtersnek as an example of Afrikaners willing to die for their freedom.

5 The Referendum

1. *Rand Daily Mail,* September 13, 1983; and *Sowetan,* September 21, 1983.

2. *Race Relations Survey* (Johannesburg: South African Institute of Race Relations), 1986.

3. *Rand Daily Mail,* August 22, 1983.

4. Ibid., September 24, 1983.

5. Ibid., October 3, 8, 10, and 22, 1983.

6. *Cape Times,* October 25, 1983.

6 The Million Signature Campaign

1. Where Lekota grew up and had family.

2. Report on Certain Events in the Trial Between the State and Patrick Baleka and 18 Others, sworn to by Willem Adolf Joubert, March 18, 1987, p. 6.

3. Supplementary Report Relating to Certain Events in the Trial Between the State and Patrick Baleka and 18 Others, sworn to by Willem Adolf Joubert, March 31, 1987, 9.

4. Ibid., 10.

5. Ibid., 12.

6. Ibid., 13.

7 Grassroots

1. Hendrick Verwoerd, author of the Bantu Education Act, 1953. Quoted in Dougie Oakes, ed., *Illustrated History of South Africa* (Pleasantville, N.Y.: Reader's Digest Association, 1988), 379.

2. Judgment, The State versus Moses Mayekiso and Others, Judge van der Walt, April 24, 1989, 7.

3. Ibid., 6.

4. Ibid., 10.

5. Ibid., 57.

6. Lekota may have been thinking of a poem by Oswald Mtshali, "A Road-gang's Cry."

> It starts
> as a murmur
> from one mouth to another
> in a rhythm of ribaldry
> that rises to a crescendo
> "Abelungu ngo'dam—Whites are damned
> Basibiza ngo Jim—They call us Jim."

Quoted in Allister Sparks, *The Mind of South Africa* (New York: Knopf, 1990), 229.

8 Violence

1. A characteristic explanation, like the other phrases Molefe quotes.

2. South Africa divides Africans by tribe and assigns them to "homelands." Some homelands are described by South Africa as independent countries, accorded recognition by no other country in the world. To control political and economic unrest, South Africa sometimes exports what it describes as "surplus people" to the homelands, where there is little work and widespread starvation. It does not recognize "homeland citizens" as South Africans. Homelands receive financial and military support from South Africa. Some homeland leaders refuse "independence." The UDF opposes grand apartheid and sees the homelands as "shock absorbers" used to buffer the whole system.

3. Molefe is quoting a phrase used by John Vorster, P. W. Botha's predecessor as State President and Prime Minister of South Africa from 1966 to 1979.

9 UDF and ANC

1. *Dawn,* the journal of Umkhonto we Sizwe, the military wing of the ANC. Quoted by van Dijkhorst. (VD:153)

2. Thomas G. Karis, "Black Politics: The Road to Revolution," in *Apartheid in Crisis,* ed. Mark A. Uhlig (New York: Vintage, 1986), 122.

3. Ibid., p. 160.

4. F. W. de Klerk, then Minister of Education. He was elected Prime Minister and President in 1989.

5. Quoted in Martin Meredith, *In the Name of Apartheid* (New York: Harper & Row, 1988), 193.

6. A veteran campaigner for human rights. Dr. Beyers Naude had been a professor at the University of Pretoria and a respected minister in the Dutch Reformed Church, the church of most apartheid supporters. In the early sixties, he recognized conflicts between his Christian faith and apartheid, and he founded the Christian Institute as an ecumenical forum for rethinking the obligations of faith in South Africa. He was soon attacked in words and by snipers. He was banned from 1977 to 1984. In 1985 after Bishop Tutu, he served as General Secretary of the South African Council of Churches.

7. A lifelong member of the Congress of Democrats, the "white" branch of the African National Congress. She was frequently banned and subject to house arrest.

10 Two Worlds in One Country

1. Quoted in Howard Barrell, "The United Democratic Front and National Forum," *South African Review* 2 (1984): 10.

14 We Might Just Push You

1. Lekota was talking in midwinter. He may have had in mind an open fire, or brazier with coals, commonly used for heating in black ghettoes where few dwellings have electricity.

16 Black Christmas

1. Thomas G. Karis, "Crisis of Legitimacy/Rising Black Confidence." Working Paper for Council on Foreign Relations, January 13, 1986.

17 In the World's Eyes

1. *Cape Times,* December 12, 1984.

2. *Rand Daily Mail,* September 10, 1984; September 29, 1984.

3. *Star,* December 25, 1985.

4. *London Times,* December 31, 1984.

5. *International Defense and Aid News Notes,* February 1985.

6. Graham Leach, *South Africa* (London: Routledge & Kegan Paul, 1986), 133.

7. Uhlig, *Apartheid in Crisis,* 203.

18 Lekota's Weekend

1. A nickname for the vehicle.

2. In May, Patrick Lephunya, Transvaal Administrative Officer of the UDF in 1985, was abducted and interrogated about his activities by four white men, two wearing ski-masks, who claimed to be agents of the National Intelligence Service. The NIS denied knowledge of the incident. *Rand Daily Mail,* March 2, 1985.

3. See chapter 12 above.

4. See chapter 13 above.

19 In Hiding

1. International Defense and Aid Fund, *Focus* 59: 6.

2. Quoting Prime Minister and State's President J. B. Vorster, Botha's predecessor.

3. Quoting P. W. Botha, Prime Minister and State's President.

20 The Trial

1. At the time Bizos was speaking to van Dijkhorst, Justice Pieter van der Walt was hearing the Mayekiso treason trial. In that trial, treason charges would be dropped, and the defendants would be acquitted, van der Walt saying that their grievances were justified.

21 History and Legitimacy

1. In 1985 a CBS reporter was killed while reporting violence between police-protected vigilantes and opponents of apartheid in the Crossroads squatter community near Cape Town. During my visit in August 1988, one reporter for *Grassroots,* an alternative newspaper in Cape Town, who had appeared on British TV, was shot and killed. Another *Grassroots* reporter was shot and blinded.

2. Van Dijkhorst uses "black" to mean African as distinct from two other groups treated different ways by South African law: the Coloureds, people of mixed lineage, and Asians, mainly people of Indian lineage. Japanese and, more recently, Chinese are considered white. When the defendants say "black," they include Coloureds and Asians in the term.

3. A leading figure in the ANC in the 1940s and 1950s. One of the leading defendants in the Treason Trial of 1956–61.

4. L. J. Blom-Cooper, quoted by Thomas G. Karis, "The South African Treason Trial," *Political Science Quarterly* (June 1961): 217.

5. Karis, "Treason Trial," 239.

6. The first policeman on the scene in Soweto was also in overall charge of what van Dijkhorst called "the Vaal Triangle situation." By 1984, Brigadier G. J. Viljoen was a colonel, and head of the riot police. Van Dijkhorst found him "an impressive witness." (VD Annexure Z, 496).

22 The Verdict

1. Edward Perkins, "Review of US-SA Relations," *Current Policy* 1189 (1989).

23 Shouting at the Crocodile

1. David Crary, Associated Press, December 15, 1989.

2. Ibid.